9.95

ADOLESCENT SUICIDE
ASSESSMENT AND INTERVENTION

ALAN L. BERMAN
and
DAVID A. JOBES

American Psychological Association
Washington, D.C.

Fourth printing February 1993

Published by the
American Psychological Association
750 First Street, NE
Washington, DC 20002

Copies may be ordered from
APA Order Department
P.O. Box 2710
Hyattsville, MD 20784

This book was typeset in Palatino by Harper Graphics, Waldorf, MD

Printer: BookCrafters, Chelsea, MI
Cover designer: Stephanie Shieldhouse
Technical editor and production coordinator: Valerie Montenegro

Library of Congress Cataloging-in-Publication Data

Berman, Alan L. (Alan Lee). 1943–
    Adolescent suicide : assessment and intervention / Alan L. Berman and David A. Jobes.
        p.   cm.
    Includes bibliographical references (p.   ) and index.
    ISBN 1-55798-107-8 : $35.00. — ISBN 1-55798-114-0 (pbk.; acid-free paper) : $17.50
    1. Teenagers—Suicidal behavior. 2. Suicide—Prevention. I. Jobes, David A.
    HV6546.B46   1991
    362.2'8'0835—dc20   91-7968
                                                                  CIP

Printed in the United States of America

Contents

Foreword

I n The Harvard Classics volume entitled *Prefaces and Prologues*, there is a selection by the distinguished French critic Hippolyte Taine (1828–1893) that makes the point that history (enduring facts and practices) is made in part by the people who write about it. In the present context, "suicidology," operationally speaking, is no less defined by the books written about it. This book by Berman and Jobes broadens, clarifies, and enhances the field of suicidology and changes it, a just noticeable difference, into a more sensitive and responsive clinical–humanistic–scientific discipline.

Around fourscore years ago, Freud held a meeting on suicide in his apartment in Vienna, with particular reference to suicide among young students. The year 1910 witnessed a resurgence of suicides, especially among students, and the schools became the most vulnerable target for public attack. In that meeting, David Ernst Oppenheim, a professor of classical languages, emphasized the emotional life of the adolescent, linking school and home. But the meeting is best remembered for Wilhelm Stekel's bold talionic formula that "No one kills himself who did not want to kill another or, at least, wish death to another." That assertion about the central role of hostility in suicide became a mainstay in psychoanalytic thinking and seemed fixed in that doctrine; indeed, it is accepted by many people even today. We have learned a great deal about suicide since then and certainly have an obviously multifaceted and wider ranging view of self-destructive phenomena. Berman and Jobes mention this 1910 meeting near the beginning of their book, and then, in a single comprehensive volume, they span the decades and bring us up to date in ways that would have popped the eyes of those earlier suicidological pioneers. This book gives us the most up-to-date findings available about the background, assessment, treatment, and prevention of adolescent suicide. Each chapter is filled with case illustrations, a catholicity of conceptual schemes, and a full bibliography—a veritable cornucopia of intellectual nutrients.

Adolescent Suicide: Assessment and Intervention is a very special book. It is both a guidebook and a textbook; it is scholarly and it is practical. In addition, it has the imprimatur of the American Psychological Association and fully exhibits the level of excellence that a reader might expect in a volume published by the major professional organization in psychology.

On a personal note: As a half-century member of the American Psychological Association and as the founder, a quarter century ago, of the much smaller and more focused American Association of Suicidology, I am doubly proud to write this foreword and to help launch this vessel of knowledge on a voyage of good effects. I urge any person—every psychologist—who, for one reason or another, has an interest in adolescent suicide to embark on an informative trip to those rare islands of Edification and Praxis.

University of California   EDWIN S. SHNEIDMAN
   at Los Angeles, January 1991

Introduction

Tom was 17, the younger of two sons of divorced parents, and a second-semester high school senior. In a matter of months, years of barely passing grades (the result of his and his mother's general lack of interest in academics) would have no more impact on Tom's life. Although not an exemplary student, Tom was an athlete of note, starring on both the school football team and wrestling squad—starring, that is, until early in the fall, when a knee injury and subsequent surgery ended his high school athletic career.

School rules prohibited him from using the available weight equipment for rehabilitating his knee and working out with his ex-teammates. With the source of his self-esteem shattered, Tom grew noticeably despondent. Over the next several months, his beer drinking escalated, and after he was caught drinking on school grounds, he was suspended for a week. Thereafter, he was prohibited from campus immediately at the end of each school day.

Friends acknowledged that Tom was depressed. To two of his buddies he talked of wanting to kill himself. One later stated that Tom spoke of "putting a gun to his head." Failing grades in two of his courses his first semester, although eliciting no observable response from Tom, surely did not help matters. He would have to complete summer school to graduate.

1

In February Tom had a physical altercation with a fellow student over some relatively trivial issue. Fighting was not typical of Tom, whose size and strength tended to win over others through intimidation. Tom began to talk obsessively to his friends about some vague threat of harm and to speak of avenging some unspecified wrong. To each friend he told a different story, changing victims, dates, and circumstances. In addition, he asked at least two girls if they would miss him if he died. One girl astutely asked if he was thinking about suicide. He responded simply, "No."

But, events were to show clearly that he had been. His obsession seemed to take on more urgency, and he spoke with some drama of planning retribution late in the week. When Tom rejected offers of friends to join him, they dismissed his story as just bravado. In school on Friday that week, Tom appeared agitated and "jumpy." That was the last anyone saw of Tom. On Friday afternoon, Tom smuggled out of his house the .22 caliber revolver his mother kept "for protection" and went deep into the woods behind his home. His body was found early that evening by some hikers. Tom had died of a contact gunshot wound to the head. Later it was noticed that in one of his school notebooks Tom had doodled "Friday Death Day—Happy Death Day." On another page he had drawn some rather primitive stick figures, the last in the series holding a gun to its head!

Until his death Tom had lived, breathed, and experienced life as did any number of his cohort. He was an imperfect kid, perhaps with a fragile ego. His decompensation occurred in a relatively short period of time. His losses were profound; his consequent depression, evident to several of his friends, exacerbated his drinking, which, no doubt, in turn caused both more loss and more despair. In retrospect Tom was too dependent on one source of self-esteem. In retrospect the loss of his athleticism became the proximate cause of his suicide; his life apparently had no other meaningful attachment. But retrospection is a gift of the future—the wisdom of hindsight. For the most part, the impact of this loss on Tom was denied or avoided by others in his life. What his friends knew and what one even questioned led not one of them to suggest that

Tom seek or receive help. Neither his mother nor his coaches—the important adults in his world—encouraged him to seek help.

Tom probably colluded in keeping that attention and help at a distance. His behaviors were not direct appeals for help, so they were easy to minimize. Tragically, the legacy of that minimization, denial, and avoidance was the unnecessary and premature loss of Tom's life and the enduring pain of his survivors.

To those who did not know Tom, his death quickly translates into a mortality statistic. He becomes yet another adolescent suicide, one of roughly 2,000 (among 15- to 19-year-olds) in the United States in the year of his death, over half of whom died by the use of a firearm or explosive.

Death is no doubt one of the most painful realities of life. The death of someone close leaves both a physical and emotional void that provokes profound feelings of grief, loss, and anger among those who survive. Yet for the most part, we are able to keep a relative emotional distance; we somehow find a way to mourn and continue.

Developmentally, we are most likely to first confront death through the loss of a grandparent or a pet, usually by natural causes of age or disease. Daily we are reminded by news reports of war and famine, of AIDS, or of drugs, crime, and homicide on our city streets. For most of us, however, death happens far away, or at some future time, or to others, especially those who lead lives of excessive risk. Thus in a predominantly youth-oriented culture, particularly among the youth of that culture, death is a topic easily avoided or denied. It is in this context that the death of a young person rapes our sensibilities, especially when that death is self-imposed (Berman and Carroll, 1984).

Suicide among young people is indeed a difficult and painful reality that many, including mental health professionals, may be tempted to avoid and deny. Yet the clinical practitioner can ill afford such avoidance or denial. Some empirical data are relevant here. One recent survey has determined that the average practicing psychologist who is directly involved in patient care has a greater than 1 in 5 chance of losing a patient to suicide some time during the course of his or her professional career

(Chemtob, Hamada, Bauer, Torigoe, & Kinney, 1988). For psychiatrists, a patient suicide will be experienced by more than one out of two practicing clinicians (Chemtob, Hamada, Bauer, Kinney, & Torigoe, 1988). Another study suggests that a psychologist in training has a 1 in 7 chance of losing a patient to suicide (Brown, 1987). On a broader level, Schein (1976) has found that suicide is the most commonly encountered emergency situation for mental health professionals. Work with suicidal patients has consistently been found to be the most stressful of all clinical endeavors (Deutsch, 1984). To come full circle, Chemtob, Hamada, Bauer, Torigoe, and Kinney (1988) report that psychologists who lose a patient to suicide experience that loss much as they would the death of a family member. And, as if this stress were not enough, one added consequence might be the threat or reality of a malpractice action brought against the clinician. Such are the grim clinical realities of working with the suicidal patient.

In this context, it is therefore paradoxical that mental health professionals actually receive so little training in the handling of this common and difficult clinical problem. Formal and ongoing suicidology training in psychiatric residencies, clinical psychology training programs, and social work and nursing programs appears to be quite limited (Berman, 1986). Survey data suggest that training in suicidology is most often expected to occur through direct clinical experiences with suicidal patients, as cases arise (Berman, 1983). Ironically, data obtained from a recent sample of clinical training directors have shown that although the study of suicide is considered a relatively important element of clinical graduate training, formal training of *any* kind in suicidology occurred in only 35% of clinical psychology doctoral programs sampled (Bongar & Harmantz, 1989)!

Accordingly, this book represents a considered attempt to replace avoidance and denial with direct focus and thoughtful examination of current knowledge relevant to theory, research, practice, and intervention in the area of adolescent suicide. Our approach to our task has been guided by three assumptions:

1. There exists a core body of empirically based knowledge in suicidology, particularly in the last decade's published research on youth suicide. This research has become increasingly

sophisticated in design and, therefore, more reliable in its find-ings and implications for practice. The typical clinician has nei-ther the time nor the interest to keep abreast of developments in this field. Our task has been to review, summarize, and integrate what is known and to translate these research-based findings into usable clinical tools. Toward this task we have relied heavily on the most recent empirical work and on well-designed and controlled research from earlier years (Berman & Cohen-Sandler, 1982).

2. By its very nature, clinical practice with the suicidal patient is difficult and anxiety-provoking. There are no consensually agreed-upon or valid, reliable risk assessment scales or other instruments that have standardized or simplified the task of assessment. There is no agreed-upon strategy for intervening in the life-and-death decision of the suicidal mind or for treating the suicidal character. Our task has been to present strategies for assessment, intervention, prevention, and postvention that the clinician can choose and apply according to individual style, theoretical orientation, and proclivity.

3. There is no typical suicidal adolescent. Tom's case is an example illustrating some risk factors captured by the nomoth-etic net and, at the same time, it is an idiographic statement. Every one of the approximately 5,000 15- to 24-year-olds who commit suicide in the United States annually presents a unique contribution to the group as a whole. And yet the group as a whole has some definable properties and attributes of import to us. We have much to learn from both the statistical set (and its scientific base) and the individual case (and the art of work-ing with it). Our task has been to preserve and integrate the science and art of clinical suicidology. In order to humanize the science of suicidology where possible, we have made every effort to liberally illustrate principles and findings with case examples.

To these ends we have organized our presentation to begin with the most emotionally distal of themes, the epidemiology of youth suicide, and end with the most emotionally impactful, personal survivorhood. The heart of this book lies in its two chapters on assessment and treatment, those of most direct clinical import to the practitioner. These chapters are nested in reviews of the theoretical and empirical contexts for understanding the suicidal adolescent and a brief integration of current, larger-scale preventive interventions. This latter focus is singularly important to today's clinician, who often is called out of the office and away from the individual patient to consult in the community on a more programmatic level.

Suicidology is a field of diversity and a rapidly growing knowledge base. We respect, even thrive on, the differing approaches brought to bear on the assessment and treatment of suicidal adolescents. We have tried to reflect what is current and promising in working with the suicidal adolescent while recognizing the spectrum of options open to the practitioner. Although we have tried in this volume to remain free from bias, we may not have succeeded absolutely. Also we are aware that what we have committed to paper today must be regarded in the context of a rapidly and continually developing literature in the field. It is just this dynamism that has made our study of suicidology both the motivation and reward for this effort.

Finally, our charge from the American Psychological Association was to accomplish our goals within the constraints of a short monograph, typical of this series of books. We hope our effort toward brevity has not shortchanged our effort toward clarity.

Case illustrations are based on actual patients. To maintain confidentiality, all names have been changed.

References

Berman, A. L. (1983). *Training committee report.* Unpublished manuscript. (Available from the American Association of Suicidology, 2459 So. Ash St., Denver, CO 80222.)

Berman, A. L. (1986). Notes on turning 18 (and 75): A critical look at our adolescence. *Suicide and Life-Threatening Behavior, 16,* 1–12.

Berman, A. L., & Carroll, T. (1984). Adolescent suicide: A critical review. *Death Education, 8*(Suppl.), 53–64.

Berman, A. L., & Cohen-Sandler, R. (1982). Childhood and adolescent suicide research. *Crisis, 3,* 3–5.

Bongar, B., & Harmatz, M. (1989). Graduate training in clinical psychology and the study of suicide. *Professional Psychology: Research and Practice, 20,* 209–213.

Brown, H. N. (1987). The impact of suicides on therapists in training. *Comprehensive Psychiatry, 28,* 101–112.

Chemtob, C. M., Hamada, R. S., Bauer, G. B., Kinney, B., & Torigoe, R. Y. (1988). Patient suicides: Frequency and impact on psychiatrists. *American Journal of Psychiatry, 145,* 224–228.

Chemtob, C. M., Hamada, R. S., Bauer, G. B., Torigoe, R. Y., & Kinney, B. (1988). Patient suicide: Frequency and impact on psychologists. *Professional Psychology: Research and Practice, 19,* 421–425.

Deutsch, C. J. (1984). Self-report sources of stress among psychotherapists. *Professional Psychology: Research and Practice, 15,* 833–845.

Schein, H. M. (1976). Obstacles in the education of psychiatric residents. *Omega, 7,* 75–82.

1

For Whom the Bell Tolls: The Epidemiology of Adolescent Suicide

*S*UICIDE IS THE THIRD LEADING CAUSE OF DEATH AMONG TEENS . . . *SUICIDE RATES AMONG YOUNG TRIPLE IN TWENTY YEARS . . . FIRE-ARM SUICIDES AMONG YOUNG INCREASE DRAMATICALLY . . .* Headlines like the above, increasingly prevalent in the popular press, result from the statistical research of epidemiologists. Epidemiology is the study of disease among populations. Generally speaking, various kinds of epidemiological investigations with different populations provide data that help determine which groups are more or less prone to (at risk for) a particular disease. Knowledge about risk factors for certain populations is then used to develop public health policies and programming to prevent diseases and promote health, especially in those populations most at risk. In the case of suicidal death, epidemiologists use information provided on death certificates to study the variations in suicide rates within and between various populations. Similarly, death certificate information may be used to investigate a variety of demographic variables relevant to suicide, such as age, gender, and race. Thus, descriptive epidemiology attempts to identify and characterize the scope of the problem by determining rates, trends, and groups at higher risk.

A risk factor is a statistically based association between some characteristic or attribute of an individual, group, or environment and an increased probability of certain diseases or disease-related phenomena (Klerman, 1987). Epidemiologically defined risk factors are of great use to clinicians to help identify high-risk patients so that they may better assess and treat these individuals.

Epidemiological methods have been used with great success to help lower death rates from heart disease and cancer. Similar approaches have increasingly been applied to deaths resulting from suicide, particularly youthful suicides. For example, epidemiological trends in youthful suicides over the last 3 decades led the U.S. Department of Health and Human Services to establish a specific federal health objective to lower the suicide rate among youth ages 15–24 by the year 1990. Similar epidemiologic studies have now defined our failure to meet that objective, leading to reestablished goals for the year 2000 (see chapter 6). Epidemiological research techniques clearly represent a major force in the study and prevention of suicide, on both macro and micro levels.

Official Statistics: Constraints and Limitations

While the epidemiological study of suicide has undoubtedly provided some of our most valuable data to date, some of the inherent constraints and limitations of the approach should be noted. Consider, for example, the constraints of the death certificate itself. The death certificate fundamentally provides the raw data of epidemiological study. Death certificates are collated by state vital statistics offices, which then summarize the data they report in order to establish both state and national mortality trends. As a primarily legal document, the standard death certificate provides only a limited amount of mostly demographic information and simply does not account for some of the most important variables that significantly bear on a suicide, such as psychological variables or premorbid history. Attempts to modify the standard document to include additional information have been met with clear resistance. Issues as mundane as the size of file drawers have been raised to oppose the expansion of the existing form (Working Group on the Classification and Reporting of Suicide, 1984)!

In a much broader sense, the interpretive value of epidemiological research may be limited in that the validity and reliability of officially reported suicide statistics have been widely questioned and debated in the literature (Jobes, Berman, & Josselson, 1987; O'Carroll, 1989; Pescosolido & Mendelsohn, 1986). The gist of this debate centers on whether official rates of suicide tend to underestimate the actual rates of suicide, thus calling into question results of epidemiological studies that use official rates.

A questionnaire survey of 195 practicing medical examiners supported reason for these doubts (Jobes & Berman, 1984). The majority (58%) of medical examiners surveyed either "agreed" or "strongly agreed" that "the actual suicide rate is probably two times the reported rate." Furthermore, when asked to rate the accuracy of mortality figures reported by the National Center of Health Statistics (NCHS) on a scale from 1 (*absolutely accurate*) to 100 (*absolutely inaccurate*), the medical examiners rated the accuracy at a mean of only 46.73.

A final consideration is that there is typically a 2- to 3-year delay in the reporting of official death statistics. The lag between the actual occurrence of a death and its official reporting is a reality-based constraint that requires that researchers continuously use out-of-date raw data.[1]

Criticisms of epidemiological data and techniques have been widely discussed in the literature and demand interpretive caution when considering these data. Nevertheless, the overwhelming strength and value of epidemiological studies of suicide clearly outweigh the various constraints and limitations inherent in this approach.

---

[1]The 1987 U.S. data on completed suicide reported in this chapter are the most recent final statistics available, at the time of writing, from the National Center for Health Statistics. *Provisional* 1988 data have been released and are referred to as well.

Adolescent Suicide Statistics

Plainly stated, this text exists largely as a direct result of epidemiological studies. The suicidal behaviors of adolescents over the past 30 years have generated a great deal of concern among public health officials, mental health practitioners, educators, and the public at large. Whereas concern is clearly warranted, hyperbole about the "epidemic" of youth suicide has led to some instances of reporting inaccurate "facts" about youth suicide, resulting in misperceptions and distortions. Let us therefore duly consider the empirical data.

In 1987 there were 4,924 officially recorded suicides for young people between the ages of 15 and 24 (National Center for Health Statistics, 1989). For every 100,000 young people in this age group, there were 12.9 suicides in 1987. This rate was only slightly lower than the high rate the prior year (1986: 13.1) and the peak rate for this age group in 1977 (13.3).

The suicide rates for 15- to 24-year-olds during the past decade have remained fairly stable, with only minor fluctuations. However, this blending of older and younger adolescent groups has an important homogenizing effect. When split into separate groups (ages 15–19 vs. 20–24), as noted in Figure 1, rates for both groups have been remarkably parallel until the late 1970s. But then, for the past decade, rates for the 15- to 19-year-old group have generally continued to rise while those of the 20- to 24-year-old group have been on a downward trend.

In 1957 the adolescent (15- to 24-year-old) suicide rate was 4.0 per 100,000. This represents a sharp contrast to the previously mentioned 1977 peak rate of 13.3. It was this striking jump in rates over these two decades that directly led to the professional and public outcry during the 1980s to prevent adolescent suicide and thereby reverse the trend. Epidemiology had begot the call for prevention!

As shown in Table 1, the overall suicide rate (per 100,000 population) for young people ages 15–24 has more than tripled (an increase of 222%) in the 30-year period between 1957 and 1987. For the same interval, the most striking increase has been for the 15- to 19-year-olds (a 312% increase). This is slightly less

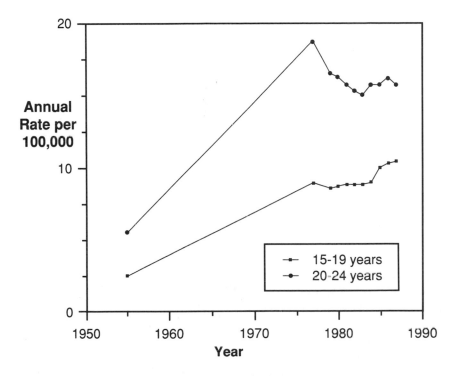

Figure 1   U.S. youth suicide rates, 1955–1987 for 15- to 19-year-olds and 20- to 24-year-olds. From "Letter to the editor" by L. A. Fingerhut and J. C. Kleinman, 1988, *Journal of the American Medical Association, 259*, p. 356.

than twice as great an increase as that experienced by the 20- to 24-year-old age group (163%).

The Study of Historical Trends

A symposium time warp. Imagine yourself sitting at a symposium on adolescent suicide called in response to media reports of an alarming increase in the incidence of youth suicide. An interdisciplinary panel of distinguished speakers has gathered to present their views and explanations for the problem and suggestions for its resolution. The panel focuses on the schools and the intensely competitive pressures of the times as sources of stress. Youth suicide is noted by some panelists to

Table 1

Suicide Rates per 100,000 Population by Age Groups Between 1957–1987

Year	Ages 15–19	Ages 20–24	Ages 15–24
1957	2.5	5.8	4.0
1987	10.3	15.3	12.9
% change	+312%	+163%	+222%

Note. From *Vital Statistics of the United States* (annual mortality summaries), U.S. Department of Health and Human Services, Hyattsville, MD: National Center for Health Statistics.

be an international problem. Others question the validity and adequacy of official statistics; and the problem of journalistic sensationalism is noted. Concerns are raised about suicide clusters, the role of suggestibility and imitation, as well as the availability of guns. Various preventive and interventive strategies are proposed and, in particular, the educational system is singled out as uniquely positioned to play a key role in prevention.

Although the themes and insights discussed at this symposium appear contemporary, what is most remarkable about this meeting is that it was held over 80 years ago! The year is 1910 and the location is Vienna, Austria. The chair of this symposium is Sigmund Freud and the distinguished panel of scholars are members of the Vienna Psychoanalytic Society. This symposium on suicide was one of the last meetings of the original "Wednesday Night Group," which was presided over by Freud and held in his living room (Berman, 1986; Friedman, 1967).

As illustrated by this meeting, reason for concern about youth suicide is not new. Figure 2 illustrates the rates of youth suicide

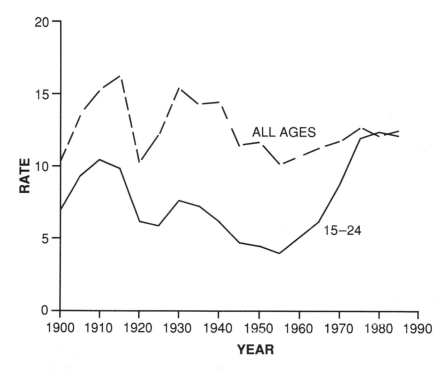

Figure 2   Suicide rates for all persons and for persons 15–24 years old per 100,000 in the United States, 1900–1985. From "The Emergence of Youth Suicide: An Epidemiologic Analysis and Public Health Perspective" by M. L. Rosenberg, Jack C. Smith, L. E. Davidson, and J. M. Conn, 1987, *American Review of Public Health, 8,* p. 420. Copyright 1987 by Annual Reviews Inc. Reprinted by permission.

in the United States over this century. Although rates tend to wax and wane over the decades, youth suicide rates in 1910 were quite comparable to rates observed in the 1970s (Rosenberg, Smith, Davidson, & Conn, 1987). A true appreciation of the epidemiology of youth suicide must therefore take into account the historical trends of the phenomenon. A true understanding of the phenomenon of youth suicide will be guided in part by the social correlates of these observed trends.

Tracking the trends. As discussed by Rosenberg et al. (1987), the early efforts at suicide surveillance among youthful populations took a variety of forms. For example, Bailey (1903) examined state registry statistics and Miner (1922) attempted to tally over 29,000 newspaper accounts of suicide. Dublin and Bunzel (1933) took yet another approach in their study of insurance records. Data obtained in the last quarter of the 19th century underscores important differences in patterns of adolescent suicide in comparison to more contemporary data.

In their review of epidemiological trends in youth suicide, Rosenberg et al. (1987) note that from 1900 to 1955, the rate of suicide for young people ages 15–24 was parallel to and about half the rate of persons of all ages (see Figure 2). In 1955, however, the rate for 15- to 24-year-olds began to steadily climb, culminating in 1978, when the rate exceeded that of all persons for the first time in the century.

Some of the most important work in the study of recent trends has been conducted by Holinger and his colleagues (Holinger, 1979; Holinger & Offer, 1981, 1982; Holinger, Offer, & Zola, 1988). This line of epidemiological research has pioneered the use of population models as well as predictive models that attempt to project anticipated rates based on historical trends. Accordingly, Holinger et al. (1988) have shown that increases and decreases in U.S. youth suicide rates have corresponded with increases and decreases in the proportion of adolescents in the U.S. population. Their consequent projection anticipates a decline in current rates until the mid-1990s, followed by an upturn in rates.

Other Causes of Death

Each year the National Center for Health Statistics publishes a variety of reports related to mortality in the United States. Reports of vital health statistics include a range of demographic information as well as data concerning the leading causes of death. According to provisional 1988 vital statistics data (National Center for Health Statistics, 1989), suicide continues to rank as the eighth leading cause of death for the entire population. For adolescents ages 15–24, suicide is the third leading cause of death (following accident and homicide, respectively). These three forms of violent death, taken together, account for the majority of all deaths in the United States of persons up to the age of 39! For Black male youth (ages 15–24) in particular, homicide is the leading cause of death (followed by accident and suicide, respectively). Increases in violent deaths by homicide and suicide for both Blacks and Whites have become a major source of concern for public health officials (see discussion by Holinger, 1979).

Demographic Data

Beyond tracking trends and causes of death, epidemiological research can provide a wealth of useful demographic information. Relevant to adolescent suicide, we will briefly consider the demographic variables of race, gender, age, geography, and socioeconomic status.

Race. Youth suicide rates in the United States have always been higher among Whites than among Blacks. However, as seen in Table 2, the rates for Black males ages 15–24 have increased most dramatically, almost tripling in the years between 1960 and 1987.[2] Similarly, the suicide rate for 15- to 19-year-old White males (who remain the modal race and sex group of completers) more than doubled over the same 1960–1987 interval. Although rates for females (see section on Gender) are now only about one fifth those for males, *both* White and Black female rates are now twice what they were in 1960.

As discussed previously, violent death in Black adolescent populations has sharply risen over the past 20 years. Unfortunately, other ethnic groups demonstrate increased risk for suicide and homicide death as well. Hispanic populations, for example, appear to be at significant risk for violent deaths (Centers for Disease Control, 1986). Similarly, American Indians represent a subgroup at very high risk for alcoholism and violent death, especially suicide (Berlin, 1987), although there are great variations in rates among tribes and reservations.

---

[2]Note that 1957 data specific to Blacks are not available, as these statistics formerly were coded under the broad heading of "non-White."

Case Illustration

As reported by Berman (1979), The Duck Valley Indian Reservation, straddling the border of Idaho and Nevada, housed a population of slightly over 1,000 mixed Shoshone and Paiute Indians during the 1970s. Between January 1970 and September 30, 1978, a period of 8.75 years, there were 38 deaths among tribal members. Fifteen of these deaths (40%) were by suicide. Correspondingly, for the United States as a whole, suicides account for about 1.5% of deaths annually. Twenty-eight (74%) of Duck Valley's deaths were nonnatural.

Duck Valley, jurisdictionally, is situated in the state of Nevada. In Nevada, the death rate from alcohol and alcohol-related causes for American Indians in the 1970s was 5 times that of non-Indians. The rate of violent death (nonnatural causes) among American Indians was 2½ times that of non-Indians. Although Duck Valley's rate of violent death was similar to that of Nevada Indians as a whole, its suicide rate was 3 times greater! Fourteen of the fifteen Duck Valley suicides were alcohol-related. The median age of these Duck Valley suicides was only 23 years. All but one were males; 11 of the 15 suicides (73%) were by firearms.

In the year 1977 alone, there were 10 deaths at Duck Valley: four suicides, two accidental deaths (one of which was alcohol-related), one homicide (the only one of the decade), two natural deaths (one of which was alcohol-related), and one undetermined death (an alcoholic, schizophrenic male with a history of three prior attempts).

Among the several explanatory causes given for such high rates of suicidal and violent death at Duck Valley were: (a) the relative youth of the male population (on average, 5½ years younger than other Nevada Indians); (b) high rates of alcoholism and depression; (c) the prevalence of guns (the typical household owned five firearms); (d) high unemployment (more than 80% for most of the year); (e) the isolation of the reservation; (f) the destruction of traditional tribal cultures; and (g) community norms of intolerance of individualism (including an antisuccess norm), nonsupport for educational achievement, nonsupport for intra- or extragovernmental leadership, a lack of help-seeking behavior, a lack of systematic help giving (resources, intrasystem communication, etc.), noninterference in others' affairs, and cultural sanctions against the direct externalization of rage against others—although passive–aggressive behavior was normative.

Gender. Overall, for youth ages 15–24, the ratio of male to female suicides in 1987 was approximately 5:1. This discrepancy represents a change from prior decades, when traditionally this

Table 2

Suicide Death Rates for Years 1960 and 1987
(per 100,000 Population)

Year	All	White male	White female	Black male	Black female
			Ages 15–24		
1960	5.2	8.6	2.3	4.1	1.3
1987	12.9	22.7	4.6	12.9	2.5
% change	+148%	+163%	+100%	+214%	+92%
			Ages 15–19		
1960	3.6	5.9	1.6	2.9	1.1
1987	10.3	17.6	4.4	8.9	2.7
% change	+186%	+198%	+175%	+206%	+145%
			Ages 20 24		
1960	7.1	11.9	3.1	5.8	1.5
1987	15.3	27.5	4.7	17.2	2.4
% change	+115%	+131%	+51%	+196%	+60%

Note. From *Vital Statistics of the United States* (annual mortality summaries), U.S. Department of Health and Human Services, Hyattsville, MD: National Center for Health Statistics.

ratio stood at about 3:1, as suicide rates for young males have grown at a much faster pace than those for young females. Conversely, it appears that adolescent females more frequently attempt suicide in comparison to males; estimated ratios range from 3:1 (Garfinkel, 1989) to 10:1 (Toolan, 1975). As will be noted, there are other considerable gender differences, particularly with regard to the differential use of weapons for completed and attempted suicide, as well as differences in predisposing mental disorders, including substance use, and in overall levels of functioning.

Age. As discussed earlier, there are some distinct age differences in suicide rates between younger (ages 15–19) and older (ages 20–24) adolescents. While the largest percentage increases are observed in the 15–19 age group, the actual rates are higher for the 20- to 24-year-old age group. According to 1987 statistics, the rate of suicide per 100,000 population was 10.3 for all 15- to 19-year-olds, whereas the rate for 20- to 24-year-olds was 15.3. Seven of every eight suicides completed by all youth 19 years old and younger in 1987 were by 15- to 19-year-olds.

Although the increases in youth suicide have been dramatic, it may be surprising to know that other age groups actually have—and historically have always had—much higher rates of suicide per 100,000 population. For example, all the age groupings above 25 have higher rates of suicide than adolescents, with the elderly, 75- to 84-year-olds, having the highest rate of all (28.9 per 100,000 in 1987). In this regard, those 65 years old and older accounted for 21% of all suicides in 1987 while comprising only 12.3% of the population. Those 24 years old and younger accounted for 15.7% of all suicides while comprising an equal proportion (16%) of the population (McIntosh, 1989). Although these differences remain, the rise in youth suicide rates can be contrasted to a decline in the rates of elderly suicide during the same period of time.

In epidemiological analyses, these relative changes in age-specific suicide rates over time are called *age effects*. Age effects may be due to changes in physiology, role, or societal-age discrimination (Wasserman, 1987). *Period effects* are changes in rates of suicide associated with historical time periods, such as differences in the social environment (economic depression, war, etc.), which exert influence on all age groups. Included as period effects are documented changes in measurement, that is, changes in the manner in which suicide is certified. For example, if those deaths currently certified as undetermined—the great majority of which are overdose deaths—were to be documented as suicides, there would be an even greater increase in the rate of adolescent suicide relative to other age groups (Jobes et al., 1987).

Cohort effects are changes in the rates of suicide throughout the lifetime of those affected who share a temporal experience, for example, those born between 1965 and 1969 versus those born between 1970 and 1974. One example of a cohort effect hypothesized by Easterlin (1978) is that cohorts of greater size will have higher suicide rates (throughout their lifetime) than smaller sized cohorts. Thus, for example, as the post–World War II "baby boomers" move toward old age, they may be expected to bring with them problems inherent in larger birth cohorts, such as higher rates of suicide. The large proportionate size of the postwar birth cohorts has provided one explanatory cause for the dramatic increases in youth suicide up to the late 1970s. Several studies (see Newman and Dyck, 1988) have found increasing suicide rates with each successive cohort during the 1950–1979 period. However, Newman and Dyck (1988) have noted that it is difficult to distinguish period from cohort effects in these studies.

Geography. Geographic and related cultural influences have been widely studied and linked to various trends in international suicide rates. In terms of youth suicide, it appears that observed increases in the U.S. rates are similar to increases observed in Western European countries (Diekstra, 1985) and other countries in other parts of the world (Lester, 1988). Youth suicide trends in international rates between 1970 and 1980 for nations with populations of at least one million that also had at least 100 overall suicides have been studied by Lester (1988). The results of this investigation revealed that suicide rates for 15- to 24-year-old youths had increased in 23 of 29 countries that met the selection criteria. However, these increases varied widely among nations, and some increases were limited to one sex. Diekstra (1989) reported increases in 15- to 19-year-old suicides in 9 of 13 countries (1970–1985), with the most dramatic increases (800%!) occurring in Ireland during this period. Noted by Diekstra were correlated social changes in Ireland in rates of illegitimacy, alcohol dependency, unemployment, crime, and divorce, suggesting that youth suicide may be associated with economic instability, a breakdown of family structure, interpersonal violence, and substance abuse. We will return to these themes in chapter 3 when we discuss research-based risk factors.

In spite of these international data suggesting general increases in youth suicide, the epidemiological comparability of international statistics has been widely questioned and debated (e.g., refer to Robins & Kulbok, 1988; Sainsbury & Jenkins, 1982).

In the United States, youth suicide rates have been consistently highest in the West and lowest in the South, North Central, and Northeastern states (Shaffer, 1988). Seiden (1983) specifically examined 15 years' data (1964–1978) for youth suicide across all 50 states and the District of Columbia. A rank ordering of states by incidence of youth suicide during the study period reflected some fascinating data. Nine of the 10 states with the highest rates were in the West. Alaska, Nevada, New Mexico, Wyoming, and Arizona ranked highest. These five states also exceeded the national average in their rates of increase in youth suicide over this study period. In contrast, all 10 of the lowest ranked states were east of the Mississippi. Among other distinctions, Seiden noted that this western region with the highest incidence of youth suicide had in common low population densities, suggesting that "undercrowding," a geographical isolation leading to social isolation, may be causally related to these high rates. Uncontrolled in this study, however, were potential confounding variables related to both suicide and low population density, that is, alcohol consumption, gender ratio, and Indian population. Additionally, these data may again represent false differences due to variability in data collection and medicolegal certification of suicide (see Nelson, Farberow, & MacKinnon, 1978). In line with this, suicide rates typically are consistently higher in urban areas than in rural areas across the country (Centers for Disease Control, 1986), where more professional and better staffed or funded medical examiners' offices (vs. lay coroner offices) are housed.

Socioeconomic status. It has been said that suicide is a truly democratic phenomenon—no racial or economic class is immune. As a generalization this has been largely true. Rates among various socioeconomic classes tend to wax and wane over time and social conditions; for example, economic deprivations and recessions will affect more those who have something to lose versus those already economically disadvantaged. Empirical data concerning the exact influence of socioeconomic status have been somewhat mixed and contradictory. The overall picture is one of no consistent relation between suicide rates and family economic status (see Maris, 1981).

Easterlin's (1980) work on relative cohort size suggests that *changes* in the economic well-being of youth—the gap between the economic aspirations and reality—lead to increased stress and consequent aggression. Specifically, the relative cohort size may serve as one measure of the supply of young labor in the economic marketplace. When an increasing number of adolescents vie for a nonincreasing supply of jobs, the cohort as a whole will experience greater stress and consequent inadequacy, depression, hopelessness, and rage. The latter may explode in the form of increased and self-directed aggression. In one test of this hypothesis, Stack (1987) confirmed this relation, but only in capitalist nations (vs. welfare capitalist nations, where full employment and redistributive measures may cushion stress).

Finally, studies of attempted suicide in youth provide little useful data regarding differences in socioeconomic status. These reports invariably are setting-specific (e.g., consecutive admissions at one urban hospital emergency room). In this example, there may be considerable class differences between the relative frequency of emergency room use for medical consequences of an attempt and the use of private physicians, from whom few data on attempters has been collected.

The When, Where, and How of Adolescent Suicide

Interpretatively, the when, where, and how of adolescent suicide tell much about the motivation and intention inherent in a young person's suicidal behavior. For example, a teenager who ingests a handful of aspirin in front of her mother following an argument is clearly different from a young man who sneaks out of his house at night, hikes into a heavily wooded park, and shoots himself in the head. Revealed in these examples are distinctly different levels of behavioral motivation, suicidal intent, and lethality of method, which place both individuals "attempting suicide" on opposite ends of the suicide behavior continuum.

The When

There have been a number of studies that have examined temporal variations in the completion of suicide (Blachly & Fairley, 1989; Lester, 1979; Zung & Green, 1974), none of which, however, have been specific to adolescence. Across all ages, suicides most often occur in the spring, during the months of March, April, and May. Monday ("Blue Monday"?) appears to be the day of the week on which most suicides occur; suicide generally occurs least often on weekends. In terms of the time of day, Hoberman and Garfinkel (1988) and Shafii and Shafii (1982) found that the majority of completed youth suicides take place in the afternoon or evening. It is important to note that some of the research in temporal trends may need to be interpreted with caution, as death certificates (from which much of the data are gleaned) may not accurately reflect when the act of suicide actually occurred. As Rich, Young, Fowler, and Rosenfeld (1984) have noted, there may be as much as a 6-day difference between the date of the act and the date recorded on the death certificate.

The Where

According to the limited data available on completers of suicide, it appears that most adolescent suicides occur in the home, where the primary means for suicide are kept. Hoberman and Garfinkel (1988) found that 70% of their sample of completers killed themselves at home and 22% killed themselves outdoors. Similar results have been reported by studies reviewing coroner's records (cf. Oregon State Health Division, 1982).

The How: Methods of Adolescent Suicide

As will be discussed more thoroughly in chapter 4, risk of suicidal behaviors is often defined as a function of psychological intention. Intention is closely linked to the choice of method to be used in an attempt or completion. In general, the more death-intentioned the behavior, the greater the potential lethality of the method selected to carry out that intention. This is especially true in the planned (vs. impulsive) use of particular methods. For example, firearms and hanging are more lethal methods than are overdose ingestions, carbon monoxide poisoning, or wrist cutting.

In addition to issues of intent and lethality, the "choice" of a method of self-destruction is strongly influenced by a number of factors working independently and in combination. As described by Berman, Litman, and Diller (1989), these include:

1. **Accessibility and readiness for use.** For example, in jail settings, where other means are limited, hanging is the predictable method of choice.

2. **Knowledge, experience, and familiarity.** Socialization to gun use and ownership, for example, is greatest in the southern United States, where gun use for suicide is also greatest.

3. **Meaning, symbolism, and cultural significance.** The preference among suicidal females (vs. suicidal males) for drug ingestion has long been theorized to be due to acculturated concerns for maintaining appearance and avoiding disfigurement. Also, drugs have long been associated with peaceful sleep, a symbolic equivalent to death.

4. **The potential suicide's state of mind.** For example, the need to communicate one's last moments of thinking appears to be associated with method selection. Peck (1986), in a study of young suicides, found that those using more passive and low-lethality methods (e.g., alcohol and barbiturates, carbon monoxide poisoning) were more likely than those using active and highly lethal methods (e.g., firearms and hanging) to leave suicide notes. Bizarre methods are used almost exclusively by psychotics.

National statistics on methods of completed suicide by youth reflect both consistency and change over time. As noted in Table

Table 3

Percentage of Total Suicides by Method for 1987

Method	All	Ages 15–19		Ages 20–24	
		Total	Male : Female	Total	Male : Female
Substances	10%	6%	1 : 7	6%	1 : 5
Gases	10%	11%	1 : 1.3	10%	1 : 1.7
Hanging	14%	19%	1.5 : 1	19%	1.8 : 1
Firearms	59%	59%	1.4 : 1	59%	1.2 : 1
Other	7%	4%	1 : 2.3	6%	1.05 : 1

Note. From *Vital Statistics of the United States* (annual mortality summaries), U.S. Department of Health and Human Services, Hyattsville, MD: National Center for Health Statistics.

3, in 1987 the overwhelming method of choice (59% of youth and of all suicides) was that of firearms and explosives. More than three fourths of these self-inflicted gunshot wound deaths were accomplished by White males. The only methods proportionately more frequently chosen by females are poisoning by ingestion of solid or liquid substances and inhalation of carbon monoxide. The drugs of choice among ingestors who complete suicide are tranquilizers and other psychotropic agents—medications prescribed either directly for the adolescent or for another family member!

As noted in Table 4, between 1967 and 1987 among 15- to 19-year-olds, there has occurred a slight increase in the relative proportion of the use of more active methods, primarily firearms and hanging, with commensurate and slight decreases in all other methods. It has been argued (Boyd, 1983) that the greater availability and accessibility of guns in the United States has had a direct, measurable, and explanatory effect on observed

Table 4

Percentage of Suicidal Methods for Ages 15–19 for Years 1967 and 1987

Method	1967	1987
Poisoning	20.5%	17%
Hanging	15.5%	19%
Firearms	55%[a]	59%[b]
Other	9%	4%
Total	100%	99%

[a]Of these, 75% were by White males.   [b]Of these, 77% were by White males. *Note.* From *Vital Statistics of the United States* (annual mortality summaries), U.S. Department of Health and Human Services, Hyattsville, MD: National Center for Health Statistics.

increases in youth suicide over these years. Recently, in a study of firearm suicides in King County, Washington, researchers Sloan, Rivara, Reay, Ferris, and Kellerman (1990) were able to document that this ready access to handguns among teenagers was associated with a somewhat higher rate of suicide.

Suicide Attempting Behaviors

As a final consideration related to the extent and nature of the problem, we must briefly address the topic of nonfatal suicidal behaviors. Whereas the prevalence and incidence of completed suicide can be established through records provided by coroners and medical examiners, attempted suicide is difficult to measure epidemiologically. Attempts requiring medical treatment may be observed and counted through emergency room admissions or cooperating physicians' offices. Those occurring in institutional settings (e.g., jails and psychiatric wards) can be tabulated. But the great majority of youth suicide attempts (about seven of every eight) are of such low lethality as to not require medical or other attention and are never reported (see Smith & Crawford, 1986). Thus data relevant to these behaviors tend to be extrapolations and estimates based mostly on self-report surveys.

In their surveys of high school students, Smith and Crawford (1986) and Harkavy-Friedman, Asnis, Boeck, and DiFiore (1987) found that approximately 60% reported having some degree of suicidal ideation and that 8–9% had made one or more suicide attempts. Estimates of the ratio of attempts to completions in adolescence stand at about 100:1 (Jacobziner, 1965), although one recent report (Garfinkel, 1989) of a more rural population of self-referred attempters places this ratio at 350:1. This discrepancy is no doubt even greater among female, particularly young female, adolescents, who rarely are found as completers and frequently account for attempters.

The *typical* youthful suicide attempter is a young female who ingests drugs at home in front of others (i.e., engages in low-lethality behavior). As will be discussed in chapter 3, however, once an attempt is made at any level of lethality, the risk for future and more serious attempts and completion increases significantly. Annual estimates of attempts range from 50,000 to 500,000 per year (Allen, 1987). One study estimated that there may be as many as 2 million young people who may have made a nonfatal attempt at some time in their young lives (Smith & Crawford, 1986). These estimates may represent only the tip of the iceberg—a sobering thought about the actual scope of the adolescent suicide phenomenon.

Conclusion

The epidemiological study of youth suicide spreads the nomothetic net across the problem of youth suicide and captures some of the defining macro variables. Its significance is in highlighting both what is happening and among whom. With the canvas so brushed, we begin to develop a picture of at-risk groups. More importantly, we can pose some beginning hypotheses, based on the social correlates of epidemiological trends. What we find common to temporal variations and differences between groups that are more versus less at risk allows us to focus our assessment and treatment efforts on those in need. We now must further attempt to understand, for example, what makes some and not other members of the class of White males at risk.

References

Allen, B. (1987). Youth suicide. *Adolescence, 22,* 271–290.

Bailey, W. B. (1903). Suicide in the United States, 1897–1901. *Yale Review, 12,* 70–89.

Berlin, I. N. (1987). Suicide among American Indian adolescents: An overview. *Suicide and Life-Threatening Behavior, 17,* 218–232.

Berman, A. L. (1979). *An analysis of suicidal and non-natural deaths among the Duck Valley Reservation Indians.* Unpublished report to the McCormick Foundation, Chicago, IL.

Berman, A. L. (1986). Notes on turning 18 (and 75): A critical look at our adolescence. *Suicide and Life-Threatening Behavior, 16,* 1–12.

Berman, A. L., Litman, R. E., & Diller, J. (1989). *Equivocal death casebook.* Unpublished manuscript, American University, Washington, DC.

Blachly, P. H., & Fairley, N. (1989). Market analysis for suicide prevention: Relationship of age to suicide on holidays, day of the week and month. *Northwest Medicine, 68,* 232–238.

Boyd, J. H. (1983). The increasing rate of suicide by firearms. *New England Journal of Medicine, 308,* 872–874.

Centers for Disease Control. (1986). *Youth suicide in the United States , 1970–1980.* Atlanta, GA: Author.

Diekstra, R. F. W. (1985). Suicide and suicide attempts in the European Economic Community: An analysis of trends, with special emphasis upon trends among the young. *Suicide and Life-Threatening Behavior, 15,* 27–42.

Diekstra, R. F. W. (1989). Suicidal behavior in adolescents and young adults: An international picture. *Crisis, 10,* 16–35.

Dublin, L. I., & Bunzel, B. (1933). *To be or not to be: A study of suicide.* New York: Smith & Haas.

Easterlin, R. (1978). What will 1984 be like? Socioeconomic implications of recent twists in age structure. *Demography, 15,* 397–432.

Easterlin, R. (1980). *Birth and fortune.* New York: Basic Books.

Friedman, P. (Ed.). (1967). *On suicide: With particular reference to suicide among young students.* New York: International Universities Press.

Garfinkel, B. D. (1989, October). *Depression and suicide among adolescents.* Paper presented at Treatment of Adolescents with Alcohol, Drug Abuse, and Mental Health Problems Conference, Alcohol, Drug Abuse, and Mental Health Administration, Arlington, VA.

Harkavy-Friedman, J., Asnis, G., Boeck, M., & DiFiore, J. (1987). Prevalence of specific suicidal behaviors in a high school sample. *American Journal of Psychiatry, 144,* 1203–1206.

Hoberman, H. M., & Garfinkel, B. D. (1988). Completed suicide in children and adolescents. *Journal of the American Academy of Child and Adolescent Psychiatry, 27,* 689–695.

Holinger, P. C. (1979). Violent death among the young: Recent trends in suicide, homicide, and accident. *American Journal of Psychiatry, 142,* 1144–1147.

Holinger, P. C., & Offer, D. (1981). Perspectives on suicide in adolescence. *Research in Community and Mental Health, 2,* 139–157.

Holinger, P. C., & Offer, D. (1982). Prediction of adolescent suicide: A population model. *American Journal of Psychiatry, 139,* 302–307.

Holinger, P. C., Offer, D., & Zola, M. A. (1988). A prediction model of suicide among youth. *Journal of Nervous and Mental Disease, 176,* 275–279.

Jacobziner, H. (1965). Attempted suicide in adolescence. *Journal of the American Medical Association, 10,* 22–36.

Jobes, D. A., & Berman, A. L. (1984). *Response biases and the impact of psychological autopsies on medical examiners' determination of mode of death.* Paper presented at the annual meeting of the American Association of Suicidology, Anchorage, AK.

Jobes, D. A., Berman, A. L., & Josselson, A. R. (1987). Improving the validity and reliability of medical–legal certifications of suicide. *Suicide and Life-Threatening Behavior, 17,* 310–325.

Klerman, G. L. (1987). Clinical epidemiology of suicide. *Journal of Clinical Psychiatry, 48,* 33–38.

Lester, D. (1979). Temporal variation in suicide and homicide. *American Journal of Epidemiology, 109,* 517–520.

Lester, D. (1988). Youth suicide: A cross-cultural perspective. *Adolescence, 23,* 955–958.

Maris, R. (1981). *Pathways to suicide.* Baltimore, MD: The Johns Hopkins University Press.

McIntosh, J. L. (1989, October). *Suicide data page: 1987* (Available from the American Association of Suicidology, Denver, CO.)

Miner, J. R. (1922). Suicide and its relation to climatic and other factors. *American Journal of Hygiene Monographs* (Series No. 2).

National Center for Health Statistics. (1989). *Monthly vital statistics report* (Vol. 37, no. 13). Hyattsville, MD: U.S. Public Health Service.

Nelson, F. L., Farberow, N. L., & MacKinnon, D. R. (1978). The certification of suicide in eleven western states. *Suicide and Life-Threatening Behavior, 8,* 75–88.

Newman, S. C., & Dyck, R. J. (1988, May). *Age, period, cohort analyses of suicide rates.* Paper presented at the annual meeting of the American Association of Suicidology, San Francisco, CA.

O'Carroll, P. (1989). A consideration of the validity and reliability of suicide mortality data. *Suicide and Life-Threatening Behavior, 19,* 1–16.

Oregon State Health Division, Center for Health Statistics. (1982). *Teenage suicide in Oregon,* Portland, OR: Author.

Peck, D. L. (1986). Completed suicides: Correlates of choice of method. *Omega, 16,* 309–323.

Pescosolido, B. A., & Mendelsohn, R. (1986). Social causation or social construction of suicide? An investigation into the social organization of official rates. *American Sociological Review, 51,* 80–101.

Rich, C. L., Young, D., Fowler, R. C., & Rosenfeld, S. K. S. (1984). *The difference between data of suicide act and recorded death certificate date in 204 consecutive suicides.* Paper presented at the annual meeting of the American Association of Suicidology, Anchorage, AK.

Robins, L. N., & Kulbok, P. A. (1988). Epidemiological studies in suicide. *Psychiatric Annals, 18,* 619–627.

Rosenberg, M. L., Smith, J. C., Davidson, L. E., & Conn, J. M. (1987). The emergence of youth suicide: An epidemiologic analysis and public health perspective. *Annual Review of Public Health, 8,* 417–440.

Sainsbury, P., & Jenkins, J. S. (1982). The accuracy of officially reported suicide statistics for purposes of epidemiological research. *Journal of Epidemiological and Community Health, 36,* 43–48.

Seiden, R. H. (1983). Death in the West: A spatial analysis of the youthful suicide rate. *Western Journal of Medicine, 139,* 783–795.

Shaffer, D. (1988). The epidemiology of teen suicide: An examination of risk factors. *Journal of Clinical Psychiatry, 49* (Suppl. 9), 36–41.

Shafii, M., & Shafii, S. L. (1982). Self destructive, suicidal behavior, and completed suicide. In M. Shafii & S. L. Shafii (Eds.), *Pathways of human development: Normal growth and emotional disorders in infancy, childhood and adolescence* (pp. 164–180). New York: Thieme-Stratton.

Sloan, J. H., Rivara, F. P., Reay, D. T., Ferris, J. A., & Kellerman, A. L. (1990). Firearm regulations and rates of suicide: A comparison of two metropolitan areas. *New England Journal of Medicine, 322* (6), 369–373.

Smith, K., & Crawford, S. (1986). Suicidal behavior among normal high school students. *Suicide and Life-Threatening Behavior, 16,* 313–325.

Stack, S. (1987, May). *The impact of relative cohort size on national suicide trends, 1950–1980: A comparative analysis.* Paper presented at the annual meeting of the American Association of Suicidology, San Francisco, CA.

Toolan, J. (1975). Suicide in children and adolescents. *American Journal of Psychotherapy, 29,* 339–344.

Wasserman, I. M. (1987). Cohort, age, and period effects in the analysis of U.S. suicide patterns: 1933–1978. *Suicide and Life-Threatening Behavior, 17,* 179–193.

Working Group on the Classification and Reporting of Suicide (1984). *Minutes of the Las Vegas meeting.* Atlanta, GA: Centers for Disease Control.

Zung, W. K. W., & Green, R. L. (1974). Seasonal variation of suicide and depression. *Archives General Psychiatry, 30,* 89–91.

2

The Theoretical Context

Intuitive Models

To talk of adolescence and of adolescents nomothetically blurs the uniqueness of every teenager in a developmental period invariably described as "caught between" childhood and adulthood. To talk of these individuals idiographically makes all the more difficult our task of arriving at general principles and universal variables. Because clinicians are often inclined to focus on the individual, it is perhaps best to begin our understanding with an idiographic approach. To that end, let us briefly introduce two adolescents.

Bill Carlson is 17, a senior in high school. A good student, hard-working, some would say "driven," Bill has achieved well and is hoping to go to either Harvard or Stanford next year. He also is hopeful that his college career will lead him to medical school and a career as a surgeon like his father.

Bill is a tall, handsome boy, attractive to girls but surprisingly shy among them. When he socializes, he prefers to hang out in groups rather than date; in these groups, he is likely to be seen deep in introspective discussions with one girl or another.

Introspection has no place on the school football team, where this past season Bill led all receivers in pass catches. Nor does he appear at all the quiet type in his new sports car, a gift from his parents on his 17th birthday. The elder of two sons, Bill has always been close to his parents, and a "good son." Perhaps for these reasons, he has been increasingly preoccupied as verbalized threats of separation and divorce become common in his parents' increasingly frequent conflicts. These worries he has kept largely to himself.

Jenny Bailes is 15, a sophomore at a large urban high school. Attractive, but about 20 pounds overweight, Jenny is mostly a loner, that is, with two exceptions. Since the beginning of this school year, she has had a relationship with a blind classmate for whom she takes notes and has helped around school. And she has just broken up with her first boyfriend, a ninth-grader who took her out on a date after weeks of awkward telephone calls.

Jenny is an average student, taking clerical subjects with hopes of getting a job as a clerk-typist at one of the insurance companies downtown upon graduation from high school. She is the fourth of seven children. Her mother is a homemaker and her father a master carpenter.

Bill and Jenny could be two kids from Anytown, U.S.A. One average, the other a star, each is prototypical, perhaps, of adolescents we have known; neither is prototypical of all adolescents. Each can be described in terms of strengths and weaknesses; each triggers impressions, associations, and value judgments within us as observers.

But Bill and Jenny are not typical adolescents. Bill's body was brought to the local medical examiner's office last week. He put his father's .22 caliber handgun to his head and ended his life in an instant. And Jenny was brought by her mother to the local hospital emergency room after she was found bleeding from both forearms, having slashed them with a razor blade.

Why? What could possibly drive these two youths to suicidal action? We might hypothesize about Bill's world being about to undergo great change, about the stress of graduating and starting to prove himself anew among a much higher level of competitors, about his lack of preparedness to deal with any threat to success or status, about his fears of losing his parents and the protection and security of a predictable family unit. We might pose the idea that his family had not taught him to deal well with loss or change, that he was too enmeshed, too close, too identified. We might wonder about his rigidity and his need to be perfect; no doubt, he even accomplished his suicide with characteristic perfection!

In contrast, it is tempting to construe Jenny's attempt as a "cry for help," a dramatic and powerful statement to her interpersonal surround that she wanted to be attended to and noticed. She was a lost child, in the middle of several siblings, not standing out, keeping her distance from others, invisible even to the one peer she had befriended. Maybe she fantasized about her recent relationship with her first boyfriend in Cinderella-like terms, only to have the dream dashed when the glass slipper fell and broke.

Then, again, we might tell you that none of the above happened, that Bill and Jenny continue on pace toward their chosen futures, each alive and thriving in his or her own way. At once, figure and ground shift. What "explained" the suicide of one now recedes into background noise to an otherwise successful career. What gave ominous meaning to the other's attempt now simply describes ongoing life challenges in an otherwise average teen's struggle toward adulthood.

In great measure, this is how we learn about suicide and suicidal behaviors. Suicide is rarely studied prospectively. Our theories, our hypotheses, our assumptions are generally built upon retrospective analyses of behaviors and character studies. The potential for uncorrectable distortion is great. Dead bodies only indirectly answer our question, "Why?" Surviving family members, friends, and others have reason for denial and selective attention in reporting to us their impressions of the decedent. Suicide notes, where available, may be misleading (Leenaars, 1988).

Even those who survive an attempt and are therefore available to give us answers do not do so in ways we believe. Hawton (1987) has reported results of interviews with hospitalized overdose patients and documented the reasons they gave for their attempts. When the same questions were posed to these patients' psychiatrists, quite different motivations were ascribed to their patients' attempts.

The reasons for these discordant views are manifold. They involve our implicit assumptions about human behavior, some predetermined thinking about suicide, our attempts to apply the nomothetic theory to the idiographic case, sometimes requiring us to shift figure and ground for our convenience. As with the blind men describing the elephant according to the shape of the trunk versus the ear versus the body, so it is that what we come to believe about suicide, what theories we construct to give meaning to "the ultimate philosophical problem" (Sartre, 1956), and how we assess and treat those who remain alive, begin with the data available to us. An understanding of this context is important to our grasp of the numerous theories of suicidal behavior from which we might choose to guide our clinical work.

Overview of Theories

Some of the most distinguished practitioners, researchers, theoreticians, and scholars in the fields of psychology, psychiatry, sociology, and biology have contributed a wide range of theories to explain suicidal behavior. Although a number of attempts have been made to develop viable and heuristic theories of suicidal behaviors, conceptually adequate and applicable theories in the field of suicidology have remained elusive. Only limited progress has been made toward the goal of constructing a comprehensive theory of life-threatening behavior (see discussions by Berman, 1986a; Comstock, 1979; Litman & Tabachnick, 1968; Tabachnick, 1971). Accordingly, most of the major theories in the suicide literature discretely describe different aspects of suicidal behaviors using the characteristic language and construct domains of a particular theoretical orientation or discipline.

The major theories of suicide may be conceptually grouped under the following headings: (a) sociological theories, (b) psychological theories, and (c) biological theories. Although many of the major theories were not specifically constructed to explain youthful suicide per se, they are nevertheless usually applicable to young people. However, some theories have been developed with youth suicide as a particular focus and will be mentioned under the appropriate conceptual headings.

Sociological Theories of Suicide

Case Illustrations

> The partially decomposed body of Frank Johnson, a 19-year-old male, was found hanging by a noose in a condemned apartment building. Residents of the neighborhood reported that Frank, a high school drop-out, was often seen loitering in the area, but kept to himself and had not been seen of late. There were no known family or friends to contact for funeral arrangements.

> Steve Jenkins was a 20-year-old part-time college student and full-time political activist. At the end of a political rally protesting apartheid in South Africa, Steve poured gasoline over himself and lit himself on fire as a "protest against racism throughout the world." Steve died as a result of first- and second-degree burns to his body.

> Kathy Thomas, a 15-year-old high school freshman, took a fatal overdose of barbiturates and was found in her bed after her mother noticed she had not gotten up for school. Kathy had been very depressed about breaking up with her boyfriend of two years. The night of her death she had seen him with another girl at a party. A bitter argument ensued in which she threatened to kill herself if he refused to get back together with her.

> Bill Carpenter, a 17-year-old juvenile delinquent, was found hanging in his room at the detention center after being arrested for a drunk driving incident in which he hit and killed three pedestrians. This arrest followed a series of previous arrests for armed robbery, assault, and possession of drugs. Hours before his death, a peer told Bill that he would probably be tried as an adult and receive a stiff prison sentence.

Each of the preceding four cases of suicide could be theoretically explained and conceptually understood in terms of Emile Durkheim's sociological theory of suicide. Durkheim's classic work *Suicide: A Study in Sociology* (1897/1951) established a model of sociological study of suicide which has led to an extensive line of research and subsequent theory construction. He argued that suicide results from society's strength or weakness of control over the individual. Durkheim identified four basic types of suicide that reflect the individual's relationship to society: egoistic, altruistic, anomic, and fatalistic.

Frank Johnson's death is an example of an *egoistic suicide*, which is thought to stem from an individual's lack of integration into society. Largely left to themselves, victims of egoistic suicide are neither connected with, nor dependent on, their community. Steve Jenkins's self-immolation is an example of an *altruistic suicide*. In altruistic suicide, the individual is overly integrated into a group so that he or she feels no sacrifice is too great for the larger group. Japanese kamikaze pilots in World War II or Islamic fundamentalists who kill themselves in the act of attacking their enemy are clear examples of altruistic suicide. Kathy Thomas's suicide would be conceptualized by Durkheim as an *anomic suicide*. The victim of anomic suicide is not capable of dealing with a crisis in a rational manner and chooses suicide as the solution to a problem. Anomic suicide occurs when the individual's accustomed relationship with society is suddenly and shockingly altered. Finally, Bill Carpenter's death is an example of a *fatalistic suicide*. Fatalistic suicides are thought to be caused by excessive societal regulation that fundamentally restricts an individual's freedom. Victims of fatalistic suicide feel that they have no viable future.

Many scholars have followed the sociological study of suicide established by Durkheim. Some have employed Durkheim's research methodology (Cavan, 1926; Henry & Short, 1954; Sainsbury, 1955; Schmid, 1928), while others have developed and extended his theoretical tradition (Douglas, 1967; Gibbs & Martin, 1964). One notable contribution is Maris's (1981) notion of "suicidal careers." Maris's empirically based theory moves away from a static, structural focus and emphasizes a dynamic, developmental model of suicide. By focusing on a multivariate analysis of a large sample of suicide completers in developing this model, Maris was able to simultaneously develop and test his primary thesis that the suicide's "career," or life history, establishes a vulnerability to suicide. Additionally, Maris's work moved traditional sociological research and theory, limited in its exclusive emphasis on societal influences, toward a broad integration with more psychological foci.

Social–psychological approaches. In order to address some of the limitations of purely sociological approaches, some recent theories attempt to synthesize both inter- and intrapersonal variables that may bear on suicidal behaviors. For example, Petzel and Riddle (1981), in an extensive review of the literature, conceptualize adolescent suicide as a social and psychological phenomenon. These authors assert that adolescent suicide is related to interactions of multiple social (e.g., family conflict, school adjustment, and social relationships) and cognitively based psychological (e.g., conceptions of death, hopelessness, intention, and motivation) factors.

Hendin's (1987) theory of youth suicide attempts to explain the phenomenon from both epidemiological and psychodynamic perspectives. Central to Hendin's perspective are trends in the demographic occurrence of youthful suicide, the relation of violence to suicide, and the impact of family influences on youth who become preoccupied with death and suicide. Hendin asserts that integrative social and psychological conceptualizations of youthful suicide provide a framework for understanding the personal meaning of life and death (and related behaviors that exist within a particular culture or subculture).

David Lester (1988a, 1988b) has proposed a social–psychological perspective that attempts to explain youthful suicidal behaviors as a function of quality of life. Lester (1984) has shown that nations with a higher quality of life have higher suicide rates, a finding that he has linked to Henry and Short's (1954) theory of homicide and suicide. These authors have asserted that when people have a clear external source of blame for their misfortune, they are more likely to be angry and assaultive, and thereby less depressed and suicidal. However, although Lester has observed the quality of life effect in other populations, he has not been able to corroborate the effect within youthful samples to a statistically significant degree (Lester, 1988a).

In a different vein, Lester (1987) has also attempted to explain youthful suicides in relation to the concept of social subcultures. Building on a case presentation, Lester describes various defining elements of a "teenage suicidal subculture." In this particular case example, the subculture was made up of five teenagers

with heavy substance abuse problems, poor parental relationships, poor self-image, shyness and dependency on peers, loss
of lovers, and a deep involvement in heavy metal rock music
and related fantasies. Lester asserts that this self-contained group
generated a great deal of suicidal preoccupation and acting out
in their student peers. Lester thus argues that this smaller group
"tapped into a suicidal vein among other students," revealing
the existence of a "peer culture" that transcends the specific
peer group. Accordingly, what we know as the natural experimentation and competition of adolescents within a peer group
or culture that becomes a suicidal subculture through social
shaping may inevitably lead young people to perform overt
suicidal acts.

Psychological Theories of Suicide

Case Illustration

> Daniel, an 18-year-old college freshman, was the eldest of
> three children. Throughout his childhood, Daniel was phys-
> ically beaten on a regular basis by his alcoholic father. Daniel
> saw himself as the protector of his younger siblings and was
> the only child his father abused. The abuse was perhaps
> related to his father's jealousy of the extremely close rela-
> tionship Daniel had with his mother, whom Daniel idealized
> as a saint. At the age of 13, Daniel chose to leave with his
> divorcing mother while his two siblings stayed in the family
> home with his father. Daniel and his mother barely scraped
> by through the subsequent years as his mother worked as a
> secretary. The family was bitterly divided and his father re-
> fused to pay his mother any alimony. Daniel's scholastic
> abilities earned him an academic scholarship at a local uni-
> versity. In the summer prior to his freshman year, Daniel's
> mother was diagnosed as having inoperable stomach cancer,
> from which she died a month prior to the start of school.
> Daniel was devastated, but was determined to attend college
> anyway to fulfill his mother's dream. His Thanksgiving visit
> to his father's home was a disaster. Daniel returned to school
> a day early. On the night of his return, Daniel called his
> father and during an argument on the phone, shot himself

in the head with a revolver he had apparently taken from his father's home. Daniel's last words to his father prior to the fatal gunshot were "I hate me and I hate you—it's time for the big payback, Dad. . . ."

The case of Daniel may be best explained by one of the various psychological theories of suicide. In contrast to the purely societal influences emphasized by sociologically oriented theories, psychological theories of suicide emphasize intrapsychic processes as well cognitive, emotional, and personality variables. The various psychological theories of suicide reflect perspectives from virtually all the major theoretical orientations in the field (e.g., psychoanalytically oriented, cognitive–behavioral, and family systems theories).

Psychoanalytically oriented theory. As with many theoretical considerations in psychology, theorizing on the psychological nature of suicide must fundamentally begin with the thoughts of Sigmund Freud. Although Freud never wrote a paper specifically about suicide, he did see a number of suicidal patients and indirectly provided some important perspectives on the topic. Freud's (1917) classic work "Mourning and Melancholia" outlines the psychological mechanisms involved in turning hostility against the self, which explains the self-reproach and suicidal ideation often seen in melancholic depressions. As summarized by Shneidman (1980), the central Freudian position on suicide was that it represents "murder in the 180th degree." Since people identify with and internalize the objects of their love with ambivalence, they may direct their own aggressive impulses against the internalized love-object whom they both love and hate.

While this concept of "retroflexed rage" was primary to Freud's considerations of suicide, Tabachnick (1971) notes that his construct of the death instinct is also implicated. As described in "Beyond the Pleasure Principle" (Freud, 1920), the death instinct represents a primary instinctual force in all living matter to return to a state of complete inertia. However, the force of the life instincts as well as societal forces and values generally interfere, albeit temporarily, with the expression of the death instinct. As it relates to suicide, the death instinct (through the superego) was seen to have the capacity to drive the ego into death (Tabachnick, 1971).

In contrast to Freud's indirect and largely contextual discussions of suicide, Karl Menninger considered suicide in more direct and comprehensive fashion. Menninger's psychoanalytic theory of suicide represents an important elaboration and extension of some of Freud's ideas, which he combined with his own seminal thoughts on the topic. Menninger's (1938) classic text *Man Against Himself* represents one of the most important, eloquent, and comprehensive theoretical considerations of suicide to date. Through discussion and case example, Menninger delineates analytic perspectives on hostility and the death instinct. Most notably, Menninger explains the psychodynamics of hostility and suicide in relationship to (a) the wish to kill, (b) the wish to be killed, and (c) the wish to die. Each of these three "wishes" is present in every suicide, Menninger argued, with one predominating in each. As is evident in Daniel's suicide, his wish to punish his father (the wish to kill) ultimately dominated, although both other motivations, the wish to die (to reunite with mother) and to be killed (self-punishment—"I hate me") are in evidence.

Menninger further elaborated the role of the death instinct through his examination of the construct as it relates to physical illnesses. Menninger also theoretically defined different forms of suicidal expression contributing to a broader conceptualization of suicidal behaviors. One form of expression described by Menninger is "chronic suicide" in which long-term life-threatening and indirect self-destructive behavior (e.g., chronic substance abuse) reveals a latent suicide death wish. Similarly, "focal suicide" reveals self-destructive impulses through focused self-destructive acts (e.g., nonlethal cutting behaviors; see chapter 3).

As discussed by Shneidman (1980), Gregory Zilboorg further refined Menninger's hypothesis, asserting that every case of suicide contains strong unconscious hostility combined with an unusual lack of capacity to love others. Zilboorg (1936) also considered narcissistic aspects of suicide, conceptualizing suicide as a primitive act in which one attempts to achieve a fantasied immortality. Asserting the role of a broken home in suicide proneness reflects both internal and external etiological influences, Zilboorg was one of the first theorists to extend conceptualizations of suicide from purely intrapsychic dynamics to the external world.

A number of the neoanalytic theorists considered both inter- and intrapsychic aspects of suicide. Adler (1958) viewed suicide as an interpersonal act: Due to insufficient social interest, a suicidal individual hurts others by inflicting injury upon himself or herself. Sullivan similarly emphasized the interactive aspects of suicide, asserting that suicide is usually an interpersonally destructive activity that reflects a hateful and hostile type of integration with others (Green, 1961). Karen Horney argued that most suicides represent a failure in social as well as individual growth, fundamentally reflecting a failure in the development of the self (De Rosis, 1961). In the Jungian tradition, Wahl (1957) hypothesized that suicide represents a desire for rebirth or resurrection to a new and better life. Suicide is conceptualized as a magical and omnipotent act of regression towards a rebirth of a new self (refer to Jung, 1959). Some suicide notes are explicit in these types of references, such as that of a 13-year-old male who wrote, "Mom and Dad, I'm going to a new life. . . . I always wanted a second chance."

Other dynamically oriented theorists have offered additional perspectives to explain the nature of suicidal behavior. Some have conceptualized suicide as a means of resolution to problems of separation and individuation (Wade, 1987). As discussed by Jan-Tausch (1963), aggressive acts and suicide attempts can lead to temporary relief of painful affect through the experience of the body as a separate self from an overenmeshed primary object relation. Wade's (1987) study of adolescent girls has indicated that relief from abandonment depression and feelings of separateness is achieved by using suicide as means for regression to the safety of an earlier symbiotic state. Thus suicide may represent a resolution of separation–individuation from parental objects, which reestablishes narcissistic equilibrium. From a slightly different perspective, Ammon (1974) asserts that suicidal acting out may be used as a mechanism to defend against feelings of separateness and depression brought on by abandonment.

Leonard (1967) has constructed a theory of suicide that similarly emphasizes separation and individuation issues of the first years of life. Inadequate resolution of this phase of development is thought to lead to a lack of separate identity, inadequate impulse control, and rigidity. Leonard theorized that these three factors may increase the individual's vulnerability to suicide later in life under certain precipitating stresses.

More recently, Smith (1985) has proposed the notion of "ego vulnerabilities" as a means of understanding suicidal behavior. Central to this perspective is the contention that death is the ego's ultimate tool of denial, in that suicide is an act that both preserves (or allows) the realization of the preferred self–other image while negating (attacking) the frustrating and devaluing object. In his reflections of psychoanalytic aspects of suicide, Rangell (1988) highlights the motives for suicide, conscious versus unconscious intention and the role of agression, and suicide as a "path to glory."

Not surprisingly, psychoanalytic constructs have been widely applied to varied and specific aspects of suicidal behavior, from implications in suicide among the elderly (Achte, 1988) to clinical risk assessment of suicide (Maltsberger, 1986, 1988) to predictive models of suicidal behavior (Leenaars & Balance, 1984). Clearly the psychoanalytic tradition, both past and present, has greatly contributed to suicide theory building and our understanding of the phenomenon.

Developmental theory. Much of the theorizing of psychoanalytically oriented scholars has been used to generate developmental perspectives that are relevant to adolescent suicidal behaviors. These theories tend to emphasize developmental issues that are unique to adolescence, such as simultaneous and competing needs inherent to this stage of life. As Berman (1984) notes, the adolescent is developmentally caught between two worlds: Needs for autonomy and independence paradoxically conflict with dependency needs and a desire to be a part of the family. Often adolescent developmental issues are interactive with the family system, which may foster a shared family regression. Ultimately, a shared family regression may lead to feelings of abandonment, rage, or both which may in turn lead to self-destructive acting out (Shapiro & Freedman, 1987).

In a broader context, Emery (1983) had discussed a developmental perspective that emphasizes identity formation through psychosocial development and epigenetic maturational processes unique to adolescence and the individual. To more fully understand the nature of adolescent depression and suicide, Emery emphasizes the importance of examining a variety of developmental dimensions. Although the unfolding of the adolescent's identity within the social context may be central (cf. Erikson, 1959), Emery asserts that cognitive, learning, and moral development must be considered as well. As the youth passes through the developmental stage of adolescence, a variety of complex psychological functions are involved in what Emery refers to as the "progression/regression ratio." Building on the work of Erikson (1959) and Bowlby (1973) Emery describes various phases in the development of adolescent identity that may include behaviors that reflect adolescent protest, despair, and detachment. Critically, adolescent attempts to struggle through the various developmental phases inherent in identity formation may lead to depressive symptomatology or suicidal behaviors.

Family systems theory. A related line of theorizing arises from the family systems perspective (Minuchin, 1974). Joseph Richman (1984, 1986) is perhaps the most noted author of the family systems approach to suicide and its application to family therapy treatment of suicidal individuals. The essence of this perspective (Richman, 1986) is that disturbances in the family structure, including role conflicts and blurring of role boundaries, dysfunctional alliances across boundaries, secretiveness and failures of communication, and rigidity with inability to accept change or tolerate crisis, have been thought to promote suicidal acting out within the family system. In their discussion of this approach, Trautman and Shaffer (1984) point out a "chicken or egg" dilemma inherent in family theory in that it is unclear whether the dysfunctional family system produces suicidal behavior or whether individual factors lead to suicidal behavior and a dysfunctional family.

Also implicated in family theories is the potential influence of parental psychopathology and the influence of conscious and unconscious wishes by the parent to "kill off" the child, which may lead to the child's suicidal acting out (Weissman, Paykel, & Klerman, 1972). Relevant to this perspective is Sabbath's (1969) notion of the "expendable child" who is driven to self-destruction by a pathogenic family system. In their review of family dynamics of adolescent suicide, Shapiro and Freedman (1987) assert that adolescent suicidal behavior may be seen as a consequence of ego deficits or faulty internalizations, but emphasize the importance of the youth's response to certain unconscious dynamics within the family system.

Behavioral and cognitive theory. A number of theorists have addressed the topic of suicide from behavioral (learning) and cognitive perspectives. From a purely behavioral perspective, Ferster (1973) provides a provocative discussion of the incidence of depression and associated suicidal behaviors in relation to environmental reinforcement contingencies. Frederick and Resnick (1971) applied the principles of learning theory to describe how suicidal behaviors are learned. These authors argued that a variety of stimulus–response relations account for the production of suicidal behaviors, and, therefore, behavior therapy approaches can be effectively used to treat suicidal individuals.

From the perspective of cognitive theory, Aaron Beck and his colleagues (Rush & Beck, 1978) have emphasized the role of cognitive errors and distorted thinking in suicidal behaviors. Beck's concept of the "cognitive triad" (negative thoughts about oneself, the future, and others) is central to the cognitive theory of suicide. Within the cognitive perspective, hopelessness has been found to be perhaps the single most relevant clinical variable implicated in suicidal behavior. Beyond theorizing, empirical investigation has indeed confirmed the importance of hopelessness as an integral feature of suicide (Beck, Brown, & Steer, 1989). Shneidman (1980, 1985) and Neuringer (1964) have contributed further elaborations of cognitive aspects of suicide in their discussions of cognitive constriction, ambivalence, rigidity, and dichotomous thinking. Again, while no comprehensive theory is offered by any one theorist, the importance of learning and cognitive theoretical considerations is clear.

Integrative psychological theory. Some psychological theories have been developed that integrate a range of perspectives and potential influences on suicidal behavior. Farber (1968), for example, conceptualizes suicide as a disease of hope in which social influences (subcultural tolerance for suicide, availability of succorance, demands for interpersonal giving, and demands for exercising competence) are interactive with psychological influence (e.g., future time perspective). Farber contends that the interrelation of perceptual, social, interpersonal, psychological, and cultural variables define the hopelessness that accounts for suicide.

Similarly, and more recently, Mack (1986) has proposed an "architectural model" of adolescent suicide. This varied and broadly comprehensive model is comprised of the following elements: the macrolevel sociopolitical context; genetic–biological vulnerability; early developmental influences; personality organization and self-esteem regulation; past and current object relationships; evidences of depression and psychopathology; the ontogeny of the relationship to death; and contemporary situation and circumstances at the time of the clinical assessment.

Baechler (1975) has proposed a "strategic theory" of suicide. As a function of genetics and learning, Baechler proposes, individuals develop stable tendencies to react in specific ways to specific situations. He argues that there are basically five ways (strategies) available to individuals to resolve any existential problem: rational (changing the conditions of the problem; e.g., compromising one's aspirations in light of blocked goals); irrational (constructing a private reality); to refuse to play, to quit (suicide); not playing by the rules (to cheat, arrive at an unlawful solution); or annihilation (to destroy the source of the problem and the self as in murder–suicide.) Suicidal solutions are likely to occur under only three conditions: when possible rational solutions are narrowed, when the number and severity of problems increase beyond capacity to "stand it," and when one's vital capacity is diminished.

From a somewhat different perspective, Edwin Shneidman has developed a novel theoretical model based on 10 common psychological variables associated with suicidal death (Shneid-

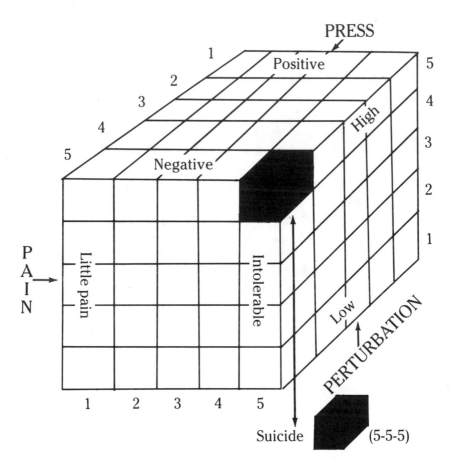

Figure 3   A theoretical cubic model of suicide. From "A Psychological Approach to Suicide" by E. S. Shneidman. In *Cataclysms, Crises, and Catastrophes: Psychology in Action*, edited by G. R. VandenBos and B. K. Bryant, 1987, Washington, DC: American Psychological Association. Copyright 1987 by the American Psychological Association. Reprinted by permission.

man, 1985). Shneidman (1988) posits that the etiology of suicide can be conceptually understood schematically in terms of a suicidal cube. The three surfaces of the cube are respectively labeled "pain," "perturbation," and "press" (see Figure 3).

Pain is described as the subjective experience of unbearable psychological pain (idiosyncratically defined by the individual) and can range from 1 (*little pain*) to 5 (*intolerable pain*). Shneidman (1985) has described perturbation as the individual's general state of emotional upset—a key psychological feature necessary for a lethal suicide attempt to occur. Perturbation is reflected in poor impulse control, agitation, and propensity for precipitous action. With regard to the schematic model, perturbation can range from 1 (*low*—mild upset) to 5 (*high*—extreme agitation and emotional upset). Finally, press is seen as everything that is done to an individual that effects an individual's response to virtually anything. As discussed by Shneidman's mentor, Henry Murray (1938), presses are those pressures and influences that affect an individual's feelings, thoughts, and behaviors. From an integrative perspective, interpersonal and societal influences on the individual could be conceptualized as presses. In terms of the schematic suicidal cube model, presses range, as well, from 1 (*positive*) to 5 (*negative*).

According to Shneidman's model, the "suicidal cubelet" (the 5-5-5 blackened portion of the cube) represents the maximum combination of pain, perturbation, and press—the most dangerous and acute suicidal risk. Shneidman asserts that no one commits suicide in a nonsuicidal combination of these three interactive components. Shneidman further asserts the uniquely psychological nature of suicide as motivated by *psychological pain*, in turn initiated and maintained by blocked *psychological needs*. This theoretical model thus defines suicide as a death fundamentally caused by a synthesis of emotional energy (upset), acute subjective intrapsychic pain, and overwhelming external pressures.

Biological Theories

In more recent years there has been a proliferation of research investigating biological aspects of suicide. Most of this research has examined a range of specific biological correlates of suicide, such as hormonal or neurotransmitter imbalances.

The most promising line of brain biochemistry research has involved neurotransmitter monoamine metabolites, particularly the serotonin metabolite 5-hydroxyindoleacetic acid (5-HIAA), and observed correlations with suicidal behavior. Noting that antidepressant treatment enhances serotonin transmission, early lines of experimental inquiry focused on the question, is serotonin transmission disordered in depression? (Asberg, 1990). Studies of depressed patients indicated a bimodal distribution of 5-HIAA in their lumbar cerebrospinal fluid (CSF), in contrast to a normal distribution in nondepressed patients. Suicidal patients, especially completers who died using violent methods, were noted to aggregate among those with low CSF-5-HIAA. Depressed (unipolar) suicide attempters had 5-HIAA concentrations 25% lower than those of controls. Similar findings have been reported among suicide-attempting nondepressed patients—those with personality disorders (e.g., criminal offenders) and schizophrenia (Asberg, 1989, 1990).

The more violent character of the suicide behavior noted among low 5-HIAA patients has given rise to the suggested relation between 5-HIAA and the control of aggressive and violent impulses and to the hypothesis that there is a biological vulnerability to suicide. To date, however, support for this hypothesis has been inconclusive. Additionally, there are no published reports of research with adolescent patient–subjects.

In a related but different vein, however, some theoretical work in the sociobiology of suicide has been developed (deCatanzaro, 1981, 1984, 1986). Focusing on the totality of biological evolution of the species, sociobiological theory emphasizes a macroscopic examination of suicide as it relates to self-preservation and natural selection within and across the species. In this theory suicide is seen as the antithesis of self-preservation. In conditions in which our "inclusive fitness," that is, the welfare of one's own genes or our reproductive potential is impeded, suicide is more likely to occur. Higher rates of suicide among terminally ill, elderly, divorced, widowed, and never-married (young) populations, for example, bolster the sociobiological position. While admittedly the sociobiological theory of suicide requires further research and development, deCatanzaro (1986) argues that an adequate general theory of suicide must consider both traditional microanalyses as well as the macrolevel of analysis inherent in the sociobiological perspective.

Summary of Suicide Theories

We have only briefly highlighted a sample of the major theoretical considerations loosely organized under the conceptual headings of sociological, psychological, and biological theories. Despite the range of perspectives that have been developed over a fairly short period of time, theory building in suicidology nevertheless remains an open frontier ready for further exploration and development. Having considered the theories relevant and specific to suicide, it is now important to conceptualize these perspectives within the larger context of adolescent development itself in order to better understand who suicidal adolescents are and who they are not.

The Developmental Context

Children are not like us. They are beings apart: impenetrable, unapproachable. They inhabit not our world but a world we have lost and can never recover. We do not remember childhood—we imagine it. We search for it, in vain, through layers of obscuring dust, and recover some bedraggled shreds of what we think it was. And all the while the inhabitants of this world are among us, like Aborigines, like Minoans, people from elsewhere safe in their own time-capsule. (Lively, 1987, pp. 42–43)

Overview

Rebellion, angst, defiance, and downright orneriness are much of what we commonly associate with adolescence. Indeed, these associations have in many ways become a fundamental part of our cultural folklore and wisdom about the adolescent phase of development. Difficult, self-absorbed, indifferent, and exclusively peer-oriented teenagers are standard fare for television situation comedies and marketing strategists. A parent's roll of the eyes on a TV situation comedy in response to a "typically adolescent" behavior is always good for a knowing laugh. Detergent companies court parent–consumers with commercials depicting a grateful mother receiving a compliment from her self-absorbed, telephone-talking, boy-crazy teenage daughter, who has just noticed how white and clean-smelling her sweatshirt is.

Adolescence is so commonly portrayed as a difficult, if not a dark and angry developmental stage, that to consider it otherwise may seem absurd to some. At first glance one might wonder why adolescents even bother to go on—depression and suicidal behaviors would be natural sequelae to the developmental issues inherent in adolescence. At second glance, however, a growing empirical literature suggests that for most young people, adolescence is *not* a fundamentally painful and conflict-ridden period, and clearly not all adolescents are suicidal. Accordingly, clinicians who work with adolescents must be able to separate fact from fiction, differentiating empirical veracity from popular cultural "wisdom."

Adolescent Psychology

In truth, much of what has become folklore about adolescence can be attributed to early and pervasive psychological theories of adolescence. But according to Sisson, Hersen, and Van Hasselt (1987), much of what passes as conventional wisdom about adolescence has never been empirically tested or validated in any scientific sense. It is perhaps surprising to note that the topic of adolescence was given practically no scrutiny at all prior to this century and has only received proper empirical attention in the past decade.

Fortunately, the field of adolescent psychology has evolved rapidly over recent years, and a great deal more theoretical perspectives and empirical data are available. Although much of the original ground-breaking adolescent theorizing came from the psychoanalytic stance, numerous other perspectives have emerged from a variety of theoretical frameworks and disciplines, including psychology, psychiatry, sociology, education, and rehabilitation. The primary theoretical models of adolescence include psychoanalytic, developmental, learning, and biological perspectives. Each respective theory contributes a unique and valuable lens through which we can better examine and understand the developmental stage of adolescence.

The classic analytic model of adolescence emphasized instinctual drives and the primacy of the genital stage of psychosexual development (Freud, 1905/1957). Subsequent analytic theories emphasized the interaction of the ego and instinctual drives, which creates anxiety and dread, Anna Freud's (1958) "storm and stress" model. More contemporary theories have de-emphasized instinctual and biological drives as the focus has shifted toward object-relations (Guntrip, 1974; Winnicott, 1965) and the development of the self (Kohut, 1971, 1977).

Developmental theories of adolescence have evolved along two major lines: (a) Erikson's (1968) psychoanalytically based psychosocial stage theory of development, which emphasizes the "identity crisis" of adolescence; and (b) Piaget's theory of cognitive development, which emphasizes the "formal operations" phase of an adolescent's cognitive development.

Learning theories of adolescence provide an empirical paradigm from which adolescent behaviors can be examined in terms of operant or classical conditioning. From this perspective, adolescence has been conceptualized as an especially significant period of learning, which may be reflected in the individuality of adolescent response styles and behaviors (Gross & Lewin, 1987).

Finally, biological theories examine the relation between the biological changes of puberty and psychological development (see Kestenberg, 1968; Peterson & Taylor, 1980)

Separating Fact From Fiction

As suggested earlier, the early and pervasive theorizing of psychoanalytically oriented scholars has greatly influenced much of what is commonly associated with the developmental stage of adolescence. Anna Freud's (1958) storm and stress model of adolescence is particularly noteworthy in its emphasis on anxiety, dread, and angst. According to Lerner (1987), the storm and stress model was built on the synthesis of instinct-oriented classic analytic theory and recapitulation theory, which argued that the adolescent reexperiences the emotional trials of the first five years of life (Jones, 1948). Accordingly, these theories fundamentally conceptualize adolescence as a period of tremendous internal anxiety, turmoil, and emotional conflict.

Even though this perspective of adolescence may seem intuitively true and may reflect commonly held cultural wisdom, the empirical data do not appear to support this view. To obtain a more accurate view of adolescence, we must therefore begin to separate empirical fact from theoretical fiction.

As suggested earlier, the fact is that the vast majority of adolescents are *not* continuously in a state of profound misery, conflict, and suicidal angst. Indeed, recent empirical data indicate that most experience at least as much happiness as misery in their daily lives. Studies conducted by Offer (1987) and Abramowitz, Petersen, and Schulenberg (1984) paint a much brighter and more balanced picture of the adolescent experience that sharply contrasts with traditional notions. According to Offer (1987), empirical data suggest that the vast majority of adolescents are well-adjusted, get along with parents and peers, adjust to social mores and values, and cope with their internal and external experience. Research addressing self-image indicates that most adolescents report a generally positive view, which continues to improve over time (Abramowitz et al., 1984).

Although such findings are leading to some reformulations of adolescent psychology, they do not suggest, however, that the adolescent experience is by any means easy. Clearly, adolescence is a period of rapid and profound, asynchronous emotional, cognitive, and physical change—a "critical transition period" (Peterson & Hamburg, 1986) during which the teenager fundamentally establishes a personal identity, explores sexual and romantic relationships, and negotiates entry into the world of adulthood. Peterson and Hamburg (1986) observe that the adult world notices these changes in the adolescent's behavior relative to the behavior of children, not relative to that of the adults they are coming to resemble. Also, they caution (and remind) us that it is important to distinguish three phases within adolescence: early, middle, and late. The early adolescent is more similar to the child and the late adolescent is more similar to the young adult.

The emerging empirically based perspectives on the adolescent experience appear to provide a more balanced and normalized view of natural developmental struggles. Adolescence is a period of increasing capacities and competencies as well as problems. The majority of adolescents successfully navigate through adolescence, learning to use developing skills to solve problems. It is a minority of adolescents who experience difficulty. For this subgroup of troubled young people, adolescent life is indeed painful and wrought with conflict. It is within this subgroup that we see the co-occurrence of deviant behaviors and psychopathologies (see chapter 3). It is within this subgroup that suicidal behaviors are most likely to occur. Thus the focus of our concern should be centered on this minority of youth who experience difficulties, who through one or more deviant behaviors or mental disorders give us warnings of their vulnerability or risk for suicidal behavior.

Fortunately, there are some novel approaches to developing better responses and interventions to promote healthy adolescent development. For example, in 1989 the Carnegie Council's Task Force on Education of Young Adolescents produced an important report of specific recommendations for restructuring the middle grade education of young people in America (Carnegie Council on Adolescent Development, 1989). Other nationally oriented public health initiatives are similarly being considered and proposed that may further promote adolescent health and development (Alcohol, Drug Abuse, and Mental Health Administration, 1989). As noted by Millstein (1989), the popular view of adolescence as a period of storm and stress is being replaced by a perspective that emphasizes the potential for constructive adaptation and maturation during this important and challenging stage of development.

Adolescents and Death

In our examination of theoretical aspects of adolescence and suicide, it may be useful to briefly consider how adolescents conceptualize death. Kastenbaum (1986, p. 13) notes that "It is in adolescence that we glimpse for the first time what we and the world *might* be." Therein lies a paradox, for in adolescence we may also realize what we might *not* be. With the completion of cognitive development and the interactions between various physical and intra- and interpersonal changes of adolescence, questions of life and death become both real and profound. Indeed, there are those who may spend the balance of their life attempting to conceal or forget a deep sense of existential vulnerability that emerges during adolescence (Kastenbaum, 1986). The pushes and pulls of life and death are commonly reflected in the music of adolescence (Attig, 1986) and in reported fears and preoccupations with nuclear war (Goodman, Mack, Beardslee, & Snow, 1983; Snow, 1984). Typically, latency-aged children and early adolescents begin to develop an increasing awareness of death as reality. Gordon (1986) refers to this process of an evolving death awareness as the wearing away of the naive child's "cloak of immortality." Through exposure, experience, and subsequent awareness the older adolescent begins to attempt to impart meaning to death (and thereby, life) in such a way as to instill a sense of hope in living. Not surprisingly, it is the absence of hope in life that is often observed as a central feature of the suicidal adolescent's inner world.

Adolescent perceptions of suicide. There have been an increasing number of empirical investigations that have examined adolescent perceptions and attitudes toward suicide. For example, one study has provided data that suggest the possibility that young people today (when compared to their parents) have a more accepting attitude toward suicide (Boldt, 1982–1983). To account for such a possibility, Baron and Byrne (1984) suggest that unlike previous generations, contemporary young people watch a great deal more television and see movies that contain many depictions of suicide.[1] A desensitization effect is therefore hypothesized: If young people are exposed to numerous portrayals of self-destruction, then the act of suicide may therefore

---

[1]Berman (1986b) reported that modern American film depicts examples of suicide attempts and completions almost three times as often as films earlier in the century.

become less mysterious, threatening, and aversive. An alternative explanation cited by numerous authors (see chapter 6) emphasizes the possibility of suicide modeling effects, by which knowledge of suicidal behaviors (particularly in young people) may foster a sense that suicide is a viable escape from unpleasant realities. Accordingly, Allen (1987) argues that death may be less real to an adolescent and suicide may be more acceptable. In effect, an adolescent may fantasize that it is possible to return to life after a suicide, just as one can return from a drug-induced escape from reality.

To better investigate specific attitudes toward suicide, one line of research has led to the construction of an instrument, the Suicide Opinion Questionnaire (SOQ). The SOQ has been used with samples of young people as well as other populations (Domino, 1980, 1981, 1985). In one recent study, for example, Domino and Leenaars (1989) used the SOQ to compare attitudes toward suicide among Canadian and American college students. Their study produced data that address suicide-related themes such as motivation, religion, impulsivity, recidivism, and various misconceptions. Results from the study suggest that college students from both countries perceive suicidal acts as manipulative, did *not* see suicide attempts as impulsive acts, and strongly endorsed the notion of that once a person makes an attempt, he or she is likely to make a second attempt. Moreover, commonly hypothesized misconceptions (e.g., see Shneidman, 1980) appeared not to be so commonly held by students in these samples. In contrast to Boldt's (1982–1983) data suggesting that young people may have an increased acceptance of suicide, almost all of the college students did not see suicide as "normal" behavior.

Reynolds and Cimbolic (1988–1989) in their recent study have examined an alternative set of suicide-related attitudes. These investigators conducted a case study experiment using a sample of college students that examined attitudes toward suicide survivors as a function of the survivor's relationship to the victim. Results of this study indicated that reactions to suicide survivors are generally negative and the relationship of survivors to victims tends to affect reactions to survivors. Specifically, children of suicide victims were seen less negatively, whereas parents of a child suicide received the most negative reactions. More will be said on the perceptions of survivors in chapter 6.

The Interpersonal Context

As a final consideration in this theory-oriented chapter, the interpersonal aspects of adolecent suicide are important to note. Intuitively, we know that a young person's suicidal behaviors will be largely influenced by their attitudes and perceptions of suicide. A young person who views suicide as an enticing and dramatic means of escape is clearly at more risk to act out self-destructively than a youth who perceives suicide as an unacceptable and abhorrent act. Critically, the formation, maintenance, and change of such attitudes and perceptions occurs within, and is interactive with, an interpersonal context.

As an example, the effects of overt and covert labeling within a family, educational, or peer group system can be devastating and may precede subsequent suicidal behaviors. Behavioral and emotional problems may lead parents to label and scapegoat their child as the family's "black sheep." Teachers may come to identitfy a struggling youth as a "problem child" or a "discipline problem." Members of an adolescent peer group may taunt and reject a disturbed cohort, tagging them with cruel names and derision. Such labeling has the potential to become self-reinforcing, leading to further negative attention seeking and self-fulfilling prophecies that a young person may become compelled to confirm. Along these lines, Bostock and Williams (1974) suggested from a behavioral perspective that suicidal behavior can be viewed as an operant that is reinforced and maintained by consequent interpersonal contingencies. This view underscores the interpersonal dilemma of a recipient of a suicidal communication. Responding to depressive or suicidal messages may reinforce the behavior, through the reward of social attention, and thereby increase the frequency of this behavior. Alternatively, to ignore the depressive or suicidal communication in an attempt to extinguish the behavior may serve to prompt feelings of rejection and more severe behavioral outcomes (e.g., an actual suicide attempt).

It is important to note that therapists are certainly not immune to labeling their patients or participating in interactive
dynamics that may be pathogenic (Berman & Cohen-Sandler,
1983). By and large, therapists expect patients to be motivated
to use offered help, follow therapeutic advice, and actively engage in the therapeutic process on their own behalf. Suicidal
patients, however, frequently do not meet such expectations.
The negativity, hopelessness, and inability to change that is
endemic to suicide is frequently interpreted and subsequently
labeled by therapists as *resistance*. Because we may blame a
patient for not changing a behavior that we may see as within
their control, there is a risk that we fail to understand the nature
of the patient's experience and thereby engage in a nonthera-
peutic interactive feedback loop. Inadvertently, a therapist's
negative responses to a patient may increase as the patient's
suicide intention increases. Therefore, the patient's irritating
behavior—perhaps the very reason that the patient needs the
therapist's help—exemplifies the process by which these individuals gradually alienate other potential helpers in their world,
thereby maintaining the depression and heightening both the
isolation and hopelessness. Accordingly, the distancing and
help-rejecting behaviors presented by suicidal patients must be
relabeled not as resistance but as the reason for treatment (refer
to chapter 5 for further discussion).

As mentioned earlier, various authors have discussed interactive issues within the family system, where a child's role can
become one of acting out the family's psychopathology (Richman, 1986; Sabbath, 1969). Peer group relationships and interactions appear to play a significant role, in that lack of peer
involvement and conflictual relationships are commonly associated with adolescent suicide (see Topol & Reznikoff, 1982).

On a more directly interactive level, there is evidence that a
peer group subculture can lead to a series of suicidal behaviors.
Robbins and Conroy (1983) cite one case example related to a
series of suicidal behaviors among members of a small peer
group of adolescents in Chappaqua, New York. In 1978 this
small suburban community experienced two adolescent suicide
deaths within a 6-month period, followed by five admissions
for suicide attempts and an admission for suicidal ideation within

7 weeks of the second suicide. The six suicidal patients were found to be a group of students from the same high school who had visited each other during their hospitalizations for suicidal behavior. The clear implication is that these youthful peers seemed to have influenced or served as models for suicidal behaviors, thus triggering subsequent imitation of suicidal acting out. Although the specifics of possible interactive or interpersonal effects remain unclear, it should be apparent that adolescent suicidal behaviors do not occur in an interpersonal vacuum.

Conclusion

We opened this chapter with the stories of Bill and Jenny, whose suicidal behaviors had some obvious and not-so-obvious explanations. Depending on the lenses we use to examine their cases, each suicidal behavior takes on a different meaning. For the sake of simplicity, it is tempting to understand suicidal behavior from a theoretical perspective; yet it appears that the most comprehensive understanding requires a sensitivity to a broad range of variables, including social, psychological, and biological influences. Moreover, it requires a larger context, that of adolescence itself and those aspects that are unique to this stage of development. To that end we have endeavored to describe what is both typical and atypical of adolescence, thus setting the stage to discern what is unique to adolescents who are suicidal. But to see these youth more clearly, we must go beyond theory and turn our focus to the empirical research upon which the validity of these and subsequent theories must depend.

References

Abramowitz, R. H., Petersen, A. C., & Schulenberg, J. A. (1984). Changes in self-image during early adolescence. In D. Offer, E. Ostrov, & K. I. Howard (Eds.), *Patterns of adolescent self-image* (pp. 19–28). San Francisco, CA: Jossey-Bass.

Achte, K. (1988). Suicidal tendencies in the elderly. *Suicide and Life-Threatening Behavior, 18,* 55–65.

Adler, A. (1958). Suicide. *Journal of Individual Psychology, 14*, 57–61.

Alcohol, Drug Abuse, and Mental Health Administration (1989). *Report of the Secretary's Task Force on Youth Suicide: Volume 1. Overview and recommendations* (DHHS Publication No. ADM 89–1621). Washington, DC: U.S. Government Printing Office.

Allen, B. P. (1987). Youth suicide. *Adolescence, 22*, 271–290.

Ammon, G. (1974). The psychodynamics of the suicide event. *Dynamische Psychiatrie, 21*, 1–19.

Asberg, M. (1989). Neurotransmitter monoamine metabolites in the cerebrospinal fluid as risk factors for suicidal behavior. In Alcohol, Drug Abuse, and Mental Health Administration, *Report of the Secretary's task force on youth suicide. Volume 2. Risk factors for youth suicide* (pp. 193–212). (DHHS Publication No. ADM 89–1622). Washington, DC: U.S. Government Printing Office.

Asberg, M. (1990, April). *The biology of suicide.* Paper presented at the 23rd annual conference of the American Association of Suicidology, New Orleans, LA.

Attig, T. (1986). Death themes in adolescent music: The classic years. In C. A. Corr and J. N. McNeil (Eds.), *Adolescence and death* (pp. 32–56). New York: Springer Publishing Company.

Baechler, J. (1975). *Suicides.* New York: Basic Books.

Baron, R., & Byrne, D. (1984). *Social psychology: Understanding human interaction* (4th edition). Newton, MA: Allyn and Bacon.

Beck, A. T., Brown, G., & Steer, R. A. (1989). Prediction of eventual suicide in psychiatric inpatients by clinical rating of hopelessness. *Journal of Consulting and Clinical Psychology, 57*, 309–310.

Berman, A. L. (1984, October 3). The problem of teenage suicide. Testimony presented before the U.S. Senate, Committee on the Judiciary, Subcommittee on Juvenile Justice.

Berman, A. L. (1986a). A critical look at our adolescence: Notes on turning 18 (and 75). *Suicide and Life-Threatening Behavior, 16*, 1–12.

Berman, A. L. (1986b, April). *Suicide and the American film.* Paper presented at the annual meeting of the American Association of Suicidology, Atlanta, GA.

Berman, A. L., & Cohen-Sandler, R. (1983, May). *The therapeutic alliance with suicidal patients: Thoughts on attributions of responsibility.* Paper presented at the annual meeting of the American Association of Suicidology, Dallas, TX.

Boldt, M. (1982–1983). Normative evaluations of suicide and death: A cross-generational study. *Omega, 13*, 145–157.

Bowlby, J. (1973). *Attachment and loss: Vol 11. Separation.* New York: Basic Books.

Bostock, T., & Williams, C. L. (1974). Attempted suicide as an operant behavior. *Archives of General Psychiatry, 31*, 482–486.

Carnegie Council on Adolescent Development. (1989). *Turning points: Preparing American youth for the 21st century.* New York: Carnegie Corporation.

Cavan, R. S. (1926). *Suicide.* Chicago, IL: University of Chicago Press.

Comstock, B. (1979). Suicide in the 1970s: A second look. *Suicide and Life-Threatening Behavior, 9*, 3–13.

deCatanzaro, D. (1981). *Suicide and self-damaging behavior: A sociobiological perspective.* New York: Academic Press.

deCatanzaro, D. (1984). Suicidal ideation and the residual capacity to promote inclusive fitness: A survey. *Suicide and Life-Threatening Behavior, 14,* 75–87.

deCatanzaro, D. (1986). A mathematical model of evolutionary pressures regulating self-preservation and self-destruction. *Suicide and Life-Threatening Behavior, 16,* 84–99.

De Rosis, L. E. (1961). Suicide: The Horney point of view. In N. L. Farberow and E. S. Shneidman (Eds.), *The cry for help* (pp. 236–254). New York: McGraw-Hill.

Douglas, J. D. (1967). *The social meaning of suicide.* Princeton, NJ: Princeton University Press.

Domino, G. (1980). Altering attitudes towards suicide in an abnormal psychology course. *Teaching of Psychology, 7,* 239–240.

Domino, G. (1981). Attitudes towards suicide among Mexican-American and Anglo youth. *Hispanic Journal of Behavioral Sciences, 3,* 385–395.

Domino, G. (1985). Clergy's attitudes towards suicide and recognition of suicide lethality. *Death Studies, 9,* 187–199.

Domino, G., & Leenaars, A. A. (1989). Attitudes towards suicide: A comparison of Canadian and U.S. college students. *Suicide and Life-Threatening Behavior, 19,* 160–171.

Durkheim, E. (1951). *Suicide: A study in sociology.* New York: The Free Press (Original work published 1897).

Erikson, E. (1959). *Identity and the life cycle.* New York: International Universities.

Erikson, E. (1968). *Identity: Youth in crisis.* New York: W. W. Norton.

Emery, P. E. (1983). Adolescent depression and suicide. *Adolescence, 18,* 245–258.

Farber, M. L. (1968). *Theory of suicide.* New York: Funk & Wagnalls.

Ferster, C. B. (1973). A functional analysis of depression. *American Psychologist, 28,* 857–870.

Frederick, D. J., & Resnik, H. L. P. (1971). How suicidal behaviors are learned. *American Journal of Psychotherapy, 25,* 37–55.

Freud, A. (1958). Adolescence. *The Psychoanalytic Study of the Child, 13,* 261–277.

Freud, S. (1905/1957). Three essays on the theory of sexuality. *Standard Edition* (Vol. 7). London: Hogarth Press.

Freud, S. (1917). Mourning and melancholia. *Standard Edition, 14.* London: Hogarth Press.

Freud, S. (1920). Beyond the pleasure priniciple. *Standard Edition, 18.* London: Hogarth Press.

Gibbs, J., & Martin, W. T. (1964). *Status integration and suicide.* Eugene, OR: The University of Oregon Press.

Goodman, L. A., Mack, J. E., Beardslee, W. R., & Snow, R. (1983). The threat of nuclear war and the nuclear arms race: Adolescent experience and perceptions. *Political Psychology, 4,* 501–530.

Gordon, A. K. (1986). The tattered cloak of immortality. In C. A. Corr & J. M. McNeil (Eds.), *Adolescence and death.* New York: Springer Publishing Company.

Green, M. R. (1961). Suicide: The Sullivanian point of view. In N. L. Farberow and E. S. Shneidman (Eds.), *The cry for help* (pp. 220–235). New York: McGraw-Hill.

Gross, A. M., & Levin, R. B. (1987). Learning. In V. B. Van Hasselt & M. Hersen (Eds.), *Handbook of adolescent psychology* (pp. 77–90). New York: Pergamon Press.

Guntrip, H. (1974). Psychoanalytic object relations theory: The Fairbairn-Guntrip approach. In S. Arieti (Ed.), *American handbook of psychiatry* (Vol. 1). New York: Basic Books.

Hawton, K. (1987). *Attempted suicide.* New York: Oxford.

Hendin, H. (1987). Youth suicide: A psychosocial perspective. *Suicide and Life-Threatening Behavior, 17,* 151–165.

Henry, A., & Short, J. (1954). *Suicide and homicide.* Glencoe, IL: Free Press.

Jan-Tausch, J. (1963). *Suicide of children 1960–1963, New Jersey Public School studies.* Trenton, NJ: NJ Public Schools, Department of Education.

Jones, E. (1948). Some problems of adolescence. In E. Jones (Ed.), *Papers on psychoanalysis.* London: Bailliere, Tindall & Cox. (Original work published 1922).

Jung, C. G. (1959). The soul and death. In H. Feifel (Ed.), *The meaning of death.* New York: McGraw-Hill.

Kastenbaum, R. (1986). Death in the world of adolescence. In C. A. Corr & J. N. McNeil (Eds.), *Adolescence and death* (pp. 4–15). New York: Springer.

Kestenberg, J. (1968). Phases of adolescence with suggestions for a correlation of psychic and hormonal organization: Part III. Puberty growth, differentiation, and consolidation. *Journal of American Academy of Child Psychiatry, 7,* 108–151.

Kohut, H. (1971). *The analysis of the self.* New York: International Universities Press.

Kohut, H. (1977). *The restoration of the self.* New York: International Universities Press,

Leenaars, A. (1988). *Suicide notes.* New York: Human Science Press.

Leenaars, A., & Balance, W. (1984). A predictive approach to Freud's formulations regarding suicide. *Suicide and Life-Threatening Behavior, 14,* 275–283.

Leonard, C. V. (1967). *Understanding and preventing suicide.* Springfield, IL: Charles C. Thomas.

Lerner, H. (1987). Psychodynamic models. In V. B. Van Hasselt & M. Hersen (Eds.), *Handbook of adolescent psychology* (pp. 53–76). New York: Pergamon Press.

Lester, D. (1984). The quality of life and suicide. *Journal of Social Psychology, 125,* 279–280.

Lester, D. (1987). A subcultural theory of teenage suicide. *Adolescence, 22,* 317–320.

Lester, D. (1988a). Youth suicide: A cross-cultural perspective. *Adolescence, 23,* 955–958.

Lester, D. (1988b). One theory of teen-age suicide. *Journal of School Health, 58,* 193–194.

Litman, R. E., & Tabachnick, N. (1968). Psychoanalytic theories of suicide. In H. L. P. Resnik (Ed.), *Suicidal behaviors: Diagnosis and management* (pp. 73–81). Boston, MA: Little, Brown and Company.

Lively, P. (1987). *Moon tiger.* New York: Harper & Row.

Mack, J. E. (1986). Adolescent suicide: An architectural model. In G. L. Klerman (Ed.), *Suicide and depression among adolescents and young adults* (pp. 55–76). Washington, DC: American Psychiatric Press.

Maltsberger, J. T. (1986). *Suicide risk: The formation of clinical judgement.* New York: New York University Press.

Maltsberger, J. T. (1988). Suicide danger: Clinical estimation and decision. *Suicide and Life-Threatening Behavior, 18,* 47–54.

Maris, R. W. (1981). *Pathways to suicide: A survey of self-destructive behaviors.* Baltimore, MD: The Johns Hopkins University Press.

Menninger, K. (1938). *Man against himself.* New York: Harcourt Brace.

Millstein, S. G. (1989). Adolescent health: Challenges for behavioral scientists. *American Psychologist, 44,* 837–842.

Minuchin, S. (1974). *Families and family therapy.* Cambridge, MA: Harvard University Press.

Murray, H. A. (1938). *Explorations in personality.* New York: Oxford University Press.

Neuringer, C. (1964). Rigid thinking in suicidal individuals. *Journal of Consulting and Clinical Psychology, 76,* 91–100.

Offer, D. (1987). In defense of adolescents. *Journal of the American Medical Association, 257,* 3407–3408.

Peterson, A. C., & Hamburg, B. A. (1986). Adolescence: A developmental approach to problems and pathology. *Behavior Therapy, 17,* 480–499.

Peterson, A. C., & Taylor, B. (1980). The biological approach to adolescence: Biological change and psychological adaptation. In J. Adelson (Ed.), *Handbook of adolescent psychology* (pp. 117–155). New York: John Wiley & Sons.

Petzel, S. V., & Riddle, M. (1981). Adolescent suicide: Psychosocial and cognitive aspects. *Adolescent Psychiatry, 9,* 342–398.

Rangell, L. (1988). The decision to terminate one's life: Psychoanalytic thoughts on suicide. *Suicide and Life-Threatening Behavior, 18,* 28–46.

Richman, J. (1984). The family therapy of suicidal adolescents: Promises and Pitfalls. In H. S. Sudak, A. B. Ford, & N. B. Rushford (Eds.), *Suicide in the young* (pp. 393–406).

Richman, J. (1986). *Family therapy for suicidal people.* New York: Springer.

Reynolds, F. M. T., & Cimbolic, P. (1988–1989). Attitudes toward suicide survivors as a function of survivors' relationship to the victim. *Omega, 19,* 125–133.

Robbins, D., & Conroy, R. (1983). A cluster of adolescent suicide attempts: Is suicide contagious? *Journal of Adolescent Health Care, 3,* 253–255.

Rush, A. J., & Beck, A. T. (1978). Cognitive therapy of depression and suicide. *American Journal of Psychotherapy, 32,* 201–219.

Sabbath, J. C. (1969). The suicidal adolescent—the expendable child. *Journal of American Academy of Child Psychiatry, 8,* 272–289.

Sainsbury, P. (1955). *Suicide in London.* London: Chapman and Hall.

Sartre, J. P. (1956). *Being and nothingness.* New York: Pocket Books.

Schmid, C. F. (1928). *Suicide in Seattle, 1914 to 1925.* Seattle, WA: University of Washington Publications in the Social Sciences.

Shapiro, E. R., & Freedman, J. (1987). Family dynamics of adolescent suicide. *Adolescent Psychiatry, 14,* 271–290.

Shneidman, E. S. (1980). Suicide. In E. S. Shneidman (Ed.), *Death: Current perspectives* (pp. 416–434). Palo Alto, CA: Mayfield Publishing Company.

Shneidman, E. S. (1985). *Definition of Suicide.* New York: John Wiley and Sons.

Shneidman, E. S. (1988). Some reflections of a founder. *Suicide and Life-Threatening Behavior, 18,* 1–12.

Sisson, L. A., Hersen, M., & Van Hasselt, V. B. (1987). Historical perspectives. In V. B. Van Hasselt & M. Hersen (Eds.), *Handbook of adolescent psychology* (pp. 3–10). New York: Pergamon Press.

Smith, K. (1985). Suicide assessment: An ego vulnerabilities approach. *The Bulletin of the Menninger Clinic, 49,* 489–499.

Snow, R. (1984). Decision making for a nuclear age. *Boston University Journal of Education, 166,* 103–107.

Tabachnick, N. (1971). Theories of self-destruction. *American Journal of Psychoanalysis, 32,* 53–61.

Topol, P., & Reznikoff, M. (1982). Perceived peer and family relationships, hopelessness, and locus of control as factors in adolescent suicide attempts. *Suicide and Life-Threatening Behavior, 12,* 141–150.

Trautman, P. D., & Shaffer, D. (1984). Treatment of child and adolescent suicide attempters. In H. S. Sudak, A. B. Ford, & N. B. Rushford (Eds.), *Suicide in the young* (pp. 307–323). Boston, MA: John Wright PSG Inc.

Wade, N. L. (1987). Suicide as a resolution of separation–individuation among adolescent girls. *Adolescence, 22,* 169–177.

Wahl, C. W. (1957). Suicide as a magical act. In E. S. Shneidman & N. L. Farberow (Eds.), *Clues to suicide.* New York: McGraw-Hill.

Weissman, M. M., Paykel, E. S., & Klerman, G. L. (1972). The depressed woman as a mother. *Social Psychiatry, 7,* 89–108.

Winnicott, D. (1965). *The maturational processes and the facilitating environment.* London: Hogarth Press.

Zilboorg, G. (1936). Suicide among civilized and primitive races. *American Journal of Psychiatry, 92,* 362.

3

The Empirical Context

Difficulties of Suicide Research

Over the last several decades, a significant acceleration of empirical research in the area of youth suicide has closely followed and paralleled reports of the dramatic increases in these behaviors (Berman & Tanney, 1984). Although an increasingly empirical focus has been encouraging and much needed, the lack of methodological rigor and evidence of spurious findings have been discouraging and problematic. A number of authors (Berman & Carroll, 1984; Berman & Cohen-Sandler, 1982; Pfeffer, 1989a; Seiden, 1969) have commented on the presence of inadequate methodologies and misleading findings inherent in much of the adolescent suicide literature.

Many investigations have either largely neglected or simply ignored basic methodological and design considerations such as adequate definitions, measures of suicidal behaviors, and use of appropriate comparison control groups (Berman & Cohen-Sandler, 1982; Pfeffer, 1989a). The lack of a commonly used nomenclature has been a consistent problem in a literature in which fundamental terms such as "suicide attempt" or "lethality" are often not operationally defined (see Resnik & Hathorne, 1973).

From an empirical perspective, suicide is indeed a very difficult phenomenon to study. Adolescent suicide research (as with any age group) is fundamentally limited by the deaths of its subjects. The people who are most important to understand are, by definition, unavailable to the suicide researcher. Use of standard scientific methodology, such as randomly selected samples or rigorously controlled experiments, is often prohibited by the unique constraints inherent in the suicide phenomenon. The subject matter, therefore, often requires the use of less than elegant approaches of study.

Many investigators retrospectively study data obtained by medical examiners and coroners as well as other data gathered through post-hoc interviews, suicide notes, or medical records. As an alternative, many suicidologists choose to study living suicide ideators or surviving attempters. However, data obtained from attempters and ideators is often not readily generalizable to completers, who represent a markedly different population (see Linehan, 1986). Prospective studies (cf. Motto, 1984), desirable from a purely scientific perspective, are difficult, if not impossible, to conduct due to ethical constraints (not allowing the death of a known individual at risk) and sample or resource considerations (affording to collect data on a sample large enough to be meaningfully interpretable).

The Statistical Approach

From a purely statistical perspective, suicidal behaviors are rare. This fact greatly limits the researcher's ability to empirically identify those demographic, sociocultural, and clinical variables that might provide the means to validly and reliably predict suicidal behaviors (a goal shared by many suicidologists). Even were we able to develop tests with high specificity and sensitivity,[1] the prediction of suicide at a definite or indefinite future time would lead to an intolerable number of false positives and false negatives, and inadequate levels of reliability (Kaplan, Kottler, & Frances, 1982; Murphy, 1983; Pokorny, 1983; Rosen,

---

[1]Sensitivity refers to the proportion of correctly identified positive cases, defined as 100 × the ratio of true positives divided by the sum of true positives and false negatives. Specificity refers to the proportion of correctly identified negative cases, that is, 100 × the ratio of true negatives divided by the sum of true positives and true negatives (Galen & Gambino, 1975).

1959). The consequences of relying on a predictive (statistical) approach, therefore, are an unacceptable number of patients on suicide watch with associated restrictions in personal liberty (false negatives) or an unacceptable number of otherwise preventable deaths (false positives). As a "low base-rate" event, valid and reliable prediction of suicide at a definite or indefinite future time is virtually impossible.

As an illustration, consider the following example (cf. Rosen, 1959). Imagine we had available for our use a 10-item checklist or "suicide assessment scale," which, given a cutoff score, could correctly identify 95% of potential adolescent suicide completers and attempters. For the sake of our discussion, let us assume that in a population of 100,000 adolescents we could expect 20 completed suicides and 2,000 attempts in any given year. Therefore, the application of our scale should lead to the correct identification of 95% of 2020 suicidal adolescents per year, or 1919 adolescents in need of early intervention and treatment. However, the same scale would incorrectly identify 5% of this population as at risk, totalling 4,899 false positives also in need of intervention. If all these youngsters were deemed in need of hospitalization for observation and treatment, we would need 6,818 beds each year!

Also, suicidal urges and behaviors are largely temporally and situationally specific. Suicidal intent is not constant within an individual. The urge to act in a self-harmful or destructive manner is state-dependent. It waxes, wanes, disappears, and returns (Murphy, 1983). The interaction of factors specific to the individual, the environment, and the situational and temporal context determine, in an idiosyncratic and dynamic manner, the if and when of both the urge to commit suicide and the action to accomplish it. Therefore, any attempt to apply a statistical model through the use of scales, questionnaires, psychological tests, and so forth to the assessment of possible suicidal behavior must account for these dynamic interactions. To date, this has not been accomplished.

The Descriptive Approach

Statistical and clinical models of assessment share a common strategy. The diagnosis of pathology or the prediction of certain behaviors depends on the similarity between that which is observed in a patient and that which is known (through the study of other patients already defined) to be associated with the diagnosis or the behavior. Thus a patient with an affective disorder may be so diagnosed because said patient has observable symptoms or characteristics that are similar to those of patients reliably and validly diagnosed as having an affective disorder.

In the context of suicide assessment, this strategy calls for an understanding of those characteristics descriptive of known suicidal individuals, that is, those who have completed suicide. Possible future suicidal individuals, then, are defined by the degree to which they share these characteristics. Furthermore, this strategy allows for an evaluative heirarchy. Levels of risk (e.g., low, moderate, high) can be established based on the degree of similarity (e.g., a weighted number of shared factors) observed. Again, this strategy at best provides a static definition of risk, that is, defining someone as "in the ballpark" and needing further observation and evaluation.

With regard to suicidal adolescents, a wide range of associated characteristics have been noted and described (cf. Berman, 1986a, 1986b; Berman & Carroll, 1984; Shaffer, 1988; Spirito, Brown, Overholser, & Fritz, 1989). Most of these factors, however, are derived from the study of low-lethality attempters (e.g., female drug ingesters who are most available for study because of their postattempt hospitalization and compliance with treatment regimens), who, as we shall see, may only slightly resemble adolescents at risk for serious self-harm or death. Thus, we may be faced with the most paradoxical of strategies— attempting to assess an adolescent at mortal risk based on characteristics common to those with minimal intent to die who engage in behaviors unlikely to produce a lethal outcome.

From the preceding discussion, it should be quite clear that the methodological and statistical problems inherent in suicide research are considerable, but not prohibitive. Increasingly, youth suicide researchers are improving their ability to address the various challenges of this topic through creative approaches and use of better methodologies and scientific rigor. In this chapter the empirical context of adolescent suicide will be reviewed and critiqued before shifting the focus to an examination of the empirical data.

Research Methodology: Review and Critique

As discussed in the preceding section, the methods of suicide research are limited to two fundamental approaches: (a) those studies that pertain to completed suicide and (b) those that pertain to attempters or ideators. As discussed by Robins and Kulbock (1986) and Stack (1987), within the study of completed suicides, the following two traditions are evident: (a) the "ecological" or macro approach, which uses large samples of aggregate data to address larger epidemiological considerations and social correlates of suicide; and (b) the "case study" or micro approach, which retrospectively examines records or interview data of individual suicides to provide important clinical data pertaining to completed suicides. Within the attempting and ideator studies, a range of methodologies are employed with inpatient and outpatient samples to describe characteristics unique to these populations.

Completed Suicide Research

Much of what is commonly thought to be known about suicide in general, and adolescent suicide in particular, actually comes from studies of relatively nonlethal attempters (Berman & Cohen-Sandler, 1982; Maris, 1981). Unfortunately, considerable differences between attempters and completers have been found such that inferences drawn from one population may not apply to the other. Therefore, the best data about completed suicides comes from studies that examine completed suicides. In that regard, a range of methodologies have been used to obtain some very valuable data about adolescents who kill themselves.

Ecological methods of research. In their review of methodological strategies in suicide, Robins and Kulbock (1986) refer to "ecological analyses" as those studies that compare officially reported suicide mortality statistics between nations, or within a nation, across various demographic variables such as age, sex, and race. A variety of trend analyses are employed to examine patterns of suicide in various populations over time.

Emil Durkheim's (1897/1951) pioneering sociological studies of national suicide rates have led to an extensive line of empirical investigation. However, Durkheim's statistical approach has also sparked an extended scientific debate among subsequent investigators about the use of officially reported suicide statistics for studying epidemiological trends and social correlates of suicide (see Jobes, Berman, & Josselson, 1987; Kreitman, 1988; Pescosolido & Mendelsohn, 1986). A great deal of concern has been expressed about the process by which suicide is investigated, determined, and subsequently reported as a mortality statistic. The variability observed in medicolegal practice (e.g., Jobes, Berman, & Josselson, 1987; Nelson, Farberow, & MacKinnon, 1978) and recording procedures (e.g., Hlady & Middaugh, 1988) has led to fundamental questions as to whether officially reported suicide statistics are a valid and reliable source of basic epidemiological data.

The resulting "social constructionist" argument asserts that the alleged underlying inaccuracies of officially reported suicide statistics invalidate research results that rely on this database (Douglas, 1967; Nelson, et al., 1978). In response to this argument, others (Pescosolido & Mendelsohn, 1986; Sainsbury & Jenkins, 1982) have argued that officially reported rates are indeed appropriate for research purposes. These authors contend that the error variation in the reporting of suicide statistics is randomized in such a way as to not invalidate comparisons made between different suicide rates or conclusions made about social correlates of suicide.

While the actual extent and impact of potential inaccuracies of suicide statistics will probably continue to be debated, the sheer weight and import of this research cannot be denied. The caution of the social constructionists may or may not be warranted, yet there is much to be offered by ecological studies. Indeed, it is fair to say that much of what is thought to be empirically known about completed adolescent suicide comes from this line of empirical investigation (see chapter 1).

Social correlate approaches. Related to demographic research of risk factors are studies that seek to determine "social correlates" of suicide. As discussed earlier, although there has been a great deal of debate about the validity and reliability of this research, the social correlate method of study has been widely used by sociologists to explain suicidal behavior in terms of social influences. One example of this approach is seen in the attempts to measure the effects of modeling of suicidal behavior, or the "Werther Effect," which is described in chapter 3. In a broad sense some of this research has followed the Durkheimian tradition with its emphasis on social integration and the influence of society (Durkheim, 1951; Gibbs & Martin, 1964; Maris, 1981). While social correlate methods of study are widely used and published, these methods are also hotly debated and criticized (Baron & Reiss, 1985; Cohen, 1986).

Case study method of research. While macro-oriented ecological research uses aggregate data to define correlates of suicide, micro-oriented case study approaches use individual data to identify more specific risk variables. A range of case-control designs have been employed to identify the most salient risk variables associated with suicidal death. Ideally, these studies use control comparison samples such as matched samples of accidental deaths or living cohorts to help distinguish those variables that are unique and specific to suicidal death. From a purely empirical perspective, retrospective designs are not as preferable as prospective designs. Practical considerations such as economic, resource, and ethical limitations, however, usually require the use of post-hoc methodologies.

Medical examiner and coroner data. Perhaps the most straightforward case study method involves the direct examination and analysis of medical examiner and coroner data. Some studies have been conducted that examine data appearing on death certificates (e.g., Brent, Perper, & Allman, 1987). Other investigators have directly examined the investigatory records of medical examiners and coroners (e.g., Hoberman & Garfinkel, 1988). An additional approach has been used to collect data relevant to suicide and accident deaths directly from medicolegal officials by having them complete a standardized data collection form following their investigation of a case (Jobes, Casey, Berman, & Wright, 1991).

Psychological autopsies. The psychological autopsy was originally developed as a method to assist in the medicolegal investigation of "equivocal" suicide cases (Litman, Curphey, Shneidman, Farberow, & Tabachnick, 1963; Shneidman & Farberow, 1961). Although the medicolegal use of the technique has been clearly demonstrated (Jobes, Berman, & Josselson,

1986), the psychological autopsy has been increasingly used as an effective and valuable research tool.

Whether used for medicolegal or research purposes, the psychological autopsy technique involves the systematic collection of psychological data through structured interviews of the decedent's family members, friends, co-workers, fellow students, and other associates. Although the specific format may vary, most investigators collect data relevant to the decedent's behavior, personality, style of coping, cognitive processes, psychiatric history, and general emotional life, so that a rich psychological mosaic of the decedent can be assembled.

As with any post-hoc analysis, use of the psychological autopsy method is wrought with potential methodological problems (Brent, Perper, Kolko, & Zelenak, 1988; Brent, 1989). For example, issues of reliability and validity are obvious when data are collected retrospectively from the recollections of grieving family members and friends. Although the inherent methodological issues are considerable, the information produced through well-controlled and rigorously conducted psychological autopsy studies have provided suicidologists with some of the most valuable data collected to date (Fawcett & Clark, 1987; Rich, Young, & Fowler, 1986; Shaffer & Gould, 1987; Shafii, Carrigan, Whittinghill, & Derrick, 1985).

Suicide notes. The systematic analysis of individual suicide notes is yet another case study method of investigation. This method of study was first systematically employed by Shneidman and Farberow (1957). More recently, Leenaars (1988, 1989) has applied some novel procedures to the study of suicide notes. Various strategies have been used to study the content of suicide notes to determine authentic versus simulated notes as well as emotional and cognitive variables that are unique to suicidal individuals.

Postmortem studies. A final case study approach is used to study potential biological markers that may contribute to suicidal behavior. Various studies of cerebral spinal fluid (Brown et al., 1982; Roy et al., 1985; van Praag, 1983) and neuroendocrine functioning (see Ostroff et al., 1982; Rich, 1986) have been conducted postmortem on individuals who have completed suicide. Although quite different in focus from psychosocially oriented studies, the range of postmortem biological studies are increasingly used and are beginning to uncover the biological substrata of suicidal behavior (for a review, see Stanley & Stanley, 1989; and see pp. 49–51, this volume).

Attempter and Ideator Research

While suicide completers are fundamentally different from attempters, attempter- and ideator-oriented research is nevertheless quite valuable. As many suicide completers have made previous attempts or have previously thought about suicide, the study of attempters or ideators can provide important data about those variables that may uniquely contribute to an eventual suicide. On a more pragmatic level, it is much easier to study suicide vis-a-vis attempters because they are still alive and able to provide data. The relative ease of studying living subjects versus deceased subjects is probably most responsible for the heavy emphasis on attempter-oriented research in the empirical literature.

Inpatient samples. Studies using adolescent inpatient samples of suicide attempters and ideators have been widely reported in the literature (Apter, Bleich, Plutchik, Mendelsohn, & Tyano, 1988; Bettes & Walker, 1986; Brent, Kalas, Edelbrock, Costello, Dulcan, & Conover, 1986; Cohen-Sandler, Berman, King, 1982a; Pfeffer, Newcorn, Kaplan, Mizruchi, & Plutchik, 1988; Robbins & Alessi, 1985). As discussed by Pfeffer (1989a), many of the original clinical reports in the literature were essentially descriptive in nature, whereas in more recent years more empirical approaches have been employed.

A common problem with a number of studies published in this literature base involves the lack of clear operational definitions (e.g., the exact meaning of "suicidal behavior," "suicide attempts," or "suicide ideation" is often left unclear). Often groups of ideators and attempters are combined as one (see Smith & Maris, 1986). Frequently studies purporting to be examinations of suicide are in truth studies more focused on symptoms and variables related to depression (where suicide is only implicated). The bulk of inpatient attempter and ideator studies attempt to determine clinical risk variables for suicide through interview and administration of psychometric instruments and measures. Some treatment-oriented studies have been conducted as well, including use of some quasiexperimental designs.

In her review of inpatient research methods, Pfeffer (1989a) points out the importance of consistent components among studies so that replication and comparison are possible. She emphasizes five major components: (a) defining and measuring suicidal behavior, (b) describing the index sample to be studied, (c) using appropriate comparison subjects, (d) using standardized measures for data collection, and (e) documenting the limitations of a research design. Although these components represent essential elements of more controlled and rigorous research, the vast majority of inpatient studies usually do not address all of these methodological considerations.

Pfeffer (1989a) breaks down youth suicide inpatient research into two primary methodological designs: cross-sectional investigations and follow-up studies. Cross-sectional designs are used primarily to investigate suicidal risk factors, the spectrum of severity for suicidal behaviors, and continuity in factors associated with preadolescent and adolescent suicidal behavior. Follow-up designs are employed to investigate the incidence of suicidal ideas and acts among previously suicidal youth and to study which factors predict repeated suicidal acts.

A limited number of treatment-oriented studies have been described in the literature. Treatment studies tend to be descriptive (e.g., Paykel, Hallowell, Dressler, Shapiro, & Weissman, 1974), with only a few employing quasiexperimental treatment outcome designs (Cohen-Sandler, 1982, Liberman & Eckman, 1981). More recent studies have focused more specifically on borderline pathology and the treatment of self-destructive acting-out behaviors (see Linehan, 1985).

Outpatient samples. Efforts have been made to gain some empirical perspective on suicidal thoughts and behaviors among "normal" (nonpsychiatric) samples. Much of this research is conducted through descriptive surveys with more accessible populations. For example, a number of investigators have surveyed high school and college students to determine the prevalence of suicidal ideation (Craig & Senter, 1972; Harkavy-

Friedman, Asnis, Boeck, & DiFiore, 1987; Hersch, 1975; Lee, 1978; Rudd, 1989; Smith & Crawford, 1986).

Some studies have measured college student attitudes toward suicide (Domino & Leenaars, 1989) and suicide survivorship (Reynolds & Cimbolic, 1988–1989), whereas other research has been conducted to develop predictive models of suicidal ideation and behavior based on data obtained from college students (Bonner & Rich, 1987). The difficulty of gaining access to "normal" subjects and participation consent from their parents greatly limits the scope of suicide research efforts with nonhospitalized populations. However, some investigators are still able to navigate through some of these difficulties to make useful contributions to the literature (Smith & Crawford, 1986; Rubenstein, Heeren, Housman, Rubin, & Stechler, 1989).

Critique of Suicide Research

Many novel and creative approaches have been applied to the study of youthful suicidal thoughts and behaviors. As discussed earlier, suicide remains a particularly difficult domain of behavior to study. Moreover, more widespread applications of empirical methodologies and scientific rigor are still rather recent, primarily appearing in the last 10 to 20 years. Having acknowledged the inherent difficulties and the relative newness of this field of study, one critical question remains: Can youth suicide data obtained thus far be trusted?

The answer is an unequivocal yes and no. Clearly, some data appear to be more reliable and valid than other data. More valid and reliable studies tend to use more rigorously controlled designs, comparison or control groups, and clear, measurable operational definitions of independent and dependent variables. In reading the suicide literature, it is important to retain a critical eye for the preceding basic methodological components. However, there are certainly less rigorously designed studies that may still provide useful data. As discussed by Berman (1986c), the systematic and scientific study of suicide is itself only in its adolescence. While adolescents may not always speak with the certainty or maturity of adults, they nevertheless have much of great value to say.

As more sophisticated designs and methodologies are developed, better and more meaningful data will no doubt be generated. The use of prospective designs, predictive models, and the integration of individual and ecological approaches represent some of the new frontiers in the study of suicide. Whereas new approaches hold great promise, past and current investigations have already provided some very important information upon which further research can be based and applications made to the clinical setting. To best understand what the adolescent science of suicidology has to say about youthful suicide, the importance of maintaining a critical eye on the evolving empirical literature cannot be overemphasized.

The quality of the empirical base in suicidology determines, in great measure, the quality of our clinical work with suicidal patients. This intimate relationship is well reflected in the science and art of assessment of the potentially suicidal adolescent. Our intent in this chapter is to review the scientific and definitional basis for what, by necessity, becomes the art of risk assessment to be discussed in chapter 4.

Suicidal Behaviors

Completed Suicide

A completed suicide is certified by a coroner or medical examiner on the basis of evidence indicating intentional, self-inflicted death. The assessment of intentionality often is difficult (Berman, Litman, & Diller, 1989) but rests on evidence that the decedent "had in mind" that the self-inflicted action would produce death. Thus, when we study retrospectively those adolescents who have completed suicide, we derive factors common to youth with high degrees of both lethality and intention to die.

In 1987, there were 251 certified suicides by youth 14 years old and younger in the United States and 4,924 suicides by those aged 15–24 (National Center for Health Statistics, 1989). To date, very little research has been published assessing, in depth, the psychological characteristics of these youth. A good example of the kind of research needed is that of Shaffii et al. (1985), who compared 20 youth suicides to a group of living controls, documenting a number of significant factors that differentiated the suicidal youth. A major study in the metropolitan New York City area by Shaffer and his colleagues (Shaffer & Gould, 1987) will soon be reported in final form. These two works taken together have yielded important data for our understanding of the suicidal adolescent, particularly as the suicidal youth is differentiated from *both* nonsuicidal controls and nonfatal attempters. For example, one finding common to these researchers' results is the frequency with which suicidal youth displayed antisocial behavior, conduct disorders or both *in contrast to* the oft-reported affective disorders seen with great frequency in less lethal suicidal youth. With some youngsters, as in the case of David, it is difficult to distinguish the core etiology, as a diagnosis of attention deficit disorder may serve to mask an underlying depression.

Case Illustration

David, a 12-year-old sixth-grader, was found dead by asphyxiation, hanging from a clothes rod in his bedroom closet. The third of four children, David had a history of hyperactivity, low frustration tolerance, and aggressive behavior. He was in frequent combative relationships with peers and often was taunted by them. As a result he was often angry and frequently in tears. In school, his inability to maintain attention to task resulted in special placement in a class for the learning disabled. He believed this further marked him as a "loser," giving rise to a continuous cycle of pain–frustration–anger and acting out. In the last week, he told his grandfather that he would kill himself "some day." His parents, when told of this comment, denied the seriousness of both his intention and his difficulties. With their knowledge, David was not complying with the recommended treatment for his diagnosed attention deficit disorder. On the day of his death, David had been excluded from eating with some classmates and, at recess, had mud thrown on a new jacket, one he especially had wanted and had appeared proud to display.

The concept of intent central to the definition of suicide posed here makes clear that a variety of self-destructive behaviors, each with increased risk for premature death, are not suicidal. For example, anorexics, drug abusers, alcoholics, and even self-mutilators and autocastrators typically do not seek a cessation of life or of conscious experience through their behavior. Each has a more focal concern (e.g., to alter one's body, to anesthetize pain, to seek pleasure, etc.) having nothing in common with a goal of ending life.

Self-Mutilation

The study of self-mutilators has been given increasing attention (Favazza, 1989; Walsh & Rosen, 1988). Self-mutilation most commonly receives clinical attention through self-inflicted wrist cuts and cigarette burns. More extreme forms, such as genital castration and eye enucleation, are indicative of major psychopathology (e.g., schizophrenia and mania). As described by Walsh and Rosen (1988), the function of mutilative cutting, for example, is to decrease tension or other intense affect, diminish a sense of alienation, or terminate dissociation ("I bleed, therefore I am"). Favazza (1989) lists a dozen different goals articulated by patients to explain their mutilative behaviors. In adolescence, the conditions that commonly trigger moderate mutilative behavior are (a) losses that reactivate earlier losses; (b) peer conflict and intimacy problems; (c) body alienation (e.g., distress over sexual identity); and (d) impulse control problems (often modeled by parents)—themes quite similar to those we find with more directly suicidal youngsters. The most frequent diagnostic frames for these patients are those of borderline personality disorder, often with a co-morbid mood disorder, and dissociative disorder.

It is important to note that self-mutilators also make serious suicide attempts. In fact, each of the conditions noted as self-destructive (e.g., eating disorders, substance abuse) are known to be associated with increased risk for suicidal behavior, perhaps as a consequence of the despair experienced when other desired goals fail to be achieved. Thus, as defined, these behaviors are dissimilar from the criterion behaviors we seek to assess as suicidal and are not *directly* suicidal (see Farberow, 1980 for an excellent compilation of articles on "indirect self-destructive behaviors"), yet they are significantly risk-related. The cases of Suzanne and Millie well illustrate the dynamics and co-morbid psychopathologies common to adolescent self-mutilators.

Case Illustrations

Suzanne, age 19, presented for outpatient treatment complaining of not coping well, of feeling "locked up" and scared. She wished to avoid repeating a hospitalization of 2 years earlier, which had been precipitated by a "hysterical spell" accompanied by visual hallucinations (menacing male figures who would make sexual advances toward her).

Suzanne had a long history of multiple somatic complaints, including dizziness, headaches, and irregular menses since puberty. She was considerably overweight, a condition for which she had entered two long-term inpatient programs to control. It was during one of these programs that her earlier hospitalization occurred. She had become increasingly agitated by her observations of polymorphous perverse sexual behavior among fellow program patients and felt a good deal of pressure to equally act out. In response she experienced fainting spells and had considerable suicide ideation.

The favorite child of her father, who appeared to dote on her, Suzanne felt a good deal of guilt over his attention. Aware of the oedipal implications, she described wanting his affection but feeling uncomfortable getting it. At the same time she described a number of self-imposed strict and rigid rules for her acceptability (to be perfect, to be healthy, to not show problems or feelings). She described her mother as a perfectionist who harped on Suzanne's lack of attractiveness as a developing female because of her weight and, in particular, her large breasts. In order to cope, Suzanne steadfastly denied her own needs and attempted to sublimate by counseling her peers, a role that reinforced her wish to hide her own pain. However, the tension of trying to meet impossible standards became overwhelming. Were she to expose herself to a peer, she would feel overwhelmingly guilty and then would hear voices that would urge her to hurt herself because she had been bad. She then would dissociate (during which time she might engage in trance writing or drawing) and, ultimately, end the dissociative episode by cutting herself or burning herself with cigarettes. Interpretively, it was noted that she would attempt to cut or burn herself only in places on her body hidden from public view (reinforcing the norm of hiding) and that this fulfilled her mother's competition with her sexuality (she would cut at her breasts and burn in the area of her uterus), as she secondarily attempted to maintain a prepubescent and dependent role in her family. Of similar interest, her only known suicide attempt was at the age of 13 with her mother's Librium pills.

Millie, age 19, presented as depressed, socially anxious, and isolated. She had no friends and saw herself as "only capable of driving others away." She did not trust others, yet desperately wished to have and be loved by a boyfriend. Although she spent considerable time alone, she was frightened of being alone. Since childhood, when she would cower at the creakings of an old house, she had repeatedly checked behind the shower curtain and under her bed before going to sleep in order to assure herself that there were no burglars in her house. Once asleep, she would have frequent nightmares.

Millie described feeling both empty and "rotten" inside. She described her parents as rigid perfectionists who were opinionated and intolerant. Her only success in being acceptable to them was through academics, at which she excelled, maintaining a straight-A average. She filled her aloneness and emptiness with bulimic binge–purge behavior, consuming 5,000 calories at a sitting. Motivated by "irresistible urges," she relieved herself of overwhelming pressure and tension by punching the walls of her apartment and by repetitively slicing her wrists. These cuts had never been severe enough to require medical intervention. Nor had she ever been psychiatrically hospitalized; she equated coming for treatment with confirmation of herself as a failure.

Attempted Suicide

What is complicating about this definitional approach is that the great majority of what gets labeled as an "attempted suicide" by definition is not. Attempted suicide is an inchoate act, that is, an attempt to commit. Thus, a true suicide attempter had both intent to die and sufficient lethality in the method to accomplish that intent, but either failed or was foiled (e.g., through rescue or intervention). Neither of these conditions pertains to the great majority of those adolescents who are treated in emergency rooms or referred for psychiatric consultation after self-harm behavior. The typical adolescent attempter is a female who ingests pills in front of her family after an argument (Trautman, 1986). In fact, the overwhelming majority of attempters are female (by a ratio of about 4:1) and, similarly, pill takers (from 71–93%: Bond, Riggs, Spirito, & Fritz, 1988; Garfinkel, Froese, & Hood, 1982; Gispert, Davis, Marsh, & Wheeler, 1987; Slap, Vorters, Chaudhuri, & Centor, 1989). These modal descriptors are quite different from those of the typical adolescent completer, who is a male gunshot wound victim (almost two thirds of all adolescent completers).

Moreover, Linehan (1985) and Cross and Hirschfield (1985) have described clear differences in the personalities of high- and low-intent attempters, with the latter appearing more deviant. Given the heterogeneity of this group, therefore, it would be helpful were research studies of adolescent attempters to distinguish different subgroups for comparative study. Some typologies have been proposed (e.g., Henderson, Hartigan, & Davidson, 1977; Peck, 1982, 1985), but discriminative research has yet to follow. One interesting exception is the work of Stephens (1985), who distinguished two polar opposite groups of adolescent female attempters: (a) those characterized by a pattern of defiance, rebelliousness, acting out, drug involvement, and indiscriminate sexuality ("cheap thrills"); and (b) those characterized by overconformity, docility, passivity, and emotional submergence ("humble pie").

As it is apparent that this is not a homogeneous group, and as it is difficult to distinguish among the variety of intentions of these adolescent attempters, and because adolescents often deny their intent upon questioning, the term *parasuicide* (Kreitman, 1977) has been adopted to denote all deliberate self-harming behaviors.

The reader should not misconstrue this disparity to imply a total lack of pattern within or overlap between groups of those who complete and those who attempt suicide in adolescence. With regard to the relationship between attempters and completers, for example, Brent (1987) has documented that those who make medically lethal attempts are similar to those who complete suicide. And as we shall note, a prior attempt has been found in psychological autopsy studies to be one of the more important risk factors among completers (Shafii et al., 1985). Also a significant number of attempters ultimately complete suicide (Goldacre and Hawton, 1985; Motto, 1984). Thus, histories of suicidal behavior may be significantly tied to risk for completion, and the lethality of an attempt is related to its intentionality (see chapter 4).

Whereas the intentionality of a completer is presumed to be that of death or ending life as it is known, such is not always the case. Some adolescents, lacking intent to die, gamble with the possibility, and lose. Others lack sufficient knowledge to calculate accurately, for example, less than toxic dosages of ingested medication. Conversely, some who intend to die are rescued, interrupted, or lack access to lethal means and therefore survive.

The intent of most adolescent parasuicides appears to be interpersonal and instrumental, for example, to mobilize or effect change in another's behavior. For many, their stated intent may not be congruent with that evaluated by a clinical interviewer. For example, Hawton, Cole, O'Grady and Osborn (1982) reported that of 50 adolescents hospitalized for deliberate self-poisoning, one third stated that they wished to die at the time of the overdose. However, the clinical interviewer believed that only seven (14%) of these patients had an intent to die.

Where intent is interpersonal and designed to effect change in another's behavior and where lethality is low, the behavior of the adolescent may involve initiating movements toward an attempt. These low-level parasuicidal behaviors are often called *suicide gestures* and are equivalent to behavioral threats (see case illustration to follow). Thus the adolescent may make hesitation cuts to the wrist or swallow a decidedly nontoxic dosage of medication in order to scare others into a different response. As is evident in Linda's case, such low-toxicity ingestions often represent attempts to exert power in a context of felt powerlessness.

Case Illustration

> Linda, age 15, argued with her grandmother, with whom
> she had lived for the 7 years since her mother died, when
> she was told she could not go on a family outing because
> she had not completed her chores. Upset, she ran to the
> bathroom thinking she would end her life. Grabbing a bottle
> of Extra-Strength Tylenol, Linda took and swallowed 6 pills.
> Later she asked her grandmother, "What would happen if
> I killed myself?" In discussing her ingestion at the hospital,
> she related that when she actually took the pills, she was
> hoping that she would get sick and, in consequence, that
> her family would change their attitude toward her.

Reliable estimates of the incidence of parasuicidal behavior
among adolescents are difficult to establish and, for the most
part, based on hospital admissions. Recent surveys of high
school students, one at an academically select New York City
public high school (Harkavy-Friedman et al., 1987) and a second
based on a sample of Midwest high school students (Smith &
Crawford, 1986) found that 8–9% admitted to one or more
"attempts." Yet, in the Midwest sample, only about 1 in 11 of
these attempters received medical attention after their attempt.
Thus, relying on hospital records leaves uncounted the overwhelming majority of parasuicides, and it appears safe to conclude that the overwhelming majority of parasuicides are of
low lethality.

Repeat Attempters

One group of parasuicides is of special interest for purposes of
assessment. This group is composed of those who engage in
chronic, habitual parasuicidal behavior. Estimates of the percentage of attempters across all ages repeating an episode within
1 year of the first attempt range from 14–26% (Reynolds &
Eaton, 1986). The majority of adult repeaters have been found
to be younger (under 30) and the frequency of repetitive attempts appears greater at younger ages (under 19; Eyman and
Smith, 1986). These patients use parasuicidal behavior as a reg-
ular means of coping with stress and are significantly demanding of the treatment system. They also appear to have more

chronic symptoms, poorer coping histories, and more family histories positive for suicidal behavior and substance abuse (Reynolds & Eaton, 1986). The chaotic and chronic dysfunctional family patterns common to lives of repeat suicide attempters is clearly evident in the case of Cassie, which follows. Although their first attempts are generally milder, once a more seriously lethal attempt is made, subsequent attempts remain seriously lethal (Eyman & Smith, 1986). Thus this group remains at high risk for completing suicide. In fact, one report from Finland indicated that after an approximately 5-year period of follow-up, 5% of adolescent repeaters had completed suicide as compared to only 1% of "first-timers" (Kotila & Lonnquist, 1987).

Case Illustration

> Cassie, age 15, was brought to the emergency room by her mother after ingesting multiple medications. Her overdose was precipitated by a fight with her mother, when Cassie was confronted with being truant from school five times in the previous week. Concurrently, Cassie's mother reported dramatic changes in Cassie's behavior and personality over the previous few months, including an escalating series of altercations with friends and a significant drop in school interest and performance. Although denying drug use herself, Cassie's boyfriend had recently been sentenced to 30 months in jail for drug possession.
>
> This was Cassie's fifth emergency room visit for self-harm behavior, since age 10, when she deliberately splashed hot grease on her arms, ending a furious fight with her older sister. This sister recently had been indicted for assault and battery. Cassie's mother has a history of hospitalizations for schizophrenia, including visual hallucinations. Her father deserted the family when Cassie was 7 years old.

Threateners

Two categories of suicidal actors and actions remain to be described in our array of defined suicidal behaviors. These involve verbal behavior, one public, the other subvocal. Those who make suicidal threats, or "threateners," are those who alert their interpersonal context, most often during crises, to the possibility of suicide. As we will learn, the great majority of attempts and completions, perhaps as much as 80%, are preceded by such threats or warnings. Conversely, the great majority of threats are not followed by actions, are often not intended to be so followed, or are deterred from being acted upon by their contingent reinforcers (e.g., desired attention from others). However, we would be remiss if the following point did not strike the reader as a déjà entendu before the end of this book: All threats and communications about suicide should be taken seriously, responded to, and evaluated as indicators of potential clinical significance and potential risk. To not do so and to be proven wrong by eventual suicidal behavior is a cost we believe to be most preventable.

Ideators

As noted earlier, transient thoughts about the meaning of life and even suicide may be normative in adolescence, with up to 63% of high school students reporting any degree of ideation (Smith & Crawford, 1986). Where ideation becomes clinically significant is where it is more than transient, possibly a preoccupation, or where it is accompanied by the possibility of being translated into action (see chapter 4).

It may be presumed, a priori, that the thought of suicide precedes suicidal behavior, although this may not be conscious for some. Although most adolescent attempters report contemplating their attempts only a relatively short time before engaging in the behavior (Hawton et al., 1982), most who make an attempt report much longer histories of wishing to die, often extending back to early childhood (Berman & Schwartz, 1990). Teenagers reporting "troubling" levels of suicidal ideation have been found more likely to also report an attempt and, compared to nonideators, more negative and total life stress, less support, and poorer adjustment (Dubow, Blum, & Reed, 1988). Suicide ideation also has an obvious and significant relation to both major depressive and borderline personality disorders, of which it is one of the defining criteria for diagnosis (American Psychiatric Association, 1987).

Relation Between Suicidal Behaviors

As noted earlier, suicidal ideation precedes threats and attempts, and a single attempt is significantly related to both a repeat attempt and completed suicide. Both retrospective and prospective studies of adolescent suicidal behavior note significant overlap among these behaviors.

In studies of completed suicides across all age groups, including youth, prior suicide attempts consistently stand out. For example, Maris (1981) found the number of prior attempts to be the predictor with the strongest beta value when comparing both attempters and completers with normal controls. With a particular focus on adolescence, Farberow's (1989) summary found prior behavior (attempts, threats, ideation, or a combination of these) to be "one of the strongest indicators of high risk in adolescents," with reported frequencies varying from 22–71% of those making subsequent attempts. Similarly, Shafii et al. (1985) concluded that a prior attempt was the single most important risk factor for ultimate completion.

Conversely, follow-up studies of teenage attempters find the rate of completed suicide to be higher than that of the general population, with rates ranging from 1–9% among males and from 1–4% among females (cf. Shaffer, 1988). Frequencies of subsequent attempts by first-time attempters range as high as 50% over a 3-year period (Stanley & Barter, 1970).

Thus, the adage that the best predictor of future behavior is past behavior appears applicable to suicidal behavior among both adolescents and adults. As Marks and Haller (1977) could not distinguish adolescent threateners from attempters, and as the preceding brief review makes clear that there is significant overlap among attempts and completions, the at-risk adolescent, first and foremost, is so identified by any of the various prior suicidal behaviors. However, as noted recently by Clark and Gibbons (1987), the association between past and future suicidal behaviors is mostly explained by the individual's predispositional attributes (from genetic to characterologic). What remains for us to identify, therefore, are those factors denoting risk that can be identified before any self-harm action occurs.

Risk Factors

Risk factors are those attributes or characteristics of the index group (i.e., suicidal adolescents) that describe membership in that group. As such, the identification of such attributes in an as yet nonsuicidal adolescent should alert us to the possibility that this adolescent may become a member of the group already identified as suicidal. These attributes will not describe all suicidal adolescents but they should identify a significant porportion of these youth. Also, identified attributes are most significant when they are derived from control group studies, that is, they differentiate suicidal adolescents from nonsuicidal adolescents.

As noted by Berman & Cohen-Sandler (1982), a finding of frequency, for example, an occurrence common to 60% of a sample of suicidal adolescents may have use for generating testable hypotheses but has little meaning as a specific risk factor if that frequency is not significantly greater than that of a relevant control group. For these reasons, we will attempt in the following delineation of risk factors to highlight only those research-based findings that have been found to discriminate suicidal adolescents from others, and to note high-frequency attributes as worthy of more controlled study.

Psychopathology and Personality Characteristics

Rich et al. (1986) studied a large cohort of completed suicides under the age of 30 in San Diego County and summarized their findings by stating that "psychiatric illness is a necessary (but insufficient) condition for suicide." Indeed, these researchers were able to retrospectively provide DSM-III diagnoses to 92% of the cases they studied. Similarly, Shaffer, Garland, Gould, Fisher, and Trautman (1988) have noted that "only a very small proportion of suicides appear free of psychiatric symptoms prior to death." Whether diagnosable or merely symptomatic, there

is wide agreement among clinical researchers that suicidal behavior is pathognomic of psychopathologic states. Crumley (1982)
has gone so far as to state that a suicide attempt by an adolescent
is a "cardinal symptom of psychiatric disorder."

Although a variety of pathologies have been noted, three
disorders predominate in reports of completed and attempted
suicide among adolescents: mood disorders, substance abuse
disorders, and conduct disorders.

Depression, both unipolar and bipolar, has been frequently
reported among both completers (Brent, Perper, Goldstein, et
al., 1988; Rich et al., 1986; Shaffer & Gould, 1987; Shafii et al.,
1985) and parasuicides (Carlson, 1983; Friedman, Corn, Aronoff, Hurt, & Clarkin, 1984; Marks & Haller, 1977), with rates
being higher among psychiatric inpatients than in medically
hospitalized samples (Spirito et al., 1989).

The relation between depression and suicidality, however,
is complex. Depression appears most directly related to suicide
ideation (Pfeffer, Zuckerman, Plutchik & Mizruchi, 1984; Velez
& Cohen, 1988). Carlson and Cantwell (1982), for example,
reported that 83% of youth with suicidal ideation showed signs
of depression. However, the great majority of depressed youth
are not suicidal. Shaffer and Bacon (1989) have estimated that
among males, the ratio of depressed to depressed suicidal adolescents is approximately 660:1. Depressives with suicidal
ideation have been differentiated from those without ideation
primarily in terms of the former having more disturbed intra-
familial relationships (Kosky, Silburn, & Zubrick, 1986). In addition, the relation between depression and suicidal ideation
may be mediated both by deficits in cognitive coping strategies
and hopelessness (see below).

Clinically associated with depression in adolescence is *sub-
stance use*. Drug and alcohol use and abuse, again, have been
found with great frequency among completers (Rich et al., 1986;
Shaffer & Gould, 1987; Shafii et al., 1985) and parasuicides
(Garfinkel et al., 1982; McKenry, Tishler, & Kelly, 1983; Riggs,
Alario, McHorney, DeChristopher, & Crombie, 1986; Robbins
& Alessi, 1985). Substance abuse histories have been noted in
15–33% of adolescent completers (Hoberman & Garfinkel, 1988;
Poteet, 1987; Thompson, 1987). In studies of adolescent sub-

stance users, suicide attempts have been found to occur at rates three times those of controls, with the "wish to die" increasing dramatically *after* the onset of substance use (Berman & Schwartz, 1990). Most importantly, substance use at the time of suicidal behavior has been found to be related to the lethality of the method used (Brent et al., 1987).

Rosenstock (1985) has reported on a 9-year longitudinal analysis of consecutive adolescent psychiatric inpatient admissions, finding *concurrent* increases in admission diagnoses of depression (350%), substance abuse (200%), and suicidal ideation (300%). Embedded as intervening variables among and common to these symptom presentations are cognitive distortions, impulsiveness, frequent and serious interpersonal loss, and family pathology. More will be said about these and related themes descriptive of the common threads between pathological states and suicidal behaviors.

Related to both depression and substance abuse disorders is the third commonly found pathology, *conduct disorder*. Shafii et al. (1985) found that 70% of their psychological autopsy subjects had exhibited antisocial behavior (vs. 24% of controls). These youth were noted to come into conflict with legal authorities and to be involved in a variety of antisocial behaviors, from shoplifting to drug selling and prostitution. Shaffer & Gould, (1987) similarly note a preponderance of antisocial behaviors among completers. The role of conduct disorder in adolescent suicidal behavior may be even greater than that of depression. Apter et al. (1988) found higher scale scores for suicidality on the K-SADS for conduct disordered adolescents than for those with major depressive disorder, even though those with conduct disorders were less depressed.

Relatedly, aggressive symptoms are common to hospitalized attempters (Garfinkel et al., 1982) and characterize one of two types of child attempters described by Pfeffer, Plutchik, and Mizruchi (1983). The importance of aggression to suicidality has been highlighted by Plutchik, van Praag, and Conte (1989), who proposed that suicide risk is heightened when aggressive impulses are triggered, then amplified by forces such as substance abuse and not attenuated by opposing forces such as appeasement from others.

Conduct disorders, depression, and substance abuse disorders frequently present co-morbidly, with the frequency and lethality of attempts increasing with the degree of co-morbidity (Frances & Blumenthal, 1989). Depression and anxiety symptoms have been noted to be co-related among samples of suicidal adolescents (cf. Bernstein & Garfinkel, 1984; Mattison, 1988), as have depression and conduct disorders (Alessi, McManus, Brickman, & Grapentine, 1984).

Related as well is borderline personality disorder, a diagnosis more common among parasuicides (Crumley, 1979). Friedman, Clarkin, and Corn (1982) found the most suicidal of their sample of adolescents to be those with both borderline pathology and depression. It is important to note that this relation was sustained even once the suicide criterion was removed from those criteria used to make the DSM-III diagnosis of borderline personality disorder.

Common to these diagnoses are symptoms of affect dysregulation, intense rage, and impulsive behavior. These and similar personality traits are commonly reported in studies of adolescent parasuicides. Hostility (McIntire & Angle, 1973; Tishler, McKenry, & Morgan, 1981), intense anger (Withers & Kaplan, 1987), impulsivity (Arffa, 1983; Crumley, 1979; McIntire & Angle, 1973), and significant acting out (Gispert et al., 1987) also have been frequently found.

Impulsivity reflects not only angry and aggressive behavior but also a low frustration tolerance and a lack of planning. In support of this, both Shaffer et al. (1988) and Hoberman & Garfinkel (1988) report that most completed suicides by adolescents are impulsive, with perhaps only about one in four giving evidence of planning.

Another cognitive–emotional variable related to these conditions is hopelessness. Based on Beck's findings with adult samples (Beck, Steer, Kovacs, & Garrison, 1985), hopelessness has been found at significantly higher levels in samples of adolescent parasuicides than in nonsuicidal controls (Spirito, Williams, Stark, & Hart, 1988; Topol & Reznikoff, 1982). However, although it is a robust finding among adult parasuicides, the relation between hopelessness and suicidality in adolescence has not been upheld universally (Asarnow, Carlson, & Guthrie,

1987; Carlson & Cantwell, 1982; Rotheram-Borus & Trautman, 1988).

As we shall note in the next chapter, there is no typical suicidal adolescent. Indeed, in addition to these primary diagnostic types, a variety of other diagnoses can be found among those adolescents at risk. Shaffer et al. (1988) note finding a subgroup of completers showing evidence of anxiety, perfectionism, and distress at times of change and dislocation. This description might best fit the high-achieving "star," whose suicide invariably shocks the community of survivors as beyond reason and worthy of front-page news coverage. Shaffer et al. also report learning disabilities and schizophrenia as characterizing completers. The most common descriptors applied to Hoberman and Garfinkel's (1988) sample of adolescent completers were: withdrawn, lonely, and supersensitive, labels remarkably similar to those Shafii et al. found in two thirds of their subjects. However, in the latter study, this withdrawn, inhibited personality was not found significantly more often among the suicides when compared to control subjects.

Behavioral Characteristics

The withdrawal noted among suicidal adolescents may be a sign of depression or a coping strategy (Spirito et al., 1989). As such, much research is yet needed to discriminate between suicidal and nonsuicidal depressed adolescents. Social isolation and social alienation, however, consistently identify the suicidal adolescent in a number of studies (cf. Farberow, 1989).

Only 10% of Hoberman and Garfinkel's (1988) sample were characterized as loners. However, more commonly, suicidal adolescents are reported to have no close friends (Khan, 1987) and less likely to have a close confidant (Topol & Reznikoff, 1982). Closely related is the finding that suicidal substance abusers, compared to nonsuicidal abusers and to normal controls, significantly more often describe their early childhood as characterized by loneliness (Berman & Schwartz, 1990). These findings are consistent with other studies that have found suicidal adolescents to be lonely and socially withdrawn (Petzel & Cline, 1978; Rubenstein et al., 1989).

Alienation from and a lessened involvement in the school milieu have also been found (Corder, Shorr, & Corder, 1982; Garfinkel et al., 1982; Gibson, 1982), but, again, may be predictive more generally of emotional disturbance (Cohen-Sandler et al., 1982a) and of depression in particular. Consistent with findings of both depression and acting-out behavior, school disciplinary problems, poorer school performance, and underachievement have all been noted among suicidal adolescents (cf. Berman & Carroll, 1984; Garfinkel & Golumbek, 1983; Shafii et al., 1985). Although many of the studies that have examined the relation between suicide and school achievement have not adequately used control groups (cf. Petzel & Riddle, 1981), one retrospective study of youthful completers found that up to 50% had some form of learning disability (Peck, 1985).

Runaway street youth have been compared to nonrunaway peers with findings of greater depression, prior and current suicidality, and other psychopathology, including substance abuse (Nilson, 1981; Yates, MacKenzie, Pennbridge, & Cohen, 1988). Stiffman (1989) found that 30% of the St. Louis area runaways she studied reported a past suicide attempt. Multiple regression analyses revealed that runaways who had attempted suicide differed from those who had not by greater substance abuse, more behavior problems, family instability (including drug abuse, suicidality, depression, and antisocial behavior) and female gender. Running away from home is inherently a sign of family conflict, a variable of significance we shall discuss. However, it is important to note that in studies of children and latency-aged youth (Pfeffer, Conte, Plutchik, & Jerrett, 1980; Cohen-Sandler & Berman, 1982), running away is a sign of emotional disturbance and is not pathognomic of suicidality. Furthermore, characteristic of these younger adolescents is a family enmeshment making it difficult for them to pull away from familial and parental problems. It has been postulated that in these families, the suicide attempt may be the youngster's way of wrenching away from a fused system (Cohen-Sandler, Berman, & King, 1982b).

Sometimes, emotionally disturbed and alienated youngsters seek a sense of belongingness in new "families," for example, cults. One form of this involves satanic worship. Bourget, Gagnon, and Bradford (1988) have documented (in a noncontrolled study) an apparently strong relation between satanic involvement and a history of suicide attempts among a small group of adolescents. As in the case of Teri, an identity—even one of deviance from the mainstream—means that one need not be isolated and alone.

Case Illustration

> Teri, age 15, had been depressed since her father died when she was 11. According to her mother, over the past 14 months her behavior had gone from "moody" to "sullen." She had become increasingly noncompliant, violated curfews, disobeyed restrictions imposed as punishments, and had run away from home on several occasions. She labeled herself as "stupid," spoke and wrote (see Figure 4) often of death and suicide, and on three occasions had cut her wrists, albeit only superficially. Her school performance had declined and she spoke now of hating school. Her peer associations were almost exclusively with other alienated teens, described by her as "punks and other anarchists."

Family and Parental Characteristics

Among the most studied of variables relating to adolescent suicide is the influence of the family, and the parental system in particular. As models, as sources of praise and reinforcement, as nurturers and caretakers, parents have obvious roles in the development of healthy and ultimately autonomous children. Where parents, individually or together, have serious conflicts or problems, the adolescent's press for autonomy and growth may be seriously interfered with.

Compared to normal adolescents, suicidal adolescents report poorer familial relationships (Slap et al., 1989) and report receiving less affection (Korella, 1972). They describe time spent with their families as less enjoyable and hold more negative views of their parents (McKenry et al., 1983).

Shafii et al. (1985), in their controlled study of suicide completers, found significantly higher levels of family turmoil, from what's the use?

I look ~~from~~ around here and all
I see,
I s a school and a world
that could do with out me.
I've gotton here but only by
Fate.
My death, I'm sure, will not come late.
I try each day to see the use
of being here.
There is none.
I try to find a meaning,
But the wars have been fought,
my battle is yet to come.
When I close my eyes the path
yoes.
When I open them again the
pain. shows.
~~I try~~ to not cry aloud,
Wouldn't matter anyway I'm lost in
this crowd.
You can pretend I don't live.
But I'll keep living till my
life gives.

Figure 4 Teri's note, found by her homeroom teacher and forwarded to her mother.

violence to suicidal tendencies. In studies of parasuicides, summarized by Pfeffer (1989b), two types of factors consistently have been associated with adolescent suicidal behavior:

1. Familial stress, particularly due to changes and threatened changes in the parental system such as loss, death, separation,

and divorce (Cohen-Sandler et al., 1982a; Corder et al., 1974; Garfinkel et al., 1982; Kosky, 1983; Miller, Chiles, & Barnes, 1982; Stanley & Barter, 1970) and a consequent lack of support for the adolescent (Stanley et al., 1970) and

2. Parental dysfunction, suicidality, and psychopathology, the latter ranging from generalized psychiatric problems to those of depression and substance abuse and including consequent aggression against and abuse and neglect of children (Cohen-Sandler et al., 1982a; Deykin, Albert, & McNamarra, 1985; Garfinkel et al., 1982; Kosky, 1983; Joffe, Offord, & Boyle, 1988; McKenry et al., 1983; Shaffer & Gould, 1987; Tishler & McKenry, 1982). Levin and Schonberg (1987) report greater exposure to family violence among a sample of attempters.

In Frieda's case, the family history reflects parental substance abuse, dysfunction, and psychopathology in all members of the family system. Although Frieda is the identified patient, her pathology has been decidedly influenced by the family system via social learning, modeling, or perhaps, genetics and biochemistry.

Case Illustration

> Frieda, age 14, came to the emergency room complaining of back pain suffered due to a jump from the third-story attic window of her house. She stated that her mother, an alleged alcoholic, had locked her in the attic as a punishment. This was the fourth visit Frieda had made to the emergency room for parasuicidal behavior, the last three having been for overdoses, all within the last 18 months. Not one of these admissions was followed by compliance with recommended outpatient therapy.
>
> Frieda had a long history of acting-out, runaway, and impulsive behaviors and of early sexual relations, including a pregnancy and abortion at age 12, which led to her initial suicidal threats. She was in constant and intense conflict with her mother. Her father had been killed while dealing drugs when Frieda was 7; her only brother had been institutionalized several times for "a nervous breakdown."

Stressful Life Events

Almost all the research on stressful life events and suicidal behavior has been with adult samples, and the few studies with youth have not used rigorous methodology (Paykel, 1989). Among suicidal adolescents, significantly increased levels of life stress have been found (Gispert et al., 1987; Rubenstein et al., 1989), particularly when compared to normal controls (Jacobs, 1971). Schotte and Clum (1982) found that college student suicide ideators reported more negative life events over a 6-month period than did nonideators. In the Rubenstein et al. (1989) study, high-school-aged adolescents who reported an attempt to hurt themselves in the previous year had stress scores 33% higher than those of nonsuicidal adolescents. The four areas of stress most associated with suicidality were concerns over sexuality, achievement pressure, family suicide, and personal (family and peer) loss. Among a large sample of middle and high school students who self-reported suicide ideation, Garrison et al. (1988) found significant associations between several measures (except "desirable") of life events and suicidality. However, these associations maintained only in cross-sectional rather than longitudinal analyses.

Among older adolescents, issues of sexuality, as noted by Rubenstein et al. (1989), may pose significant stress and risk for suicidality. Harry (1989) notes, for example, that homosexuals of both sexes are 2 to 6 times more likely to attempt suicide than are heterosexuals and that risk for an attempt is greatest during the period of coming to terms with "coming out," typically about the age of 18–19.

Gay youngsters, such as Barry, are particularly vulnerable to questions of acceptability and experiences of rejection at a point in their development where their sexual and personal identities are particularly fragile.

Case Illustration

> Barry, age 17, was found at 2:30 a.m., breathing with great difficulty. At the emergency room he was agitated and

confused to the point of incoherence. It was discerned that he had ingested approximately 60 appetite stimulant pills prescribed to him just three days before. In his bedroom was found a suicide note addressed to his 15-year-old cousin, who had recently come to live with him. In the note, Barry spoke of his "feelings exploding" in referencing his homosexual passion for his cousin. It appeared that he had made sexual advances toward his cousin and that these had been rejected. This rejection precipitated the current overdose.

In their controlled study of parasuicidal children, age 5–14, Cohen-Sandler et al. (1982a) found that suicidal children experienced more stressful life events than did hospitalized depressed and psychiatrically disturbed, nondepressed children. Stress was consistently greater for the suicidal youth from early childhood through latency age, and particularly in the year preceding hospitalization. The suicidal group experienced greater losses and significant changes, primarily in the parental and caretaker system (i.e., death of a grandparent; separation, divorce, remarriage, or hospitalization of a parent) and psychological trauma (e.g., witnessing the father attempt to murder the mother). In Stanley et al. (1970), parental loss through separation and divorce was significant for suicidal adolescents when it occurred prior to the age of 12. What we must note in these findings of family instability are the probable impacts on youth ultimately at risk, that is, increased social isolation, feelings of rejection and a consequent lack of trust, rage, and an absence of nurturant caregivers and effective models for problem solving.

Paykel (1989) concludes his review by noting that there is a dearth of studies employing careful methodology and controlled comparisons of recent life events of suicidal (vs. nonsuicidal) youth. Uncontrolled studies suggest high rates of stress in the lives of adolescent attempters. It is important to keep in mind that other variables may mediate between stress and suicidality (e.g., psychopathology and cognitive coping strategies), rather than result from stressful life events.

Cognitive Strategies

The very occurrence of suicidal behavior in a context of life stress strongly implicates the absence or ineffectiveness of behavioral controls (coping strategies) and alternative cognitive problem solving. Adult suicide has often been described as problem-solving behavior (Beck, Rush, Shaw, & Emery, 1979) based on distorted patterns of thinking. In addition to patterns already discussed (impulsivity and hopelessness), the focus has been on dichotomous (polarized) thinking, rigidity, inflexibility, and constriction (Levenson & Neuringer, 1971; Neuringer, 1976).

Deficits in problem-solving skills among suicidal children (Asaranow et al., 1987; Cohen-Sandler & Berman, 1982; Orbach, Rosenheim, & Hary, 1987) and adolescents (Hynes, 1976; Trautman, 1987) have also been documented, particularly in terms of generating fewer alternative solutions to situations of interpersonal conflict. Corder et al. (1974) found suicidal adolescents to feel less control over their environment. Consequently, they responded with greater rigidity and more attempts to structure. At the more extreme end, Tishler et al. (1981) found that their sample of suicidal adolescents displayed poorer reality testing and more psychotic thinking.

The reader interested in the extensive literature on cognitions and suicidal behavior might consult Arffa (1983) and Ellis (1986). For our purposes, it is important to note that the adolescent deficient in these problem-solving skills is more likely to distort his or her perception of problem situations, narrow the range of alternatives to deal with the situation, express greater hopelessness, and behave with more impulsivity. Again we are stuck with a chicken-or-egg type problem etiologically, as these observations may reflect either the cause or the effect of psychopathology.

Imitation and Suggestibility

Exposure to the suicidal behavior of another person in the social networks or the families of completers (Shafii et al., 1985) or attempters (Garfinkel et al., 1982) appears more common to these groups than to controls. Attempters (such as Darlene) and ideators identified through high school surveys of non-patient adolescents report more frequently knowing of a peer, friend, or family member who had attempted suicide (Harkavy-Friedman et al., 1987; Smith & Crawford, 1986).

Case Illustration

> Darlene, age 15, ingested 30 Naldecon tablets after hearing that her "best friend" had attempted suicide (by overdose) earlier in the day. Darlene had shown signs of a depressive disorder, including insomnia, weight loss, and suicide idea-tion, for 3 weeks since problems began developing with her boyfriend. One of her presenting problems was that she had no friends.

As we have noted, a family history of suicide should be considered significant as an alerting sign to suicide risk in ad-olescence. Murphy and Wetzel (1982), after reviewing the lit-erature, estimated that 6–8% of those who attempted suicide had a family history of suicide. The most significant findings regarding family history of suicidal behavior are with adult samples. As one example, Roy (1983) found that of 243 psy-chiatric inpatients with a definite history of suicide in a first- or second-degree relative, almost half had attempted suicide, more than half had a depressive disorder, and more than a third had a recurrent affective disorder. In a 7½-year follow-up, 3% of these patients had completed suicide. Both identi-fication and genetic explanations have been posed to explain these findings.

Exposure to another's suicide may be considered an accel-erating risk factor among those already predisposed to be at risk. That is, exposure by itself is not sufficient to cause a suicide that otherwise would not have occurred. Two sources of re-search provide a basis for this perspective: studies of media influence and cluster studies.

Suicide Clusters and Media Influence

When suicidal events occur close together in space and time or when suicidal events share characteristics (e.g., a similarity of method), beyond what would be normally expected in a given community, such connections suggest an influence among events or triggering by one or more of the preceding events. In epidemiology, such a closely grouped series of phenomena is termed a "cluster," and with regard to suicide has been further defined by the Centers for Disease Control as requiring *three or more* events in the series, although some have criticized this definition as not precise enough epidemiologically (Clark, 1989).

The primary mechanism by which exposure effects a follow-up suicide is through imitation or modeling. The degree to which the second person identifies with or feels similar to the model has been suggested as a possible modifier of the degree of influence exerted (Davidson & Gould, 1989; Davidson, Rosenberg, Mercy, Franklin, & Simmons, 1989).

Adolescents, in general, are highly susceptible to suggestion and imitative behavior, as these are primary modes of social learning and identity formation. To a disturbed youngster, particularly one with preexisting suicidal impulses and diffuse ego boundaries, the perceived attention given to a suicidal event might easily lead to any of several irrational cognitions. Most powerful among these is the belief that the attention and notoriety given to the preceding suicide will be achieved by their own *and* that, even in death, they somehow will be able to appreciate that attention. Where the model suicide is that of a star, one believed to have everything going for him or her, the model's suicide may precipitate or exacerbate a sense of hopelessness ("If he or she couldn't hack it, what chance do I have?") or be permission-giving ("If you feel like you think I did, here's the way to solve your [our] problem").

Where exposure to another's suicide has been used to explain such phenomena, such exposure may be *direct*, where the subsequent suicidal youngster actually knew the victim of a preceding suicide, or *indirect*, where knowledge was garnered through word of mouth, news, or fictional accounts.

The majority of research studies have been in the area of indirect exposure, with the focus on nonfictional and fictional media accounts of suicide as stimuli. As summarized by Berman (1989a) and Davidson and Gould (1989), the effect of publicized suicides on imitative behavior has been most consistently documented in studies of the nonfictional, print, and television news media. Primarily based on the work of sociologist David Phillips, the significant increases in suicides noted after publication of front-page suicide stories has been termed the "Werther effect," referring to an alleged rash of imitative youth suicides following publication of Goethe's *The Sorrows of Young Werther* in 1774.

Other researchers have extended Phillips's work and reported that stories of celebrity suicides, particularly those of entertainment celebrities, had the most significant effect and that that effect was specific to those in a similar social role (Berman, 1989a). Thus for example, Phillips (1985) reported that in the month following Marilyn Monroe's suicide there was an extraordinary increase (12%) of suicides nationwide, particularly among young females. Similarly, Berman (1987) was able to demonstrate a statistically significant increase in gunshot wound suicides in Los Angeles County in the 7 days following comedian Freddie Prinze's suicide by gunshot wound in 1977. The most recent work in this area (Kessler, Downey, Milavsky, & Stipp, 1988), using more refined methods of analysis, has raised some critical questions about whether any observed effect on teenage suicides is indeed imitative.

Several reviews are recommended for the interested reader (Berman, 1989a, 1989b) with regard to studies of the media and imitative suicide. For our purposes it is sufficient to note that there is no conclusive evidence that there is a media (fictional or nonfictional) impact on subsequent suicides among the young. For example, more recent studies (Berman, 1988; Kessler et al., 1988; Phillips & Paight, 1987) have found no evidence of imitative effects of television presentations on suicide, in contrast to earlier and widely publicized reports of aggregate increases in youth suicide after such presentations (Gould & Shaffer, 1986; Schmidtke & Hafner, 1988).

Where effects have been documented, and these are mostly on an idiopathic level, the mechanisms proposed to explain such influences are those of imitation and identification. Social modeling principles apply where the initiator simultaneously displays an answer to life's problems through suicide and indirectly gives permission for suicide by making suicide an acceptable alternative to living a life of pain. When the initiator is a star such as a celebrity, role model, or perceived leader of a social network, a loss of hope follows the suicide, expressed in the following query: What hope do lesser beings have if he or she (the class president, Marilyn Monroe, my father) could not hack it? That hopelessness paired with other reasons for predisposed risk now potentiates that risk.

With regard to the impact of fictional presentations of suicide, the evidence is more controversial and less conclusive (see Berman, 1989a; Gould, Shaffer, & Kleinman, 1988). Most importantly, as all these studies involve large groups and examine aggregate effects, concluding that any individual suicide was imitative of a stimulus model may be an "ecological fallacy" (Davidson, Rosenberg, Mercy, Franklin, & Simmons, 1989).

Davidson et al. (1989) have reported the first systematic and matched case-control investigation of both direct and indirect exposure in two clusters of teenage suicides that occured in Texas in the 1980s. A total of 14 suicides were involved, the majority ($N = 12$) were male and gunshot wound victims (54%). Unexpectedly, neither direct nor indirect exposure to suicide was found to be associated significantly with these suicidal deaths, although the suicidal youths were more likely to have known someone closely who had died violently. Case subjects, on the other hand, shared a number of characteristics known to be associated with suicidal vulnerability. In particular, they were more likely to have made prior threats or attempted suicide; to have been hospitalized for mental disorder or a substance abuse problem; to have communicated about death or suicide or have said "last goodbyes"; to have behaved in physically self-damaging ways; to have been arrested; to have shown recent deterioration in performance or relationship; and to have had instability and change in their family life. The suicidal youths were, moreover, described as easily hurt and to have suffered the recent loss of a boyfriend or girlfriend.

Clark (1989) has criticized the Davidson et al. (1989) cluster study as inadequate as a test of the issue of exposure, because matched control subjects from the same community, grade, and so forth would, therefore, be equally exposed to the same direct and indirect models of suicide. Irrespective of evidence of exposure, there is little dispute that clusters do occur and that suicidal youths within a cluster have known risk factors that can identify them with some precision.

Means of Death

As noted in chapter one, the majority of both male and female adolescent suicide completers die by firearms and explosives, with handguns predominating. Hanging is second most frequent among males, ingestion among females. The overwhelming majority of parasuicides use ingestion of pills as their preferred method of attempt, with analgesics and prescribed medications (for self or parent), such as antidepressants and tranquilizers, most frequntly used (Worden, 1989).

There are a number of factors that have been posited to explain the choice of method used. These are:

1. Availability and accessibility (i.e., ease to obtain)
2. Sociocultural acceptance (i.e., normative use)
3. Knowledgeability (i.e., familiarity with use)
4. Social or behavioral suggestion (e.g., modeling)
5. Saliency (e.g., suggested by publicity)
6. Personal, symbolic meaning of act or setting (e.g., a landmark jumping site such as the Golden Gate Bridge)
7. Intentionality and rescuability (if intent is high, methods of choice will be those most lethal, most efficient, and least likely to be interfered with).

Given a context for suicidal action, that is, an otherwise predisposed youth in a situation of precipitating stress, the ready availability or accessibility of a method of suicide may be a sufficient triggering mechanism to promote impulsive suicidal behavior. In this sense it is imperative that a focus on methods of possible use by the adolescent be considered along with other sociopsychological risk factors.

Protective Factors: Contraindications to Risk

It seems inherently obvious and tautological that the absence of risk factors noted above should serve to protect the adolescent from self-harm potential. Garmezy (1985) has specifically written on such protective factors in his discussion of "stress-resistant" children. Garmezy notes three categories of protective factors that increase resilience and adaptive capacity: (a) dispositional attributes such as self-esteem, feelings of autonomy and control, and a view of life as predictable and basically positive; (b) family cohesion and warmth and the absence of family discord and neglect; and (c) the availability and utilization of external supports and resources.

Rubenstein et al. (1989) recently reported on a study of 300 public high school students focusing on protective interpersonal variables. They found support for the hypothesized relationships between certain familial and peer variables and decreased suicidality. In particular, adolescents who perceived their families to be more cohesive and adaptable and their friendships to be more positive and integrative (i.e., they belonged as a valued member of a peer group), were less suicidal.

A Note on Suicide Notes

The mind of the completed suicide is perhaps no more open to direct observation immediately prior to death than through the study of notes left behind. Furthermore, it is axiomatic that suicide notes found prior to any self-harm behavior should be considered pathognomic of lethal self-harm behavior, even though we have no way of estimating what proportion of suicide note-writers do not follow through with their suicide.

Again, almost all published study of suicide notes has focused on adult note writers. Leenaars (1988) has reviewed all of this work for the interested reader. Turning his focus to the young adult suicide note writer, Leenaars (1989) comments that young adults are different from older adult writers in degree, not in the presence or absence of observed patterns. Sex differences are noted as well. For example, young adult women are more concerned than men about their object relations; in contrast, men express more concern about ego functioning.

The first systematic research of suicide notes left by adolescents has been reported by Posener, LaHaye and Cheifetz (1989), studying 17 note writers (10% of sample) between the ages of 10 and 20. Analyzing their content from a psychoanalytic perspective, Posener et al. found these notes to show frequent themes of love (see Figure 5), aggression turned inward, and ambivalence toward an object, with a feeling of inner badness often cited as a reason for the suicide. Furthermore, notes written by the younger subjects made more references to the hereafter and displayed more psychotic disorganization and more magical thinking.

Common Themes: Risk Factors

Embedded in the foregoing summary of research-based risk factors are some common themes. Attention to these "between the lines" issues makes the intuitive process of assessment, the art of risk assessment (see chapter 4), rest appropriately on its scientific foundation. Concurrently, it allows the clinician to move away from an overly concrete focus on a checklist of risk factors, only a few of which will describe any one suicidal adolescent.

It is difficult to describe these common themes succinctly or in any ordered fashion, as many of them operate synergistically. It is difficult to describe these themes in terms of necessary and sufficient conditions as, for the most part, none of them are either necessary or sufficient. It is difficult to propose a schematic model, for example that of interlocking Venn diagrams proposed by Blumenthal and Kupfer (1989), as such schemata tend to concretize dynamic processes. In the context of this premise, it is therefore easiest simply to list and summarize these themes as follows:

1. A negative personal history. Early life events and stressors such as narcissistic injuries, significant skill deficits (particularly interpersonal and social), negative models for coping, and a

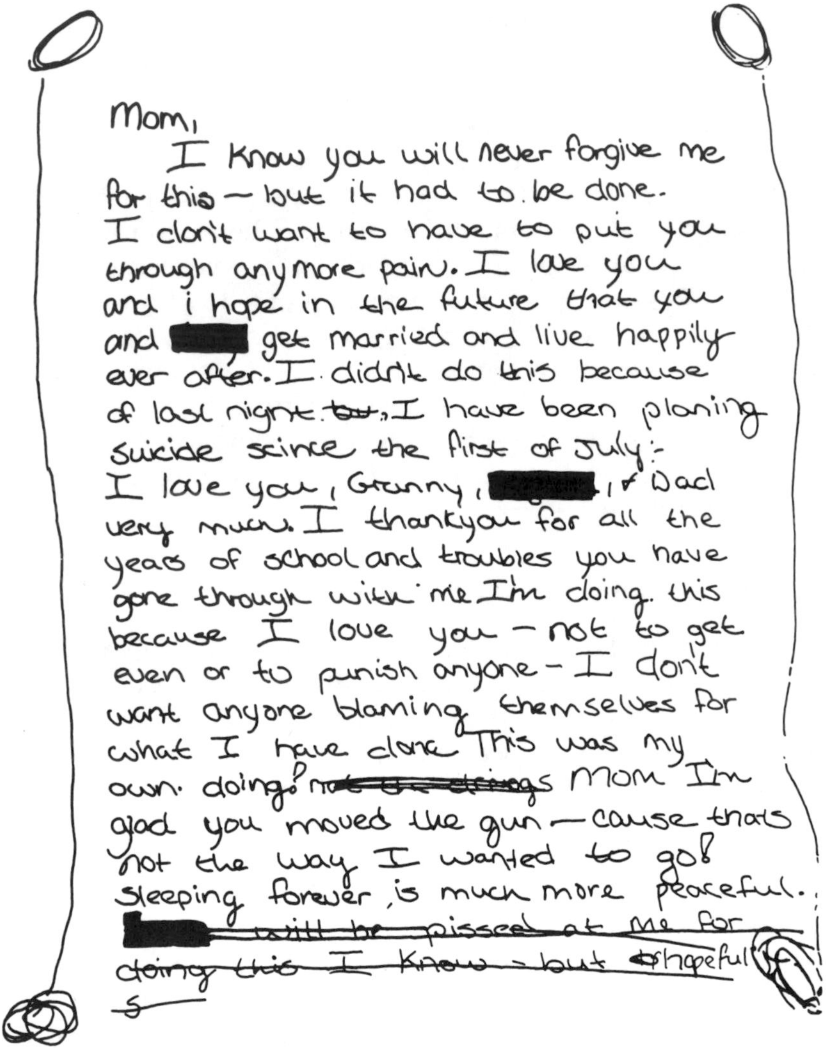

Mom,
    I know you will never forgive me for this — but it had to be done. I don't want to have to put you through anymore pain. I love you and i hope in the future that you and ▮▮▮ get married and live happily ever after. I didn't do this because of last night ~~too~~, I have been planing suicide since the first of July. I love you, Granny, ▮▮▮, & Dad very much. I thankyou for all the years of school and troubles you have gone through with me I'm doing this because I love you — not to get even or to punish anyone — I don't want anyone blaming themselves for what I have done This was my own doing. ~~not~~ ~~the~~ ~~things~~ Mom I'm glad you moved the gun — cause thats not the way I wanted to go! Sleeping forever is much more peaceful. ▮▮▮ ~~will be~~ pissed at me for ~~doing this~~ I ~~know~~ ~~but~~ ~~hopeful~~

Figure 5 Suicide note left by 17-year-old girl who ingested approximately 50 barbiturates.

genetic–biochemical vulnerability. Obviously, family history of suicidality and parental psychopathology are central to this theme. Also, prior self-harm behavior in response to real or anticipated losses is noteworthy.

2. **Psychopathology and significant negative personality attributes.** Evidence of sufficient symptomatology or personality characteristics to define either an Axis I or II diagnosis or attributes that diminish healthy attachments to systems, structures, or object relations. Particularly important are co-morbid psychopathologies including or exacerbated by significant substance abuse. Examples of personality attributes of concern would be aggression, low frustration tolerance, loneliness, and impulsivity.

3. **Stress.** Environmental, psychosocial affect-arousing stimuli that threaten the adolescent's ability to maintain self-esteem and to cope effectively. Often these stressors are anticipated, rather than real, but pose unacceptable rejection, humiliation, or feared punishments.

4. **Breakdown of defenses; affect and behavior dysregulation.** Evidence of cognitive rigidity, irrationality, thought disturbance, loss of reality testing, irrationality; acute behavioral change, including initiated or heightened substance abuse, panic, heightened anxiety, disorientation, and rage.

5. **Social and interpersonal isolation and alienation.** Behavioral withdrawal, isolation, and alienation from typical attachments; help rejecting and noncompliant behavior; antagonism toward alliances with systems, authority, or mainstream associations; alternative identifications with fringe and marginal groups identified by their alienation from main-line society.

6. **Self-deprecatory ideation, dysphoria, and hopelessness.** Statements of unhappiness, pessimism, and irritability; feelings of worthlessness, uselessness, and stupidity; negative views of self, and inability to derive pleasure or to be pleased by others; death-related and suicidal fantasies.

7. **Method availability, accessibility, and knowledgeability.** With sufficient impulse toward self-destructive action or with intent to die or to use self-harm for some instrumental or interpersonal gain, an adolescent may find the availability and accessibility of a weapon—one that he or she knows how to use—an irresistible call to action.

Conclusion

In philosophy, empiricism is a doctrine stating that all knowledge derives from experience. In the behavioral sciences, experience (observations) must be provable by experiment. Within the context of both limited observation of suicidal adolescents and significant methodological difficulties in adequately studying these youth, it is perhaps remarkable that we have come so far in so short a time in deriving empirically based risk factors. Our experience thus far ought to encourage us that significantly more refined observations, and their practical application, are within our grasp.

As we increasingly focus our lens, both the contours and the nuances of our subject matter sharpen under our gaze. Our task now shifts to the dynamic interplay of these risk factors and the assessment of possibilities we wish to prevent.

References

Alessi, N. E., McManus, M., Brickman, A., & Grapentine, L. (1984). Suicidal behavior among serious juvenile offenders. *American Journal of Psychiatry, 141,* 286–287.

American Psychiatric Association. (1987). *Diagnostic and statistical manual of mental disorders* (ed. III-R) Washington, DC: American Psychiatric Association Press.

Apter, A., Bleich, A., Plutchik, R., Mendelsohn, S., & Tyano, S. (1988). Suicidal behavior, depression, and conduct disorder in hospitalized adolescents. *Journal of the American Academy of Child and Adolescent Psychiatry, 27,* 696–699.

Arffa, S. (1983). Cognition and suicide: A methodological review. *Suicide and Life-Threatening Behavior, 13,* 109–121.

Asaranow, J. R., Carlson, G., & Guthrie, D. (1987). Coping strategies, self-perceptions, hopelessness and perceived family environments in depressed and suicidal children. *Journal of Consulting and Clinical Psychology, 55,* 361–366.

Baron, J. N., & Reiss, P. C. (1985). Same time, next year: Aggregate analysis of mass media and violent behavior. *American Sociological Review, 50,* 347–363.

Beck, A. T., Rush, A., Shaw, B., & Emery, G. (1979). *Cognitive therapy of depression*. New York: Guilford Press.

Beck, A. T., Steer, R. A., Kovacs, M., & Garrison, B. (1985). Hopelessness and eventual suicide: A 10-year prospective study of patients hospitalized with suicidal ideation. *American Journal of Psychiatry, 142*, 559–563.

Berman, A. L. (1986a). Adolescent suicide: Issues and challenges. *Seminars in Adolescent Medicine, 2*, 269–277.

Berman, A. L. (1986b). Helping suicidal adolescents: Needs and responses. In C. Corr & J. McNeil (Eds.), *Adolescence and death* (pp. 151–166), New York: Springer.

Berman, A. L. (1986c). A critical look at our adolescence: Notes on turning 18 (and 75). *Suicide and Life-Threatening Behavior, 16*, 1–12.

Berman, A. L. (1987, May). *Suicide and the mass media*. Paper presented at the annual meeting of the American Association of Suicidology, San Francisco, CA.

Berman, A. L. (1988). Fictional depiction of suicide in television films and imitation effects. *American Journal of Psychiatry, 145*, 982–986.

Berman, A. L. (1989a). Mass media and youth suicide prevention. In Alcohol, Drug Abuse, and Mental Health Administration, *Report of the Secretary's Task Force on Youth Suicide Prevention: Volume 3. Prevention and interventions in youth suicide* (pp. 276–284). (DHHS Publication No. ADM 89-1623). Washington, DC: U.S. Government Printing Office.

Berman, A. L. (1989b). Interventions in the media and entertainment sectors to prevent suicide. In Alcohol, Drug Abuse, and Mental Health Administration, *Report of the Secretary's Task Force on Youth Suicide: Volume 4. Strategies for the prevention of youth suicide* (pp. 186–194). (DHHS Publication No. ADM 89-1624). Washington, DC: U.S. Government Printing Office.

Berman, A. L., & Carroll, T. A. (1984). Adolescent suicide: A critical review. *Death Education, 8*(Suppl.), 53–64.

Berman, A. L., & Cohen-Sandler, R. (1982). Childhood and adolescent suicide research: A critique. *Crisis, 3*, 3–15.

Berman, A. L., Litman, R. E., & Diller, J. (1989). *Equivocal death casebook*. Unpublished manuscript, American University, Washington, DC.

Berman, A, L., & Schwartz, R. (1990). Suicide attempts among adolescent drug users. *American Journal of Diseases of Children, 144*, 310–314.

Berman, A. L., & Tanney, B. (1984, May). *Taking the mystery out of research*. Paper presented at the annual meeting of the American Association of Suicidology, Anchorage, AK.

Bernstein, G. A., & Garfinkel, B. D. (1984). School phobia: The overlap of affective disorders and anxiety disorders. *Journal of the American Academy of Child Psychiatry, 23*, 235–241.

Bettes, B. A., & Walker, E. (1986). Symptoms associated with suicidal behavior in childhood and adolescence. *Journal of Abnormal Child Psychology, 14*, 591–604.

Blumenthal, S. J. & Kupfer, D. J. (1989). Overview of early detection and treatment strategies for suicidal behavior in young people. In Alcohol, Drug Abuse, and Mental Health Administration, *Report of the Secretary's Task Force on Youth Suicide: Volume 3. Prevention and interventions in youth suicide* (pp. 239–252). (DHHS Publication No. ADM 89-1623). Washington, DC: U.S. Government Printing Office.

Bond, A., Riggs, S., Spirito, A., & Fritz G., (1988, March). *Adolescent attempts in a pediatric emergency room.* Paper presented at the annual meeting of the Society of Adolescent Medicine, Seattle, WA.

Bonner, R. L., & Rich, A. R. (1987). Toward a predictive model of suicidal ideation and behavior: Some preliminary data in college students. *Suicide and Life-Threatening Behavior, 17,* 50–63.

Bourget, D., Gagnon, A., & Bradford, J. M. (1988). Satanism in a psychiatric adolescent population. *Canadian Journal of Psychiatry, 33*(3), 197–202.

Brent, D. A. (1987). Correlates of medical lethality and suicide attempts among children and adolescents. *Journal of the American Academy of Child and Adolescent Psychiatry, 26,* 87–91.

Brent, D. A. (1989). The psychological autopsy: Methodological considerations for the study of adolescent suicide. *Suicide and Life-Threatening Behavior, 19,* 43–57.

Brent, D. A., Kalas, R., Edelbrock, C., Costello, A. J., Dulcan, M., & Conover, N. (1986). Psychopathology and its relationship to suicidal ideation in childhood and adolescence. *Journal of American Academy of Child Psychiatry, 35,* 666–673.

Brent, D. A., Perper, J. A., & Allman, C. J. (1987). Alcohol, firearms and suicide among youth: Temporal trends in Allegheny County, Pennsylvania, 1960–1983. *Journal of the American Medical Association, 257,* 3369–3372.

Brent, D. A., Perper, J., Goldstein, C., Kolko, D., Allan, M., Allman, C., & Zelenak, J. (1988). Risk factors for adolescent suicide: A comparison of adolescent suicide victims with suicidal inpatients. *Archives of General Psychiatry, 45,* 581–588.

Brent, D. A., Perper, J. A., Kolko, D. J., & Zelenak, J. P. (1988). The psychological autopsy: Methodological considerations for the study of adolescent suicide. *Journal of the American Academy of Child and Adolescent Psychiatry, 27,* 362–366.

Brown, G. L., Ebert, M. E., Goyer, P. F., Jimerson, D. C., Klein, W. J., Bunney, W. E., & Goodwin, F. K. (1982). Agression, suicide, and serotonin: Relationships to CSF amine metabolites. *American Journal of Psychiatry, 139,* 741–746.

Carlson, G. A. (1983). Depression and suicidal behavior in children and adolescents. In D. P. Cantwell & G. A. Carlson (Eds.), *Affective disorders in childhood and adolescence.* New York: Medical and Scientific.

Carlson, G. A., & Cantwell, D. P. (1982). Suicidal behavior and depression in children and adolescents. *Journal of the American Academy of Child Psychiatry, 21,* 361–368.

Clark, D. C. (1989). Impact of television news reports. *Suicide Research Digest,* *3*, 1–2.

Clark, D. C., & Gibbons, R. D. (1987). Does one nonlethal suicide attempt increase the risk for a subsequent nonlethal attempt? *Medical Care,* *25*(Suppl.), S87–S88.

Cohen, J. (1986). Statistical approaches to suicidal risk factor analysis. *Annal,* *New York Academy of Sciences, 487,* 34–41.

Cohen-Sandler, R. (1982). Interpersonal problem-solving skills of suicidal and nonsuicidal children: Assessment and treatment. Unpublished doctoral dissertation, American University, Washington, DC.

Cohen-Sandler, R., & Berman, A. L. (1982, April). *Teaching suicidal children how to problem-solve in non-suicidal ways.* Paper presented at the annual meeting of the American Association of Suicidology, Dallas, TX.

Cohen-Sandler, R., Berman, A. L., & King, R. (1982a). Life stress and symptomatology: Determinants of suicidal behavior in children. *Journal of the American Academy of Child Psychiatry, 21,* 178–186.

Cohen-Sandler, R., Berman, A. L., & King, R. (1982b). A follow-up study of hospitalized suicidal children. *Journal of the American Academy of Child Psychiatry, 21,* 398–403.

Corder, B. F., Schorr, W., & Corder, R. F. (1974). A study of social and psychological characteristics of adolescent suicide attempters in an urban disadvantaged area. *Adolescence, 9,* 1–6.

Craig, L., & Senter, R. L. (1972). Student thoughts about suicide. *Psychological Record, 22,* 355–358.

Cross, C. K., & Hirschfield, R. M. A. (1985, Sept.). *Role of life stressors and attributes in suicide.* Paper presented at New York Academy of Sciences Conference on Psychobiology of Suicidal Behavior, New York.

Crumley, F. E. (1979). Adolescent suicide attempts. *Journal of the American Medical Association, 241,* 2404–2407.

Crumley, F. E. (1982). The adolescent suicide attempt: A cardinal symptom of a serious psychiatric disorder, *American Journal of Psychotherapy, 36,* 158–165.

Davidson, L., & Gould, M. S. (1989). Contagion as a risk factor for youth suicide. In Alcohol, Drug Abuse, and Mental Health Administration, *Report of the Secretary's Task Force on Youth Suicide: Volume 2. Risk factors for youth suicide* (pp. 88–109). (DHHS Publication No. ADM 89-1622). Washington, DC: U.S. Government Printing Office.

Davidson, L. E., Rosenberg, M. L., Mercy, J. A., Franklin, J., & Simmons, J. T. (1989). An epidemiologic study of risk factors in two teenage suicide clusters. *Journal of the American Medical Association, 262,* 2687–2692.

Deykin, E. Y., Albert, J. J., & McNamarra, J. (1985). A pilot study of the effect of exposure to child abuse or neglect on adolescent suicidal behavior. *American Journal of Psychiatry, 142,* 1299–1303.

Domino, G., & Leenaars, A. A. (1989). Attitudes toward suicide: A comparison of Canadian and U.S. college students. *Suicide and Life-Threatening Behavior, 19,* 160–171.

Douglas, J. (1967). *The social meaning of suicide*. Princeton: Princeton University Press.

Dubow, E. F., Blum, M. C., & Reed, J. (1988, April). *Adolescent life stress, social support, and suicidal ideation*. Paper presented at the annual meeting of the American Association of Suicidology, Atlanta, GA.

Durkheim, E. (1951). *Suicide*. New York: The Free Press. (Original work published 1897.)

Ellis, T. E. (1986). Toward a cognitive therapy for suicidal individuals. *Professional psychology: Research and Practice, 17*, 125–130.

Eyman, J., & Smith, K. (1986). Lethality trends in multiple suicide attempts. In R. Cohen-Sandler (Ed.), *Proceedings of the Nineteenth Annual Meeting of the American Association of Suicidology* (pp. 75–77). Denver, CO: American Association of Suicidology.

Farberow, N. L. (Ed.). (1985). *The many faces of suicide: Indirect self-destructive behavior*. New York: McGraw-Hill.

Farberow, N. L. (1989). Preparatory and prior suicidal behavior factors. In Alcohol, Drug Abuse, and Mental Health Administration, *Report of the Secretary's Task Force on Youth Suicide: Volume 2. Risk factors for youth suicide* (pp. 34–55). (DHHS Publication No. ADM 89-1622). Washington, DC: U.S. Government Printing Office.

Farberow, N. L. (Ed.). (1980). *The many faces of suicide: Indirect self-destructive behavior*. New York: McGraw-Hill.

Favazza, A. R. (1989). Why patients mutilate themselves. *Hospital and Community Psychiatry, 40*, 137–145.

Fawcett, J., & Clark, D. (1987). *A psychological autopsy study of adolescent suicide*. Unpublished investigation funded by the Fry Foundation, The W. T. Grant Foundation, and the Arie and Ida Crowne Memorial.

Frances, A. & Blumenthal, S. J. (1989). Personality as a predictor of youth suicide. In Alcohol, Drug Abuse, and Mental Health Administration, *Report of the Secretary's Task Force on Youth Suicide: Volume 2. Risk factors for youth suicide* (pp. 160–171). (DHHS Publication No. ADM 89-1622). Washington, DC: U.S. Government Printing Office.

Friedman, R. C., Corn, R., Aronoff, M. S., Hurt, S., & Clarkin, J. F. (1984). The seriously suicidal adolescent: Affective and character pathology. In H. S. Sudak, A. B. Ford, & N. B. Rushforth (Eds.), *Suicide in the young* (pp. 209–226). Boston, MA: John Wright PSG, Inc.

Galen, R., & Gambino, S. (1975). *Beyond normality: The predictive value and efficiency of medical diagnoses*. New York: John Wiley & Sons.

Garfinkel, B. D., Froese, A., & Hood, J. (1982). Suicide attempts in children and adolescents. *American Journal of Psychiatry, 139*, 1257–1261.

Garfinkel, B. D., & Golumbek, H. (1983). Suicidal behavior in adolescence. In H. Golumbek & B. D. Garfinkel (Eds.), *The adolescent and mood disturbance*, (pp. 189–217). New York: International Universities Press.

Garmezy, N. (1985). Stress-resistant children: The search for protective factors. In J. E. Stevenson (Ed.), *Recent research in developmental psychopath-*

ology: Journal of Child Psychology and Psychiatry Book Supplement No. 4 (pp. 213–233). Oxford: Pergamon Press.

Garrison, C. Z., Jackson, K. L., Schluchter, M. D., Geller, B., Marsteller, F., Tse, J., & Hallman, M. (1988, April). *Predictors of suicide ideation in adolescents.* Paper presented at the annual meeting of the American Association of Suicidology, Washington, DC.

Gibbs, J. P., & Martin, W. T. (1964). *Status integration and suicide.* Eugene, OR: University of Oregon Press.

Gibson, A. H. (1982). Adolescent suicide attempts: An examination of critical factors in the school milieu. *Dissertation Abstracts International, 42,* 4559B.

Gispert, M., Davis, M. S., Marsh, L., & Wheeler, K. (1987). Predictive factors in repeated suicide attempts by adolescents. *Hospital and Community Psychiatry, 38,* 390–393.

Goldacre, M., & Hawton, K. (1985). Repetition of self-poisoning and subsequent death in adolescents who take overdoses. *British Journal of Psychiatry, 146,* 395–398.

Gould, M. S., & Shaffer, D. (1986). The impact of suicide in television movies: Evidence of imitation. *New England Journal of Medicine, 315,* 690–694.

Gould, M., Shaffer, D., & Kleinman, M. (1988). The impact of suicide in television movies: Replication and commentary. *Suicide and Life-Threatening Behavior, 18,* 90–99.

Harkavy-Friedman, J. M., Asnis, G. M., Boeck, M., & DiFiore, J. (1987). Prevalence of specific suicidal behaviors in a high school sample. *American Journal of Psychiatry, 16,* 313–325.

Harry, J. (1989). Sexual identity issues. In Alcohol, Drug Abuse, and Mental Health Administration, *Report of the Secretary's Task Force on Youth Suicide: Volume 2. Risk factors for youth suicide* (pp. 131–142). (DHHS Publication No. ADM 89-1622). Washington, DC: U.S. Government Printing Office.

Hawton, K., Cole, D., O'Grady, J., & Osborn, M. (1982). Motivational aspects of deliberate self-poisoning in adolescents. *British Journal of Psychiatry, 14,* 286– 291.

Henderson, A. S., Hartigan, J., & Davidson, J. (1977). A typology of parasuicide. *British Journal of Psychiatry, 131,* 631–641.

Hersch, S. P. (1975). Suicide: Youth's high vulnerability to it. *Mental Hygiene, 59,* 23–25.

Hlady, W. G., & Middaugh, J. P. (1988) The underreporting of suicides in state and national records, Alaska, 1983–1984. *Suicide and Life-Threatening Behavior, 18,* 237–244.

Hoberman, H. M., & Garfinkel, B. D. (1988). Completed suicide in children and adolescents. *Journal of the American Academy of Child and Adolescent Psychiatry, 27,* 689–695.

Hynes, J. J. (1976). An exploratory study of affective future time perspective of adolescent suicide attempters: Relationship to clinical identification of lethality and its implications for postvention. *Dissertation Abstracts International, 37,* 1404A–1405A.

Jacobs, J. J. (1971). *Adolescent suicide,* New York: John Wiley & Sons.

Jobes, D. A., Berman, A. L., & Josselson, A. R. (1986). The impact of psychological autopsies on medical examiners' determination of manner of death. *Journal of Forensic Sciences, 31,* 177–189.

Jobes, D. A., Berman, A. L., & Josselson, A. R. (1987). Improving the validity and reliability of medical–legal certifications of suicide. *Suicide and Life-Threatening Behavior, 17,* 310–325.

Jobes, D. A., Casey, J. O., Berman, A. L., & Wright, D. G. (1991). Empirical criteria for the determination of suicide. *Journal of Forensic Sciences, 36,* 244–256.

Joffe, R. T., Offord, D. R., & Boyle, M. H. (1988). Ontario child health study: Suicidal behavior in youth age 12–16 years. *American Journal of Psychiatry, 145,* 1420–1423.

Kaplan, R. D., Kottler, D. B., & Frances, A. J. (1982). Reliability and rationality in the prediction of suicide. *Hospital and Community Psychiatry, 33,* 212–215.

Kessler, R. C., Downey, G. D., Milavsky, J. R., & Stipp, H. (1988). Clustering of teenage suicides after television news stories about suicides: A reconsideration. *American Journal of Psychiatry, 145,* 1379–1383.

Khan, A. U. (1987). Heterogeneity of suicidal adolescents. *Journal of the American Academy of Child and Adolescent Psychiatry, 26,* 92–96.

Korella, K. (1972). Teenage suicide gestures: A study of suicidal behavior among high school students. *Dissertation Abstracts International, 32,* 5039A.

Kosky, R. (1983). Childhood suicidal behavior. *Journal of Child Psychology and Psychiatry, 24,* 457–468.

Kosky, R., Silburn, S., & Zubrick, S. (1986). Symptomatic depression and suicidal ideation: A comparative study with children. *Journal of Nervous and Mental Disease, 174,* 523–528.

Kotila, L., & Lonnquist, J. (1987). Adolescents who make suicide attempts repeatedly. *Acta Psychiatrica Scandanavica, 76,* 386–393.

Kreitman, N. (1977). *Parasuicide.* New York: John Wiley & Sons.

Kreitman, N. (1988). The two traditions in suicide research (the Dublin lecture). *Suicide and Life-Threatening Behavior, 18,* 66–72.

Lee, E. E. (1978). Suicide. *Personnel and Guidance Journal, 12,* 200–204.

Leenaars, A. (1988). *Suicide notes.* New York: Human Sciences Press.

Leenaars, A. (1989). Are young adults' suicides psychologically different from those of other adults? *Suicide and Life-Threatening Behavior, 19,* 249–263.

Levenson, M., & Neuringer, C. (1971). Problem-solving behavior in suicidal adolescents. *Journal of Consulting and Clinical Psychology, 37,* 433–436.

Levin, L., & Schonberg, K. (1987). Familial violence among adolescents who attempt suicide. *Journal of Adolescent Health Care, 8,* 302.

Liberman, R. P., & Eckman, T. (1981). Behavior therapy vs. insight-oriented therapy for repeated suicide attempters. *Archives of General Psychiatry, 38,* 1126–1130.

Linehan, M. (1985, Sept.). *Descriptive studies of suicidal acts.* Paper presented at New York Academy of Sciences Conference on Psychobiology of Suicidal Behavior, New York.

Linehan, M. (1986). Suicidal people: One population or two? *Annals New York Academy of Sciences, 487*, 16–33.

Litman, R. E., Curphey, T., Shneidman, E. S., Farberow, N. L., & Tabachnick, M. D. (1963). Investigations of equivocal suicides. *Journal of the American Medical Association, 184*, 924–929.

Maris, R. (1981). *Pathways to suicide.* Baltimore, MD: The Johns Hopkins University Press.

Marks, P. A., & Haller, D. L. (1977). Now I lay me down for keeps: A study of adolescent suicide attempts. *Journal of Clinical Psychology, 33*, 390–400.

Mattison, R. E. (1988). Suicide and other consequences of childhood and adolescent anxiety disorders. *Journal of Clinical Psychiatry, 49*(Suppl. 10), 9–11.

McIntire, M., & Angle, C. (1973). Psychological "biopsy" in self-poisoning of children and adolescents. *American Journal of Diseases of Children, 126*, 42–46.

McKenry, P. C., Tishler, C. L., & Kelly, C. (1983). The role of drugs in adolescent suicide attempts. *Suicide and Life-Threatening Behavior, 13*, 166–175.

Miller, M. L., Chiles, J. A., & Barnes, V. E. (1982). Suicide attempters within a delinquent population. *Journal of Consulting and Clinical Psychology, 50*, 491– 498.

Motto, J. A. (1984). Suicide in male adolescents. In H. S. Sudak, A. B. Ford, & N. B. Rushforth (Eds.), *Suicide in the young* (pp. 227–243). Boston, MA: John Wright PSG, Inc.

Murphy, G. E. (1983). On suicide prediction and prevention. *Archives of General Psychiatry, 40*, 343–344.

Murphy, G., & Wetzel, R. (1982). Family history of suicidal behaviour among suicide attempters. *Journal of Nervous and Mental Diseases, 170*, 86–90.

National Center for Health Statistics. (1989). DHHS, Mortality Statistics Branch. Annual Summary. Hyattsville, MD: U.S. Public Health Service.

Nelson, F. L., Farberow, N. L., & MacKinnon, D. R. (1978). The certification of suicide in eleven western states. *Suicide and Life-Threatening Behavior, 8*, 75–88.

Neuringer, C. (1976). Current developments in the study of suicidal thinking. In E. S. Shneidman (Ed.), *Suicidology: Contemporary developments* (pp. 229–252). New York: Grune & Stratton.

Nilson, P. (1981). Psychological profiles of runaway children and adolescents. In C. F. Wells & I. R. Stuart (Eds.), *Self-destructive behavior in children and adolescents* (pp. 2–39). New York: Van Nostrand Reinhold.

Orbach, I., Rosenheim, E., & Hary, E. (1987). Some aspects of cognitive functioning in suicidal children. *Journal of the American Academy of Child and Adolescent Psychiatry, 26*, 181–185.

Ostroff, R., Giller, E., Bonese, K., Ebersole, E., Harkness, L., & Mason, J. (1982). Neuroendocrine risk factors of suicidal behavior. *American Journal of Psychiatry, 139*, 1323–1325.

Paykel, E. S. (1989). Stress and life events. In Alcohol, Drug Abuse, and Mental Health Administration, *Report of the Secretary's Task Force on Youth Suicide: Volume 2. Risk factors for youth suicide* (pp. 110–130). (DHHS Publication No. ADM 89-1622). Washington, DC: U.S. Government Printing Office.

Paykel, E. S., Hallowell, C., Dressler, D. M., et al. (1974). Treatment of suicide attempters: A descriptive study. *Archives of General Psychiatry, 32,* 487–491.

Peck, M. L. (1982). Youth suicide. *Death Education, 6,* 29–47.

Peck, M. L. (1985). Crisis intervention treatment with chronically and acutely suicidal adolescents. In M. L. Peck, N. L. Farberow, & R. E. Litman (Eds.), *Youth suicide* (pp. 112–122). New York: Springer.

Pescosolido, B. A., & Mendelsohn, R. (1986). Social causation or social construction of suicide? An investigation into the social organization of official rates. *American Sociological Review, 51,* 1986.

Petzel, S., & Cline, D. (1978). Adolescent suicide: Epidemiological and biological aspects. In S. Feinstein & P. Giovacchini (Eds.), *Adolescent psychiatry,* (Vol. 6, pp. 239–266). Chicago: University of Chicago Press.

Petzel, S. V., & Riddle, M. (1981). Adolescent suicide: Psychosocial and cognitive aspects. *Adolescence, 9,* 343–398.

Pfeffer, C. R. (1989a). Studies of suicidal preadolescent and adolescent inpatients: A critique of research methods. *Suicide and Life-Threatening Behavior, 19,* 58–77.

Pfeffer, C. R. (1989b). Family characteristics and support systems as risk factors for youth suicide. In Alcohol, Drug Abuse, and Mental Health Administration, *Report of the Secretary's Task Force on Youth Suicide: Volume 2. Risk factors for youth suicide* (pp. 71–81). (DHHS Publication No. ADM 89-1622). Washington, DC: U.S. Government Printing Office.

Pfeffer, C. R., Conte, H. R., Plutchik, R., & Jerrett, I. (1980). Suicide behavior in latency-age children: An outpatient population. *Journal of the American Academy of Child and Adolescent Psychiatry, 19,* 703–710.

Pfeffer, C. R., Newcorn, J., Kaplan, G., Mizruchi, M. S., & Plutchik, R. (1988). Subtypes of suicidal and assaultive behaviors in adolescent psychiatric inpatients: A research note. *Journal of Child Psychology and Psychiatry, 30,* 151–163.

Pfeffer, C. R., Plutchik, R., & Mizruchi, M. S. (1983). Suicidal and assaultive behavior in children: Classification, measurement, and interrelations. *American Journal of Psychiatry, 140,* 154–157.

Pfeffer, C. R., Zuckerman, S., Plutchik, R., & Mizruchi, M. S. (1984). Suicidal behavior in normal school children: A comparison with child psychiatric inpatients. *Journal of the American Academy of Child and Adolescent Psychiatry, 23,* 416– 423.

Phillips, D. P. (1985). The Werther effect. *The Sciences, 25,* 33–39.

Phillips, D., & Paight, D. J. (1987). The impact of televised movies about suicide: A replicative study. *New England Journal of Medicine, 317,* 809–811.

Plutchik R., van Praag, H. M., & Conte, H. R. (1989). Correlates of suicide and violence risk: III. A two stage model of countervailing forces. *Psychiatry Research, 28,* 215–225.

Pokorny, A. D. (1983). Prediction of suicide in psychiatric patients. *Archives of General Psychiatry, 40,* 249–257.

Posener, J. A., LaHaye, A., & Cheifetz, P. N. (1989). Suicide notes in adolescence. *Canadian Journal of Psychiatry, 34,* 171–176.

Poteet, D. J. (1987). Adolescent suicide: A review of 87 cases of completed suicide in Shelby County, TN. *American Journal of Forensic Medicine and Pathology, 8,* 12–17.

Resnik, H. L. P., & Hathorne, B. C. (Eds.). (1973). *Suicide prevention in the 70's* (DHEW Publication No. HSM 72-9054). Washington, DC: U.S. Government Printing Office.

Reynolds, F. M. T., & Cimbolic, P. (1988–1989). Attitudes toward suicide survivors as a function of survivors' relationship to the victim. *Omega, 19,* 125–133.

Reynolds, P., & Eaton, P. (1986). Multiple attempters of suicide presenting at an emergency department. *Canadian Journal of Psychiatry, 31,* 328–330.

Rich, C. L. (1986). Endocrinology and suicide. *Suicide and Life-Threatening Behavior, 16,* 219–229.

Rich, C. L., Young, D., & Fowler, R. C. (1986). San Diego suicide study I: Young vs. old subjects. *Archives of General Psychiatry, 43,* 577–582.

Riggs, S., Alario, A., McHorney, C., DeChristopher, J., & Crombie, P. (1986). Abuse and health related risk-taking behaviors in high school students who have attempted suicide. *Journal of Developmental-Behavioral Pediatrics, 7,* 205–206.

Robbins, D. R., & Alessi, N. E. (1985). Depressive symptoms and suicidal behavior in adolescents. *American Journal of Psychiatry, 142,* 588–592.

Robins, L. N., & Kulbock, P.A. (1986). Methodological strategies in suicide. *New York Academy of Sciences, 487,* 1–15.

Rosen, A. (1959). Detection of suicidal patients: An example of some limitations in the prediction of infrequent events. *Journal of Consulting Psychology, 18,* 397–405.

Rosenstock, H. A. (1985). The first 900: A 9 year longitudinal analysis of consecutive adolescent inpatients. *Adolescence, 20,* 959–973.

Rotheram-Borus, M. J., & Trautman, P. D. (1988). Hopelessness, depression and suicidal intent among adolescent suicide attempters. *Journal of the American Academy of Child and Adolescent Psychiatry, 27,* 700–704.

Roy, A. (1983). Family history of suicide. *Archives of General Psychiatry, 40,* 971–974.

Roy, A., Ninan, P., Mazonson, A., Picker, D., van Kammen, D., Linnoila, M., & Paul, S. (1985). CSF monoamine metabolites in chronic schizophrenic patients who attempt suicide. *Psychological Medicine, 15,* 335–340.

Rubenstein, J. L., Heeren, T., Housman, D., Rubin, C., & Stechler, G. (1989). Suicidal behavior in "normal" adolescents: Risk and protective factors. *American Journal of Orthopsychiatry, 59,* 59–71.

Rudd, M. D. (1989). The prevalence of suicidal ideation among college students. *Suicide and Life-Threatening Behavior, 19*, 173–183.

Sainsbury, P., & Jenkins, J. S. (1982). The accuracy of officially reported suicide statistics for purposes of epidemiological research. *Journal of Epidemiology and Community Mental Health, 36*, 43–48.

Schmidtke, A., & Hafner, H. (1986). Die vermittlung von selbstmordmotivation und selbstmordhandlung durch fictive modelle. *Nervearzt, 57*, 502–510.

Schmidtke, A., & Hafner, H. (1988). The Werther effect after television films: New evidence for an old hypothesis. *Psychological Medicine, 18*, 665–676.

Schotte, D. E., & Clum, G. A. (1982). Suicide ideation in a college population: A test of a model. *Journal of Consulting and Clinical Psychology, 50*, 690–696.

Seiden, R. H. (1969). *Suicide among youth—A review of the literature, 1900–1967* (Suppl. to the *Bulletin of Suicidology*). Washington, DC: U.S. Government Printing Office.

Shaffer, D. (1988). The epidemiology of teen suicide: An examination of risk factors. *Journal of Clinical Psychiatry, 49*(Suppl. 9), 36–39.

Shaffer, D., & Bacon, K. (1989). A critical review of preventive efforts in suicide, with particular reference to youth suicide. In Alcohol, Drug Abuse, and Mental Health Administration, *Report of the Secretary's Task Force on Youth Suicide: Volume 3. Prevention and interventions in youth suicide* (pp. 31–61). (DHHS Publication No. ADM 89-1623). Washington, DC: U.S. Government Printing Office.

Shaffer, D., Garland, A., Gould, M., Fisher, P., & Trautman, P. (1988). Preventing teenage suicide: A critical review. *Journal of the American Academy of Child and Adolescent Psychiatry, 27*, 675–687.

Shaffer, D., & Gould, M. (1987). A study of completed and attempted suicide in adolescents (Progress report, Grant No. MH 38198). Rockville, MD: National Institute of Mental Health.

Shafii, M., Carrigan, S., Whittinghill, J. R., & Derrick, A. (1985). Psychological autopsy of completed suicide in children and adolescents. *American Journal of Psychiatry, 142*, 1061–1064.

Shneidman, E. S., & Farberow, N. L. (1961). Some comparisons between genuine and simulated suicide notes in terms of Mowrer's concepts of discomfort and relief. *Journal of General Psychology, 56*, 251–256.

Slap, G. B., Vorters, D. F., Chaudhuri, S., & Centor, R. M. (1989). Risk factors for attempted suicide during adolescence. *Pediatrics, 84*, 762–772.

Smith, K., & Crawford, S. (1986). Suicidal behavior among "normal" high school students. *Suicide and Life-Threatening Behavior, 16*, 313–325.

Smith, K., & Maris, R. (1986). Suggested recommendations for the study of suicide and other life-threatening behaviors. *Suicide and Life-Threatening Behavior, 16*, 67–69.

Spirito, A., Brown, L., Overholser, J., & Fritz, G. (1989). Attempted suicide in adolescence: A review and critique of the literature. *Clinical Psychology Review, 9*, 335–363.

Spirito, A., Williams, C., Stark, L. J., & Hart, K. (1988). The Hopelessness Scale for Children: Psychometric properties and clinical utility with normal and emotionally disturbed adolescents. *Journal of Abnormal Child Psychology, 16,* 445–458.

Stack, S. (1987). The sociological study of suicide: Methodological aspects. *Suicide and Life-Threatening Behavior, 17,* 133–150.

Stanley, E. J., & Barter, J. T. (1970). Adolescent suicide behavior. *American Journal of Orthopsychiatry, 40,* 87–96.

Stanley, M., & Stanley, B. (1989). Biochemical studies in suicide victims: Current findings and future implications. *Suicide and Life-Threatening Behavior, 19,* 30–42.

Stephens, B. J. (1985). Cheap thrills and humble pie: The adolescence of female suicide attempters. *Suicide and Life-Threatening Behavior, 17,* 107–118.

Stiffman, A. R. (1989). Suicide attempts in runaway youth. *Suicide and Life-Threatening Behavior, 19,* 147–159.

Tishler, C. L., McKenry, P. C., & Morgan, K. C. (1981). Adolescent suicide attempts: Some significant factors. *Suicide and Life-Threatening Behavior, 11,* 86–92.

Tishler, C. L., & McKenry, P. C. (1982). Parental negative self and adolescent suicide attempts. *Journal of the American Academy of Child Psychiatry, 21,* 404–408.

Thompson, T. R. (1987). Child and adolescent suicide in Manitoba. *Canadian Journal of Psychiatry, 142,* 1061–1064.

Topol, P., & Reznikoff, M. (1982). Perceived peer and family relationships, hopelessness, and locus of control as factors in adolescent suicide attempts. *Suicide and Life-Threatening Behavior, 12,* 141–150.

Trautman, P. (1986). *Referral failure among adolescent suicide attempters.* Unpublished manuscript, Columbia University, New York.

Trautman, P. (1987, October). *Adolescent suicide attempters: Deficits in cognitive style or anhedonia?* Poster presented at the annual meeting of the American Academy of Child and Adolescent Psychiatry, Los Angeles, CA.

van Praag, H. M. (1983). CSF 5-HIAA and suicide in non-depressed schizophrenics. *Lancet, ii,* 977–978.

Velez, C. N., & Cohen, P. (1988). Suicidal behavior and ideation in a community sample of children: Maternal and youth reports. *Journal of the American Academy of Child and Adolescent Psychiatry, 27,* 349–356.

Walsh, B. W., & Rosen, P. M. (1988). *Self-mutilation.* New York: Guilford Press.

Withers, L. E., & Kaplan, D. W. (1987). Adolescents who attempt suicide: A retrospective clinical chart review of hospitalized patients. *Professional Psychology: Research and Practice, 18,* 391–393.

Worden, J. W. (1989). Methods as a risk factor in youth suicide. In Alcohol, Drug Abuse, and Mental Health Administration, *Report of the Secretary's Task Force on Youth Suicide: Volume 2. Risk factors for youth suicide* (pp. 184–192). (DHHS Publication No. ADM 89-1622). Washington, DC: U.S. Government Printing Office.

Yates, G. L., MacKenzie, R., Pennbridge, J., & Cohen, E. (1988). A risk profile comparison of runaway and non-runaway youth. *American Journal of Public Health, 78,* 820–821.

4

Assessment of Risk: Early Detection

The vast majority of young people who kill themselves provide a variety of verbal and nonverbal clues about their imminent suicidal behavior to those in a position to notice. Indeed, Brent et al. (1988) found in their sample of adolescent completers that 83.3% had made suicidal threats to others in the week prior to their death. Perhaps one of the most tragic aspects of adolescent suicide is that suicidal clues and threats are often not taken seriously, are denied, or are simply missed by potential respondents. Accordingly, intervention in and the prevention of an adolescent suicide often fundamentally depend on the awareness and sensitivity of key people in the young person's life who seriously respond to obvious or veiled suicidal cues and make referrals to those who can help.

Once observed as suicidal, the adolescent at risk must be referred for professional assessment and treatment. Those who might first notice suicidal cues (e.g., friends and family) are usually *not* mental health professionals and may not be aware of the process of making an appropriate referral to a professional. Therefore, the journey an adolescent must make between feeling, contemplating, and expressing suicidal impulses and being subsequently referred for professional assessment and treatment may be dangerously circuitous or, more tragically, never made. Prior to our discussion of the clinical assessment of suicide risk, it is important that we briefly consider both the source and context of a referral that leads to that assessment.

The Referral Source

As we will note in chapter 5, adolescents rarely initiate direct help seeking. The majority of suicidal youth receive help through the referrals of others. Virtually anyone that comes into contact with a suicidal adolescent may be exposed to a suicidal threat that could lead to a referral. However, those who most commonly make a referral are those who have the most contact with a young person, such as friends, family members, or teachers. Others with less frequent contact may nevertheless be uniquely situated to detect and refer a suicidal youth. Some common "gatekeepers" include school administrators, guidance counselors, juvenile justice officials (e.g., judges, lawyers, probation officers), religious leaders (e.g, priests, ministers, rabbis), or health professionals. Physicians (pediatricians) in particular are often in a position to detect depressive symptomatology and associated suicidal feelings (Cohen-Sandler & Berman, 1980).

One ironic note is that those individuals who are probably most often exposed to suicidal threats may be the least prepared to respond responsibly. According to the Brent et al. (1988) study, up to half of the adolescent completers who made a threat made their suicidal intentions known only to a peer or sibling. Unfortunately, suicidal threats expressed only to a peer or sibling may not lead to appropriate referrals to a professional. This may be true particularly when a youthful subculture emphasizes the importance of maintaining confidences (i.e., keeping secrets from adult authority figures). Accordingly, our preventive outreach efforts with young people have aimed to drive home the idea, that it is better to lose a friendship because of sharing such a secret with an adult than to lose a friend to suicide because of keeping such a secret.

The Referral Context

The context or circumstances of the referral vary widely as there is no one pathway whereby a suicidal adolescent comes to be seen by a mental health practitioner. Perhaps most commonly, school officials or parents refer an adolescent to a professional when they detect noticeable depressive symptoms, suicidal threats, or acting-out behaviors. In a school setting, for example, an internal referral to a school psychologist or guidance counselor may occur when a teacher notices that a top student has failed three consecutive quizzes and appears lethargic and sad. The school psychologist or counselor may then assess and treat the student or refer him or her to another professional. Alternatively, a parent may seek out treatment for his or her child at a community mental health center in response to the child's vague suicidal threats and recent substance abuse.

Although perhaps less common, other individuals may also facilitate a potentially life-saving referral. An astute pediatrician finding evidence of an eating disorder and superficial cut marks on the wrists of a child in a physical examination may recommend to the parent referral to a private practitioner. A compassionate judge may detect emotional difficulties underlying a juvenile's petty crime and recommend a psychological evaluation and treatment. A child protection worker sent into the home of a reported child abuser may suspect a risk of suicidal acting out in the child–victim and accordingly recommend an assessment.

Clearly there are an infinite number of ways that a troubled adolescent may come to be seen by a clinician. The early detection and subsequent referral to a professional provides some important preassessment data that bear on the adolescent's resources, potential for compliance (see chapter 5), and ability to seek and receive help. It therefore behooves the clinician to consider briefly both the source and the context of the referral before conducting the actual assessment of suicide risk.

Case Illustration

> Susie, an 18-year-old first-semester college freshman, is re-
> ferred by her art professor to the University Counseling Cen-
> ter. On intake, she reports feeling depressed and believes
> she is unable to take her upcoming final exams. She states
> that she has been sleeping poorly and is unable to concen-
> trate on her studies. She eats infrequently and lightly and
> has lost several pounds in the last month without intention
> to do so. She describes herself as listless. Furthermore, she
> notes that she has withdrawn from friends and avoided prac-
> tically all contact. A friend, who accompanied her to the
> center, corroborates that Susie has not returned phone calls
> and has refused offers to talk. Her communications, when
> offered, have reflected a preoccupation with death and dying;
> her jokes have been morbid. Susie states that she, indeed,
> has been obsessed with thoughts of death, preferring a
> "peaceful ending" to a life of pain. She does not believe she
> will be alive by Christmas. Her major semester project for
> art, which led to her referral, was a painting of a young
> female sprawled at the foot of a tall building. It was entitled
> *Susie-cide.*

The experienced clinician may have little difficulty noting the
presence of both a diagnosable affective disorder and suicidal
ideation, as in the case of Susie. But perhaps the most difficult
and anxiety-provoking aspect of a clinical evaluation is that of
assessing whether, at some future time, there is risk for suicidal
behavior. Research has documented a significant relation between depression and suicide ideation; but, the association between these factors and future suicide attempt behavior is limited
(Carlson & Cantwell, 1980). Thus the presence of an affective
disorder, even one with concurrent suicide ideation, is not sufficiently discriminative to allow a dynamic assessment of risk
for future, potentially lethal behavior.

At the same time, such a case presentation well illustrates
the concept of early detection. Clinicians alert to risk factors
associated with suicidal behavior in adolescence (chapter 3)
must use this awareness to "red flag" (Blumenthal & Kupfer,
1989) youth at risk for future suicidal behavior. Such attention

allows for further assessment and identification of a youth at risk. In turn, such an identification is, obviously, the first step toward offering that youth treatment which, if accepted and implemented successfully, should lead to the prevention of suicidal death (Eddy, Wolpert & Rosenberg, 1989).

The Need for Multifocal Assessment

Kaplan, Kottler, and Frances (1982) presented short videotaped interviews of 16 inpatients and outpatients to a panel of mental health professionals, asking these professionals to make several ratings, among which was the risk of a suicide attempt within the next week. The intraclass reliability for risk of suicide attempt was 0.57, with this risk assessment based largely on the patient's reported "imminence of suicidal feelings," a felt-pressure or urgency to kill himself or herself. The predicted lethality of attempts so rated achieved an intraclass reliability of only 0.36, suggesting that clinicians have little rational basis on which to predict specific outcomes of expected actions. In spite of such a low level of precision, such assessments, taken together, determine in good measure our decisions to act on behalf of our patients to protect them from expected self-harm of potentially lethal consequences.

The assessment of the at-risk patient obviously is fraught with difficulty. However, with attention to multiple frames of risk assessment and a step-wise screening procedure similar to those proposed by Rotheram (1987) and Blumenthal & Kupfer (1989), we believe that clinicians can make reasoned judgments of risk leading to both reliable early detection and appropriate treatment planning.

In truth, the assessment of suicidality involves the following multiple assessments:

1. Imminent Risk. The most important aspect of the assessment of risk is temporal, that is, evaluating imminent versus long-term risk of self-harm behavior. Near-term, acute risk may determine the need for hospitalization or other significant crisis intervention responses.

2. Lethality and Intent. A second and related evaluation is that of lethality and intent. The desired and expected consequences of a contemplated behavior may determine, in good measure, what actual behavior will occur and, therefore, the predictable consequences of that behavior. Related to the assessment of intent is an understanding of the meaning, purpose, or goal of the suicidal behavior. A functional analysis of the motive and meaning of suicidal behavior is essential also to establish treatment goals for the adolescent.

3. Predisposing Conditions and Precipitating Factors. An adequate assessment must delineate and clarify what made the adolescent suicidal and, if relevant, what made risk turn into self-harmful action.

4. Psychopathology. To the extent that the presence of symptoms or diagnosable psychiatric disorders contribute to suicidality, their assessment allows for diagnosis-specific treatment strategies to be considered and instituted.

5. Compliance. The assessment interview is the first contact the adolescent has with a potential help-giving individual or system; thus it also is the first of possibly many interviews in which the adolescent is in the role of patient. His or her cooperation with the interviewer may signal what can be expected with regard to his or her compliance with future therapeutic recommendations.

6. Coping Skills and Resources. Any assessment of risk must address contraindications to self-harm behavior. The availability of both internal (e.g., cognitive) and external (e.g., interpersonal) resources needs to be determined. Included here is an understanding of the adolescent's ambivalence, that is, his or her reasons for staying alive.

Assessment Areas

Imminent Risk

The assessment of short- versus long-term risk for suicidal behavior in adolescence begins with observation of alerting signs for risk. Alerting signs indicate that the adolescent is "in the ballpark," that is, deserving of closer scrutiny because he or she shares some commonality with those who have come before. There are two approaches to establishing commonality: (a) risk factors and (b) typology.

The presence of one or more research-based risk factors, such as a family history of suicide, exposure to suicidal behavior of a peer or sibling, acting out, substance abuse, hopelessness, and depression should signal the interviewer that there is a context for the consideration of suicide by the adolescent (i.e., risk). As noted in chapter 3, there are over 50 separate and overlapping, empirically derived risk factors that have been described as discriminative of suicidal adolescents (see Berman & Carroll, 1984; Berman, 1986a, 1986b; Shaffer, 1988; Spirito, Brown, Overholser, & Fritz, 1989 for other reviews). The clinician should be as informed of these findings as possible and should recognize that significant new reports are increasingly forthcoming as researchers begin to attend to the problem of adolescent suicide.

The typological approach focuses more on diagnostic similarities based on clusters of research-based findings. As outlined in chapter 3, the following diagnostic groups appear to be commonly found among suicidal adolescents and thus are to be considered more at risk for suicidal behavior than others:

1. The *depressed* adolescent, readily diagnosed using research-based criteria;

2. The *substance-abusing* adolescent, who may turn to drugs or alcohol to anesthetize depression;

3. The *borderline* or *schizotypal* adolescent, who has a history of rage, impulsivity, and interpersonal instability;

4. The *antisocial*, *acting-out*, or *conduct-disordered* adolescent, whose behavior signals a lack of alliance with or allegiance to healthy objects and systems;

5. The *marginal*, *isolated loner*, who exists on the fringes of a peer system, separate from a peer system, or in groups of marginal others (e.g., with other runaways);

6. The *rigid*, *unifocal perfectionist*, the "star" who operates with depressogenic logic when threatened with not achieving at self- or other-demanded levels of performance;

7. The *psychotic* adolescent, whose behavior is governed by either command hallucinations or an intense panic in anticipation of a self-perceived decompensation; and

8. The *in-crisis* adolescent, whose stress-provoked behavior is driven by impulsivity and irrationality.

Communications. As noted at the beginning of this chapter, the possibility of imminent suicidal behavior may be, and often as well is, signalled by verbal or behavioral messages. Adolescents, in particular, although less frequently writers of suicide notes than adults, communicate in words, school essays, poems, diaries, journals, and artwork (like Susie's) a preoccupation with themes of death, dying, afterlife, or suicide. Questions about death or suicide, asked out of context or with more than ordinary interest, or communicated dreams about death should alert the observer to follow up with appropriate concern. When such signals are present, the interviewer should explore for further evidence of suicide ideation, especially the existence of a plan and the possibility of rehearsal behavior (e.g., the hoarding of pills, knowledge of how to secure a lethal weapon).

It is essential to establish this approach to all suicidal communications, i.e., that they deserve, no less require, further inquiry and through such inquiry the possibility of interventive response. Clinicians, given to analytic and interpretive readings of patient communications, should be careful not to prematurely interpret an adolescent's communication as signaling suicidal risk or not. All communications need to be placed in a contextual frame best supplied by the adolescent himself or herself and by that adolescent's history.

The following illustrative communications describe the range and variety of these messages, from poems to journal entries to drawings. The reader should note that each was a signal, meant for observation and discovery.

Case Illustrations: Suicidal Communications

Cheryl, age 17, wrote the following poem for her high school English class three days prior to her overdose attempt:

A Plea

My world is a lonely world
A world devoid of love, laughter, and life
A world full of despair and darkness. . .
A world in need of a knife

My life is a lonely life
No more friends or happiness do I have
The only thing left in my life
is cold, dark loneliness and sadness

No need for worry
No need for despair
Don't worry for her life
For Cheryl is already dead inside
The job has been done by her knife.

Patty, a 15-year-old repetitive wrist-cutter, kept a journal in which she frequently wrote introspectively and self-disclosingly of her pain. After being gang raped on her birthday, about which she told no one, she wrote the following passage expressing her despair and emptiness, then cut herself:

The house. The house was once happy, when the man had his wife and children. Now it is empty . . . except for the old man. Once he was young and happy. He was at peace. Now he is alone. When his wife died, and then, when his son died, he felt rage. Then he felt sad. Now he can no longer feel the pain. Now he is empty. Nothing lasts, everything can be taken away. Soon the old man will die and the house will be sad. Maybe he will find peace in the skies. No one cares about the house.

The following letter was sent to the central office of the American Association of Suicidology after the association's name and address appeared as a trailer to a public service television announcement about teen suicide:

I am 12 years old and I don't know if I have the power to live much longer. My parents pay attention to my 15-year-old sister. She blames everything on me and I don't know anything about it and I get into trouble. My teachers know I'm thinking about it cause I starve myself and I cut in my skin. My teachers had a conference with my parents about it. I've told two of my friends about it, one doesn't believe me, the other tells me "Don't do it." If things don't change, I will commit suicide. I have the date marked on my calendar. I get the feeling that my parents don't want me. They say they love me but I know they don't. So that is why I'm going to commit suicide. I'm going to give them a present on my birthday.

Barb, a 19-year-old college sophomore who acknowledged being depressed, brought her diary to her new therapist, suggesting that his reading of it might give him added insight into her problems. After only two meetings, during which Barb presented herself in a most guarded manner, speaking in a monotone and only in response to directives and questions, he was eager to have such an opportunity to read her written thoughts. When he turned to her most recent entries, dated the evening before this session, instead of introspective writing he found drawings on facing pages (see Figures 6 and 7).

The parents of an 18-year-old college freshman found a college spiral notebook their son left after being home from school over Christmas break. In it they discovered a poem which alerted their concern. In consultation, they related that their son had always lived recklessly (e.g., he had been stopped over five times for speeding), had run away from home several times during his adolescence, and had been in more than a few physical altercations with his father. Although they had found a bong in his bedroom, they had accepted his denial of drug use and his explanation that he was merely "holding it for a friend."

Our admonition to the reader to avoid premature interpretation is most evident here, as the brief background given on this adolescent leaves open several competing meanings of his written words. These range from that of a suicidal message to that depicting the thrill of the behavioral gambler (excessive risk-taker) to that of masturbatory fantasy. Furthermore, we do not know for sure that this communication even reflects his own thinking, as there yet exists the possibility, albeit remote, that it is related to academic course work or was transcribed from some other source. As always, we are left with the need for more information. The poem follows:

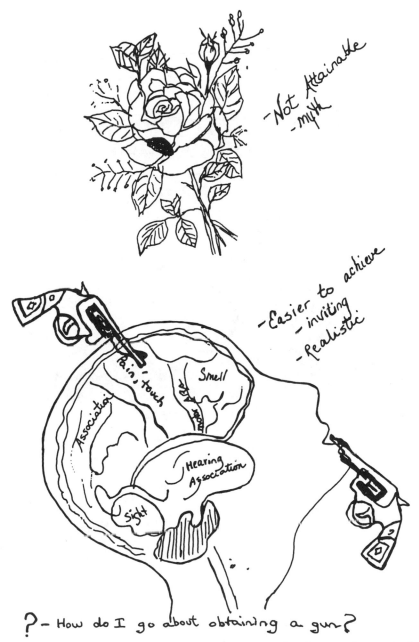

Figure 6   First of two pages in Barb's journal reflecting her suicide ideation.

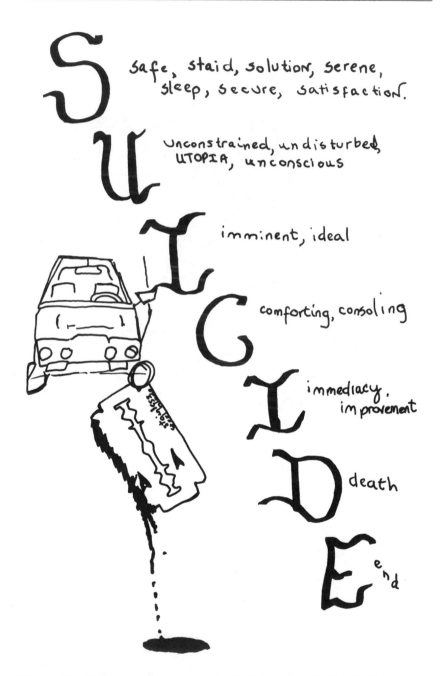

Figure 7   Corresponding page in Barb's journal. Original drawing has bright red ink dripping off of razor blade.

My search continues for a blade.
   A razor's edge to skin the fox
to determine the entrail's configuration,
   to ascertain the color of his blood.

My hand jerks down and immortality
   rises within my soul. With fright
the dial sweeps from left to right
   propelling me toward ecstasy again.

My eyes scrutinize the frictionless surface.
   A meticulous search for the final obstacle
that will jettison my corporeal body
   from reality to hell, via mutilation.

But I will not have existed without fear,
   a surname for insanity, delight.
In my final, wild ride I change dimensions
   entering through a violent, scarlet porthole.

Behavioral Communications. The possibility of suicidal behavior appears greatest, and is most difficult to predict temporally, when there are signs of poor impulse control and rage. A number of the diagnostic types noted in the previous section have in common a lack of control over expression of impulse. In particular, a history of assaultive, violent behavior implicates strongly the potential for such behavior without directionality. Often, suicidal adolescents have been observed to be as rageful toward others as toward themselves, giving evidence of the free-floating nature of their aggression. For example, Cairns, Peterson, and Neckerman (1988) compared a sample of emotionally disturbed, assaultive children (ages 4–18) with histories of serious suicide attempts to a matched sample of nonattempters and found no difference between the groups on the frequency or severity of *other*-directed violence. As in the following case, free-floating rage also exerts a most powerful interpersonal control.

Case Illustration

Leon, age 11, was brought to the emergency room after threatening to ingest his mother's Valium. Since his parents' divorce 3½ years ago, Leon began developing symptoms of

> anxiety and depression, including frightening nightmares. Recently, he attempted to hit his mother with a table lamp, yelling, "I want to kill you!" For the past month he had been carrying a kitchen knife, threatening others to "stay away from [me]!"

Where impulsivity and rage are documented, or where there exists a loosening of controls due to pathology or substance abuse, and when there exists a context to believe that suicidal intent is present (see next section), risk for near-term suicidal behavior is high. In concert with a readily available or accessible method, the possibility of imminent suicidal behavior is great, as is the need for hospitalization to protect the adolescent from himself or herself.

The most significant of behavioral markers or communications is prior suicidal behavior, with perhaps 9% of those once attempting going on to complete suicide within 10 years (Motto, 1984). Shaffer and Gould's (1987) preliminary report of New York area completers found 21% of males and 33% of females to have a history of attempt. Prior suicidal behavior is more clinically significant to a current assessment when it is relatively recent, relatively lethal, death-intentioned, not responded to with clinical intervention, or the last in a sequence of repeated parasuicidal behaviors.

Other behavioral messages are often direct substitutes for verbal communications. For example, termination behaviors such as will writing, giving away favored possessions, and making preparations for death are infrequently observed but clear markers when they do occur.

One indirect behavioral sign of note is that of acute behavioral change. Even in adolescence there are relatively stable behavioral patterns. Significant changes in behavior, particularly those out of character and persistent that are otherwise unexplained, demand a context of understanding. Absent that understanding, the possibility exists that the behavior is masking and concurrently signaling a significant mood shift (depression or anxiety), any of a number of predisposing pathologies (e.g., substance abuse), or some cognitive disturbance in need of further evaluation.

Lethality and Intent

As previously noted, the level of sophistication in both definition and research in suicidology makes it yet impossible for us to adequately establish risk factors particular to levels of lethality. In spite of this, an assessment of lethality, the expected medicobiological consequence of a performed or contemplated act, is important in order to determine evaluated dangerousness to self and the proper response to that evaluation. High lethality refers to the significant possibility of life-threatening impact of self-harm behavior. As a corresponding reference point, low lethality refers to minimal medical danger consequent to self-inflicted action.

An excellent resource for understanding the concept of lethality has been presented by Smith, Conroy, and Ehler (1984). Based on the likely impact of specific actions and modified by the circumstances of the intended action (e.g., probable rescuability), these researchers have provided the clinician with a defined procedure for scaling lethality of attempts or planned actions that does not rely on the patient's stated intent. Ratings of lethality are made on an 11-point equal interval scale having nine anchor points ranging from 0.0 (*death is an impossible result*) to 10.0 (*survival only by fortuitous circumstance and rigorous intervention*). Ease of use and reliability of ratings are enhanced by illustrative examples, by method (e.g., ingestion, cutting) for each anchor point. For example, an attempt contemplated by a patient having small doses of potentially lethal medication (e.g., six Tuinal) is rated 2.0; one ingesting 15–20 lithium carbonate tablets is rated 3.5. Ratings of suicidal behavior above scale point 3.5 are considered "serious." The following case example illustrates a highly lethal attempt (10.0 on this scale) because of his use of a shotgun, in spite of the high probability of rescue and the stated nonlethal intent:

Case Illustration

> Sam was 17 when he approached the front stoop of his girl-friend's house with a borrowed shotgun in hand. Angered by her threat to end their year-long relationship, he intended

to prove to her how much he loved her. As he claimed later, he had "carefully researched" just where to aim the shotgun in order not to hit any vital organs. After ringing her doorbell and hearing her approaching footsteps, he shot himself in the abdomen. As planned and gambled, he survived his wounds, spending close to 3 weeks in the hospital recovering.

The following two cases would be rated 7.0 and 1.0, respectively, on the Smith et al. (1984) Lethality of Suicide Attempt Rating Scale:

> Bob, age 15, was severely reprimanded by his grandmother when he returned from being with his girlfriend because he had told no one where he was. (His grandmother, who had raised him almost from birth after his mother had abandoned him, had grown increasingly anxious about Bob ever since his first suicide attempt, which had occurred over one year earlier, soon after his father, a PCP abuser, announced he was leaving.) Feeling totally unsupported, Bob went to his bedroom to listen to his stereo. He soon complained of a headache and asked for some aspirin. At the hospital, he reflected back on the next several minutes as "blank"; but, at best count, he took 72 aspirin, telling no one until he later developed shortness of breath and called out to his grand-mother, who called for emergency medical treatment.

> Patrice, age 16, attempted to kill herself by ingesting six tetracycline pills in order to avoid being sent by her father to live with his sister in another state. Patrice had a long history of behavioral problems, including substance abuse, runaway behavior, truancy, sexual promiscuity, and two prior overdoses. Additionally, she had been repeatedly assaulted by her substance-abusing boyfriend.

The case of Patrice is illustrative of the distinction between lethality and intent, where the former is low but the intent and its predisposing conditions are serious. As we noted earlier, Brent (1987), in a study of correlates of medical lethality of child and adolescent suicide attempts, has stated that ". . . the role of suicidal intent as a determinant of the medical lethality of the attempt appears robust" (p. 90). Intent refers to the purpose or goal of the self-harm behavior. When the goal is to escape a painful condition or context by seeking a condition of nonpain (i.e., by wanting death), intent is high. Similarly, when the motive of suicidal behavior is passage to a new existence, such as reuniting with a deceased love object, going to a desired afterlife, or being reborn, the likelihood of death (as the end of bodily life) being sought through high lethality behavior is great. Such was the obvious consequence of Timmy's magical thinking.

Case Illustration

> Timmy, age 14, left a note to his parents to explain his suicide by hanging. After reading *Watership Down*, a novel about and written from the perspective of rabbits, he wrote that he wanted to die in order to transform himself into a rabbit.

In adolescence, most often the stated intent of a suicidal motive is both interpersonal and instrumental. That is, the wish is to alter life circumstances, to communicate an otherwise unaccepted message, to mobilize or to change others, to coerce others' behavior through threat or guilt, or to seek revenge. As in the case of Hank, that these intentions are not death-seeking does not necessarily diminish the possibility that the adolescent will bet his survival or sacrifice his life in order to accomplish any of these ends. The functional analysis of such motives, however, is most important to therapeutic planning should the adolescent be available for such intervention.

The clinician, furthermore, needs to attend well to the meaning of suicidal behavior or intent as expressed by the adolescent. Hawton (1987) has documented that reasons given by overdose patients to explain their attempts are quite different from those ascribed to these behaviors by the patients' psychiatrists. These discrepancies do not define one or the other view as more valid but rather that for the sake of empathic communication, pairing, and rapport, we should listen carefully to our patients. When one so attends, themes of escape and relief, control and power frequently appear. The latter two motives often are described when the adolescent is asked if he or she has any fantasies of how others would react were he or she to die. In general, the intended goals of suicidal behavior involve attempts to replace the experience of pain, helplessness, hopelessness, or powerlessness—affects and cognitions common to the suicidal state.

Predisposing Conditions and Precipitating Events

Case Illustration

> Kathy's early years were marked first by her father's abandonment of his family before she was born and the subsequent rage her mother could not hide—rage at her husband for leaving and at Kathy for being "too old" to abort.
>
> Forced to work, Kathy's mother delivered Kathy and her sister to her own mother, who lovingly raised the girls throughout their early years. When Kathy was 10, her father returned and kidnapped the girls from their grandmother's house. During the next 2 years, Kathy was frequently and severely abused physically by her father; and twice she was nearly strangled to unconsciousness by her sister, who years later would be diagnosed and institutionalized as a paranoid schizophrenic. When Kathy was found and returned to her mother's custody, she learned of her grandmother's precipitous death 3 months earlier. Believing that her mother neither loved nor wanted her, still suffering the effects of her abuse, and now, deeply mourning the loss of the only person by whom she felt valued, Kathy openly expressed her wish to join her grandmother. On her 13th birthday, Kathy ingested a drug cocktail of some 85 pills culled from her mother's medicine chest.

As evidenced by Kathy's case, most suicidal adolescents have suffered serious blows to their self-esteem, their sense of self, and their ability to cope, often because of years of conflictual or stressful experience. Family history is an essential aspect of an adequate assessment of suicidal risk. Familial–genetic, biophysical, sociocultural, psychopathological, and related factors determine the context for how an adolescent will respond to later demands for adjustment.

Clarification of the acute events or stressors precipitating past suicidal crises can have great predictive value in understanding subsequent times of increased risk. Common among the significant precipitants found in studies of adolescent suicidal behavior are interpersonal conflicts (e.g., a disciplinary crisis with parents or arguments with peers) and events that pose or threaten loss (e.g., rejection), failure, guilt, humiliation, or punishment. Seventy percent of attempts and completions reported by Brent et al. (1988) were precipitated by interpersonal conflict. Hoberman and Garfinkel (1988) found that precipitating arguments with parents were most often about drug use, parenting issues, academic performance, and dating. School problems, disappointments, and problems with the police were also commonly found.

In Kathy's case, her early experiences predisposed her to be especially vulnerable later in adolescence to precipitating loss, abuse, and rejection.

> Kathy was rescued and briefly hospitalized after her ingestion attempt. For the next several years, she ambivalently chose life as she struggled to find a stable and healthier sense of self. She was bright and found some self-worth through academic successes. However, she was understandably unable to trust and, consequently, formed few significant friendships—until her senior year in high school, when she met Carl, with whom she had her first significant love relationship. But Carl soon showed *his* instability. As arguments and coercion replaced the blush of first love, Kathy attempted to break off the relationship with Carl. Carl responded by severely beating and raping Kathy. At 2 a.m. the following morning, Kathy entered her mother's car in the closed garage of her home and ran the engine, hoping that the carbon monoxide fumes would bring her the peace of death. In a single behavior, she was protesting a life in which she felt helplessly entrapped and a future that promised only more of the same. She felt compelled by an urgent and intense need to end her pain.

Stories such as Kathy's tragically are all too common among those reporting for emergency medical treatment consequent to a suicide attempt. Rowena's case, perhaps, is typical of how chaotic, pathological, and despairing these lives often are.

As noted in chapter 3 and as illustrated by Rowena's case, it is often difficult to distinguish the suicidal adolescent from the matrix of family turmoil, violence, and pathology that predispose her to be suicidal.

Case Illustration

> Rowena, age 16, made her third visit to the emergency room in 2 years after ingesting 48 Extra Strength Tylenol (500 mg.) behind a locked bathroom door (lethality rating = 7.0). Each of her prior visits was for a suicide attempt, one by overdose and the other by ingestion of rubbing alcohol. The current attempt was in response to an argument with her sister, the latest in a series of disputes beginning with her being punched in the face by her father and stabbed with a pair of scissors by her mother 9 days prior to this admission. On intake, Rowena stated unequivocally that she hoped to die (high intent).
>
> Rowena was the younger of two girls born to her father, an unemployed heroin abuser, and her mother, who abandoned her after several years of early physical abuse. At the age of 14, when her father threatened to kill her, Rowena was removed by court order to a group home. At the time of the current incident, she lived with her grandmother and sister. Her father, forbidden by the court to see Rowena, lived downstairs with his second wife. At the time of admission, Rowena had been suspended from school because of repetitive assaultive behavior toward her peers.

Psychopathology

As suggested by both empirically derived risk factors and the typology of suicidal adolescents discussed in the previous section, a number of mental disorders describe the suicidal adolescent. Often, not one disorder is apparent; frequently, disorders are co-morbid, such as borderline personality and mood disorders, as illustrated by Kathy's case. At times, one set of symptoms or behaviors may shadow an underlying disorder, such as a teenager's increasing alcohol or drug abuse used to drown out an underlying depression. Certain diagnoses have been clearly associated with increased rates of suicide (e.g., mood disorders, schizophrenia, and alcohol abuse among adults; conduct disorders, mood disorders, and substance abuse among adolescents). More importantly, certain diagnoses indicate the need for pharmacotherapeutic intervention, thereby regulating, for example, a thought disorder or bolstering behavioral control.

As noted in our chapter on risk factors (chapter 3), a number of studies have documented that diagnosable mental disorders characterize the overwhelming majority, perhaps as much as 90%, of adolescent suicidal behaviors (cf. Brent, 1987; Rich, Young, & Fowler, 1986; Shaffer & Gould, 1987; Shafii, Carrigan, Whittinghill, & Derrick, 1985). Shaffer and Gould (1987) found psychiatric symptoms among all but a small proportion of completers and also found that approximately one half of all suicides had had previous contact with a mental health professional. In an older sample (ages 15–29) of Swedish completers (Runeson, 1989), only one of 58 cases did not have either an Axis I or Axis II diagnosis, and 72% had a history of prior care from a mental health professional.

The most prevalent DSM-III-R Axis I diagnoses, among a wide range reported across many studies of both attempters and completers, appear to be conduct disorder, mood disorder, and substance use disorders. However, concomitant disorders are common, such as mood and substance abuse disorders (Brent et al., 1988; Shafii, Steltz-Lenarsky, Derrick, Beckner, & Whittinghill, 1988); different studies report markedly different prevalences of the same disorder [e.g., only 2% of Hoberman & Garfinkel's (1988) sample of completers were classified as having bipolar affective disorder as compared to the 22% observed by Brent et al. (1988)]; Axis II diagnoses are commonly observed and occur concomitant with both substance abuse and mood disorders but are difficult to diagnose in adolescents (e.g., borderline personality disorder); and some symptom presentations commonly observed, such as intense anxiety during an acute crisis or rigid perfectionism in the high-achieving student, may not be sufficient to meet defined criteria for the diagnosis of a mental disorder such as anxiety disorder (Mattison, 1988; Shaffer, Garland, Gould, Fisher, & Trautman 1988).

Case Illustrations

Major depressive disorder. Carla, age 12, was admitted to the intensive care unit unconscious and unstable after ingesting eight of her mother's 50 mg. Elavil tablets, an unknown quantity of amytryptaline, and approximately 20 tablets of Tylenol #3. This attempt, her first, came after arguing with her father over chores and restrictions imposed because her grades were so bad. She reported going to the medicine chest and ingesting everything she could find because "it became too much" and she "did not want to live."

For the previous month, she had displayed a noticeable change of mood, behaving with more instability and depression, feeling worthless and hopeless. In this period she had lost her appetite and had dropped two dress sizes. She increasingly had isolated herself, staying alone in her room. Her school performance, for which her father had restricted her, had declined from Bs the previous term to Ds. Both her mother and maternal grandmother had histories of affective disorder.

Conduct disorder. Mila, age 15, was admitted to the emergency room in a delirious, disoriented, agitated, and combative state after ingesting multiple medications, including an estimated 16 160 mg Flexoril tablets. This was her third known parasuicidal behavior, all by ingestion, in 18 months. Mila had a long record of delinquent activity that included occasional fights and the stabbings just two weeks earlier of two boys who were beating up her older brother. Because of this latter offense, she had been removed to a group home, in which she allegedly was propositioned sexually; this incident led to her anxious and tearful return home just hours prior to this attempt.

Borderline personality disorder. Stan, age 20, tested his outpatient therapist by phoning him at 4:00 a.m. on Sunday morning, stating, "I just took all of them, you quack, quack, quack" and hanging up. A 3-day hospitalization ensued for amytryptaline overdose. In explaining his attempt, Stan related that he had been criticized by his boss and had stayed up all night drinking, hating himself and everyone else. Feeling alone, empty, "a failure at everything," his rage knew no boundaries.

Stan had a long history of intense rage, directed primarily at his mother, who he claimed sexually provoked him throughout his adolescence, but also at his father for not protecting him from "the witch." He felt chronically empty, anxious, and hopeless. He harbored considerable confusion over his sexual identity, frequently testing homosexual urges under the influence of alcohol, but disowning them when sober. His therapist reported that Stan often behaved provocatively, idealizing him one moment and denigrating him the next. His chronic tension and self-deprecatory rumination made concentration difficult, resulting in much inefficient work performance. Additionally, his uneasiness with others allowed only transient relationships to develop, proof to Stan of his unworthiness.

Dual diagnoses: major depressive disorder with psychotic features and alcohol abuse. Larry, age 18, became depressed, hopeless, and increasingly suicidal after breaking up with his girlfriend while home from college over Christmas break. He blamed himself for the breakup, as he had been dating other girls at school during his first term away. With his return to school, he found himself increasingly unable to attend to and concentrate on his studies. Additionally, he felt anhedonic and anergic, had poor appetite and insomnia with early morning awakening, feelings of helplessness, hopelessness, and low self-esteem. He began to drink heavily, binging three to four nights a week until he blacked out. His academic performance deteriorated considerably. Associated with these changes, he felt paranoid and had visual hallucinations and ideas of reference.

As his depression worsened and he increasingly felt suicidal (he purchased razor blades in anticipation of cutting himself), Larry sought the counsel of a pastoral counselor, who recommended hospitalization. After 2 days, however, his parents signed him out against medical advice and returned him to their care at home. Within a week, he overdosed with an unknown quantity of his prescribed medications. Several days after his second hospital admission, he was still unable to give a coherent history of what happened.

Coping Skills and Resources

Suicidal behavior may be construed as an end result of despair and hopelessness, self-contempt, rage, and the unavailability of sustaining resources (Maltsberger, 1986). Alternatively stated, the risk of suicidal behavior is lessened when the youngster has available both internal (e.g., cognitive) and external (e.g., interpersonal) resources for coping successfully with stress and conflict.

The availability and accessibility of interpersonal resources and supports are essential, first, in the short-term monitoring of an in-crisis adolescent and, second, in the long-term alliances that inherently reduce the adolescent's intolerable feelings of aloneness while increasing the likelihood of rational problem solving to deal with the suicidogenic context.

The cognitive strategies used by the adolescent determine the degree to which alternative routes to desired goals can be considered and possibly accomplished. What problem-solving strategies have been employed in the past or applied to the current problem? How rational or irrational is the adolescent in attempting to cope with the current problem? How able is the adolescent, in the interview condition, to employ cognitive rehearsal, to think heirarchically, to assess self, and to tolerate ambivalence?

Noting that ambivalence is a common affect of the nonfatal completer or ideator, it is helpful for the clinician to focus with the adolescent on what has kept him or her alive to this point. Linehan, Goodstein, Nielsen, and Chiles (1983) have presented an instrument, The Reasons for Living Inventory (RFL), of some use in this assessment. Multivariate analyses of the RFL indicated that the RFL differentiated suicidal from nonsuicidal adults, with individuals reporting prior suicidal behavior having fewer important reasons for living.

Compliance

Crucial to the decision not to hospitalize a youth in crisis is the assessment of that youth's compliance with recommended out-patient treatment regimens. Perhaps as crucial to that compliance is the support of family members in effecting compliance. Past behavior may again be the best predictor of future behavior. The issue of compliance will be more fully discussed in chapter 5.

Information essential to the assessment of compliance is available in the assessment interview itself. One of the better measures of possible future compliance is the adolescent's cooperation with the assessment interview. In contrast, an angry, resistive, difficult-to-interview youngster evidences in his or her behavior an inability to form an alliance with a gatekeeper to the helping system. Motto's report (1984) that future adolescent male completers—significantly more often than controls—were rated as having a negative or ambivalent attitude toward the psychiatric interviewer at the time of intake underscores the importance of the adolescent's interpersonal alliances to the overall assessment of risk.

Similarly, the adolescent's willingness to form a short-term, renewable "no-suicide agreement" in order for therapeutic interventions to be instituted signals whether help offered can be help received. Such agreements or "contracts" are verbal or written statements of expectancy and contingency for both patient and therapist and serve as a first step to a treatment plan (see chapter 5). It should be noted, however, that agreements formed with some patients cannot be reasonably accepted. Adolescents with a history of lying and distrustful relationships with authority, evidence of a thought disorder, or patterns of emotional and behavioral reactivity (e.g., panic, impulsivity) simply are often unable to comply readily with such an agreement (Boggiano, 1988).

Case Illustration (continued)

> When Sam (see p. 138) entered outpatient treatment, he denied his suicidal intent in describing his shotgun attempt. Reports by others of his frequent suicidal threats and a year-long history of alcohol abuse similarly were denied. A combative and manipulative relationship with a rigid, authoritarian father served as a prototype for the transference with which he entered therapy. In this context, his response to

an offer of a no-suicide agreement—"I am here, aren't I?"—
understandably was the best he could give.

The Screening of Suicidal Risk

With attention to the foregoing observations, the clinician now
has sufficient data to make reasoned judgments of the adolescent's potential for acting in a self-harmful manner and for
developing a treatment plan. As the cliche goes, "A good surgeon does not need to make a large incision": The better the
assessment, the easier it is to develop interventive strategies.

The screening of risk represents the following series of increasingly significant questions regarding the potential for lethal outcome:

Level A: Does this patient have the potential for self-harm?

Level B: Might this patient possibly harm himself or herself?

Level C: If self-harm is possible, what is the probability of
self-harm behavior, and what are the circumstances, degree of
lethality, and imminence involved?

Levels of Risk

Level A risk. The first screen represents the "red flag" level of
assessment, wherein the patient presents with one or more risk
factors in his or her history or current life experience. For example, these might include a family history of suicidal behavior,
a history of prior attempt, family psychopathology, or the exposure to suicidal behavior of a peer. Additionally, current
diagnosed psychopathology or symptomatic behavior (e.g.,
depression, acting-out behavior, substance abuse), behavioral
patterns that signal underlying problems (e.g., a rigid cognitive
style, heightened anxiety), or high levels of observable stress
or familial conflict should alert the clinician to pay close attention to the possibility of suicidal behavior.

Level B risk. The possibility of suicidal behavior increases
dramatically when there is evidence that death, dying, or, explicitly, suicide is on the patient's mind. Expressions of ideation
and communications of these ideas through words, writings,
drawings, poems, questions about death out of context, preoc-

cupations with images of death (including obsessional fascination with death-related rock music), or behavior signaling an
identification with deceased objects, should alert the clinician's
signaling system (and probably produce some stomach discomfort!).

Ideas in themselves are not dangerous. However, in the context of poor impulse control, ideas can readily turn into behaviors. By analogy, sexual fantasies and attractions are considered
healthy expressions of libido. However, lacking appropriate
controls, such fantasies can be acted upon inappropriately, intrusively, impulsively, and, possibly, even violently.

Several of the diagnoses commonly seen among suicidal adolescents signal a common theme regarding poor impulse control. Substance abusers, borderlines, antisocial personalities,
and psychotics, for example, will display difficulties controlling
their behavior. Any evidence of impulsiveness, rageful, assaultive behavior toward others, or high degrees of anxiety
suggest a potentially dangerous lack of control.

Two other variables are particularly significant in screening
the possibility of suicidal behavior at this level. The first, cognitive constriction, reflects a rigid, inflexible ideational life. The
adolescent whose thinking is constricted will tend to dichotomize observations, to use a binary system with which to construe
problems and solutions, to develop what suicidologists refer to as
"psychological myopia" or "tunnel vision." If life is bad, then
this rationale dictates that death is the option. Gray areas,
alternative solutions, and compromise positions are not tolerated. One extreme form of this constriction is hopelessness.
Hopelessness, when expressed as the patient's dominant way
of construing self, others, and the future, is a signal of severe
cognitive rigidity and constriction. Without the flexibility to
perceive portholes in a wall, otherwise seen as increasingly
entrapping the adolescent, both panic and despair are likely to
increase. It should be noted, however, that recent research
(Rotheram-Borus & Trautman, 1988) has reported no empirical
support for hopelessness as a predictor of intent in a sample
of adolescent *minority* female attempters.

Similarly, evidence of social isolation or alienation suggests
that the adolescent is lacking needed buffers, objects with whom

catharsis may occur or from whom support can be received. When the family context is one of unavailability, nonsupport, or pathology (particularly involving abuse or violence), the adolescent must turn elsewhere. When peers are themselves troubled or identified by their discongruency with family (e.g., other runaways or substance abusers) or marginality (e.g., heavy metal rock-and-rollers), the support available to the adolescent at risk is colored by the effects of these problems (e.g., low self-esteem, substance abuse).

Level C risk. Whether a self-harmful intent will be acted upon, given the foregoing levels of risk, at this level depends on a number of situational and characterological factors. Suicide risk may be situationally specific, that is, may wax under conditions of threat and stress and wane when the adolescent is removed from those conditions. It is for this reason that brief hospitalization may serve to temporarily reduce risk, and discharge back to unresolved conditions of stress may bring the patient back to the emergency room as a result of a repetitive suicidal behavior.

The availability and accessibility of a method of self-harm, under conditions of a developed suicidal intent or reason for suicidal behavior, may be sufficient stimulus for suicidal behavior to occur. On impulse, an individual lacking ego controls will view the gun in the nightstand or vials of pills as sirens irresistibly beckoning an end to pain. Alternatively, those who develop a plan for their suicide must include a method sufficient to accomplish their ends. That method undoubtedly will be that most accessible or readily obtainable and about which the potential suicide has some knowledge or experience. Brent et al. (1988) have documented that 70% of completed suicides who had a gun available to them in their house used that gun to effect their death.

Absent intense panic or a psychotic break, potential suicides tend to choose methods of suicide that are syntonic with their character. For example, those characterologically in need of presenting well to others, and conversely intolerant of not looking good, will rarely choose a method that promises disfigurement. Similarly, planful types do not choose methods common to impulsive characters, like young children (e.g., running into oncoming traffic).

Characterologically, suicidal actions occur either on impulse, in a moment of provocation by an individual predisposed to act self-harmfully; or planfully, as an end result of a developed and organized set of actions designed to accomplish suicidal goals. Thus, individuals giving evidence of suicidal predisposition and the inability to avoid acting suicidally or evidence of a concrete and specific plan including a lethal weapon of self-destruction must be taken most seriously. Included in the former group must be those adolescents displaying command hallucinations. Also, those who are intoxicated and threatened with humiliation or punishment, such as the typical jail suicide, must be closely watched. With regard to the latter group, the clinician should be alert to the availability or obtainability of the method, the planned conditions of its use (rescuability), and the likely consequences of its use (lethality).

When a suicide note already has been drafted, risk is imminent. As stated earlier, notes are written in the past tense or from the perspective of death having been accomplished. The discovery of such a document prior to suicidal action is an undeniable signal of imminent risk.

Contraindications

Suicidal adolescents never present in such a way as to lead clinicians to unequivocally assess risk. Juxtaposed to both situational and characterological conditions suggesting levels of risk are a number of factors that must be considered as potentially abating risk. As described earlier in our discussion of multifocal assessments, these include available coping skills and resources as well as a positive history of compliance. Where there is a future time perspective including a desired object or goal; where the adolescent demonstrates some ability to tolerate frustration, to assess his or her emotional state as on a continuum that varies according to situation and time; where there is a good history of compliance and a nonhostile, nonrejecting cooperation with the intake interviewer, there exists an increased likelihood that imminent risk is not present.

Garmezy and Masten (1986) note that despite exposure to stressful events, some individuals maintain competencies. Among the "protective factors" that help adolescents resist stress, Garmezy (1985) lists (a) self-esteem, (b) feelings of control, (c) a view of the environment as predictable and life as basically positive, (d) the ability to elicit positive responses from the environment, (e) having a close personal bond with at least one family member, and (f) a positive school environment. Rubenstein, Heeren, Housman, Rubin, and Stechler (1989) recently examined such protective factors. These researchers reported that in particular, family cohesion and adaptability offset the effects of increased stress in the lives of at-risk youngsters. Thus it is imperative that risk assessment screens reflect an awareness of both risk and protective factors in arriving at judgments of both imminent and long-term risk for suicidal behavior.

Imminent Risk

Richman (1986) summarizes four characteristics common to the assessment of suicide risk: (a) the exhaustion of personal resources such as hope and energy and the breakdown of usual defenses, (b) the exhaustion of familial resources, (c) a state of intolerable stress, and (d) the perception of suicide as a viable solution. These reflect a focus similar to our common theme—the breakdown of typical defenses and consequent lack of control, interpersonal alienation or isolation, and cognitive constriction under conditions of situational stress or predisposing pathology. Given these conditions, the individual has options to attempt to change intolerable conditions but lacks resources to make mature choices. Thus limited, more primitive coping patterns emerge, primarily those of flight (suicidal death) or fight (suicidal behavior to affect others, perhaps changing their behavior). Where these ends are readily accomplished through self-harm behavior, we have the risk of imminent suicide.

Hospitalization

Assessment represents the first step in the process of treatment and, if done well, eases the transition into successful treatment. By understanding the psychological state of the potential suicide, the interviewer is in position both to effect the necessary external controls in order to reduce the likelihood of a self-inflicted, lethal solution to current problems *and* to provide the adolescent with the initial hope that these problems may be resolvable through any of a number of nonlethal interventions. In this sense, the assessment interview should be interactional. It serves both as an opportunity to observe and gather necessary information and as a structuring vehicle to stabilize the adolescent through feedback, shared conceptual understanding, and empathy.

Should intent and the risk of imminent suicide remain high in spite of initial interventions, hospitalization should be considered in order to provide sufficient sanctuary and time to achieve stabilization. This consideration should be based on other observations as well, such as (a) high levels of unresolvable stress, the presence of a thought disorder (e.g., delusions or command hallucinations), or impending ego decompensation; (b) other symptoms of loss of control (e.g., disorientation, dissociation, high impulsivity); (c) high levels of rage, panic, or uncontrollable violent behavior; (d) the absence of a supportive family or surrogate interpersonal system able to monitor and maintain sufficient watch over the adolescent through the period of crisis (or the presence of an abusive, substance-abusing, or seriously mentally disordered parent); or (e) the unobtainability of an alliance in the context of assessed risk for suicidal behavior (cf. Comstock, 1977). Landau-Stanton and Stanton (1985) pose three additional criteria: (a) an attempt is made by a male, (b) a family history of completion, or (c) an attempt made in secret, that is, clearly not a cry for help from significant others. These authors further argue that an overnight hospitalization may be warranted even in low-lethality attempts in order to lessen intensity and pressure in the adolescent's life. Clearly, hospitalization has both benefits and costs (see chapter

5 for comparisons of inpatient vs. outpatient treatment) that need to be weighed carefully on a case-by-case basis. The decision to hospitalize, as in John's case, is demanded when help seeking for either medical or psychological need is necessary but not voluntarily acted upon.

Case Illustration

John, age 19, a college sophomore transfer student, slashed his wrists and forearms with a razor blade after being rebuffed by his roommate. He later reported that he had been feeling down and had wanted to talk, but his roommate angrily demanded that he be left alone. Feeling more depressed, rageful, and worthless as a result, John proceeded to slash his arms eight or nine times in front of his roommate. When his roommate continued to show no concern, John wrote "I HATE ME!" in blood on the walls of their apartment, then locked himself in his bedroom. It was not until the following afternoon, when his roommate returned from classes and noticed that John's door was still shut and locked and that John was not responsive to his calls, that the police were called to forcibly open the door. Conscious but groggy, John was taken by the police for emergency evaluation.

On intake, John's wounds were considered superficial and bleeding had stopped. John then denied feeling depressed but did state that he felt alone and lonely, that he had no one to share his feelings with (in transferring colleges, he also left his ongoing outpatient therapy). He stated that he had no friends, that he could not talk with his parents, and that his suicide attempts—he claimed the current one to be his fifth, but the first resulted in a hospitalization—were attempts to get away from his loneliness. Mental status evaluation found John to have slightly depressed affect, but no vegetative signs of depression. He was fully oriented and showed no signs of a thought disorder. Insight was rated as limited and judgment impaired. He was admitted for protective observation and milieu therapy with provisional diagnoses of dysthymic disorder (Axis I) and avoidant personality disorder (Axis II).

Initially, John was under close observation with nursing checks every 15 minutes. He participated in nursing counseling, ward activities, and group therapy. After 3 days of hospitalization, he was considered stabilized and improved and showed no signs of continued risk. He was discharged contingent on meeting with or accepting a referral from his outpatient therapist. (We will continue our discussion of John's case, describing his treatment in chapter 5).

The Psychometric Assessment of Suicide Risk

As noted in chapter 3, questionnaires and scales purporting to measure suicide risk produce an unacceptable rate of false positives (Hawton, 1987). Though undesirable, this is an expected outcome when a test with acceptable specificity is applied to a population with a low base rate for the target event (suicidal behavior) being measured. Additionally, few if any scales have been constructed primarily on adolescent populations; most are so face-valid that they appear merely to substitute on paper questions for clinical interview questions; and most instruments are best at identifying those adolescents reporting suicide ideation, the relation between ideation and future suicidal action requiring significantly more data to understand.

These problems notwithstanding, there remains a place for scaling techniques in the assessment of risk among adolescent populations. As Reynolds (1987) has noted, distressed youth, if asked specifically, will honestly report on their distress. Because adolescents rarely are self-referred, the use of screening instruments has the potential to detect youth at risk both prior to (as in a general population screening) and in the early stage of any direct process of assessment. The use of screening instruments is particularly relevant if the adolescent is unlikely to respond to direct clinical interview.

The National Institute of Mental Health (Lewinsohn, Garrison, Langhinrichsen, & Marsteller, 1989) has reviewed 29 scales purporting to assess suicidal behavior in adolescents. The great majority of these instruments were developed for research, not clinical, purposes. This extensive review describes each scale and documents its essential psychometric properties. In addition, many of the problems already discussed, such as insufficient attention to issues of validity, unclear purposes, and unevaluated specificity, sensitivity, and efficacy studies are noted as recommendations for future work in the development of more efficient and clinically useful instruments.

Costello and Angold (1988) have reviewed self-report and parent-report measures of depressive symptoms in children and adolescents of use in the preliminary screening or in the documentation of symptom change. They iterate Lewinsohn et al. (1989) in their cautionary that these scales have better research than clinical properties as presently developed.

A second excellent review of assessment instruments for suicidal adolescents may be found in Eyman, Mikawa, and Eyman (1990). These authors have included in their analysis studies of more traditional psychological tests, specifically the MMPI and the Rorschach. Two studies have now been published using the MMPI with adolescents who had attempted suicide. Marks and Haller (1977) found scales one and five higher among adolescent male attempters than among controls and scales two and three higher among female attempters than among controls. However, more recently, Spirito, Faust, Myers, and Bechtel (1988) did not find a single MMPI profile to differentiate female attempters from a control group of hospitalized, emotionally disturbed nonattempters. Including studies with adults, Eyman et al. (1990) conclude that the MMPI has not yielded a "reliable and clinically useful prediction of suicide." In a similar vein, data on the Rorschach, at best, suggest that a multiple (vs. single) sign approach might have potential usefulness; however, studies to date show unacceptably high false positive and false negative rates and inadequate ability to discriminate groups.

Biological Markers

With increasing focus on biological correlates of suicide (see chapter 2), markers identifying those at risk on the basis of a high rate of cortisol nonsuppression by dexamethasone or a low concentration of 5-HIAA in the cerebrospinal fluid, for example, might be especially useful in samples of patients in which such analyses can be conducted. However, to date there is no compelling reason to do so.

Casat and Powell (1988) have reviewed available studies on the use of the dexamethasone suppression test (DST) in children and adolescents with psychiatric disorders. Pooled data indicated that for adolescent patients with major depressive disorder, DST sensitivity, specificity, and positive predictive power were all too low to justify the routine clinical use of the DST.

Shaffer et al. (1988) reviewed studies of CSF 5-HIAA, all using *adult* patient subjects. In spite of numerous, as yet unresolved problems, including the lack once more of study regarding sensitivity or specificity and the lack of study with adolescent samples, they are optimisitic that routine CSF monitoring after an attempt may be useful in the prevention of subsequent suicidal behavior where patients with abnormally low levels are given special care.

Assessment by Paraprofessionals and Referral Guidelines: Training Tips

We began this chapter by noting that nonclinicians, paraprofessionals, or adolescent peers are often "first finders" of suicidal messages and that knowledge of some simple rules for making appropriate assessment referrals to the mental health system may be quite beneficial to fostering early detection and treatment. Clinicians in a position to consult with and train these groups (e.g., hotline and school personnel) need to consider helping the community make effective referrals. To aid in this process, it behooves such groups to have designated ahead of time those who are familiar and comfortable with treating suicidal adolescents. Professionals who can be trusted to work well with this population ought to be so designated first by the referral source, whose experience has been positive, or secondly on the recommendation of trusted others. Also, it is imperative that nonprofessionals know the limits of their competence. As should be apparent from the preceding two chapters, the problems of suicidal adolescents should not be telescoped into mere temporal exaggerations of everyday problems of living. It takes a well-trained psychotherapist to work with these issues and with the interpersonal struggles the suicidal adolescent typically brings to treatment. Those with insufficient training should be involved only to the point of gathering sufficient information to make an effective assessment on which a referral can be based.

Paraprofessionals need to be trained in communication and interview skills to the point of understanding some simple do's and don'ts and knowing what kind of information is most pertinent to effect a referral. Learning to be calm in an anxiety-provoking interaction, not to negate or apply verbal pablum to the affect or reasons espoused by a suicidal youngster for their suicidal thoughts or impulses, not to engage in a philosphical or moral debate, and so forth takes considerable practice and supervised training. Learning to collect assessment data, particularly on the persistence, duration, and intensity of the adolescent's suicidal urges, predisposing and precipitating conditions for these urges, and sufficient background data regarding available interpersonal supports demands an awareness of what to ask as well as to how to ask. These practices should be construed as *skills* by those responsible for training, monitored consistently through supervision, and bolstered by repeat training opportunities over time.

Conclusion

The assessment of the adolescent at risk for suicidal behavior has been likened to finding a needle in a haystack. By being alert as to what to observe and by observing alertly, the size and brilliance of that needle increase, thereby correspondingly increasing the likelihood of its discovery. Translating the metaphor into practical application requires that the clinician first be alert to risk factors as alerting signs. With a focus on multiple assessments and a screening system with which to sift observations, the clinician becomes both capable of making reasoned judgments regarding the need for intervention and integral to the process of that intervention.

The assessment of suicide risk in adolescence is central to treatment planning—first, because treatment requires a live body and second, because much of the foregoing assessment analysis provides the clinician with invaluable data with which to establish meaningful goals for treatment. As noted at the outset of this chapter, the suicidal urge is not static; neither, therefore, can the assessment of that urge be static. In addition to its importance to early intervention, the assessment of suicidal risk should be made and documented with frequency during ongoing treatment, especially at times of impending transition, heightened stress, or changes in environmental supports. With such attention, it is presumed a priori that treatment will continue to have the time and opportunity to make a noticeable difference in the lives of these youngsters.

References

Berman, A. L. (1986a). Helping suicidal adolescents: Needs and responses. In C. Corr & J. McNeil (Eds.), *Adolescence and death* (pp. 151–166). New York: Springer.

Berman, A. L. (1986b). Adolescent suicide: Issues and challenges. *Seminars in Adolescent Medicine, 2,* 269–277.

Berman, A. L., & Carroll, T. A. (1984). Adolescent suicide: A critical review. *Death Education, 8*(Suppl.) 53–64.

Blumenthal, S. J., & Kupfer, D. J. (1989). Overview of early detection and treatment strategies for suicidal behavior in young people. In Alcohol, Drug Abuse, and Mental Health Administration, *Report of the Secretary's Task Force on Youth Suicide. Volume 3. Preventions and interventions in youth suicide* (pp. 239–252). (DHHS Publication No. ADM 89–1623). Washington, DC: U.S. Government Printing Office.

Boggiano, W. E. (1988, April). *When should we accept a "no suicide" pact.* Paper presented at the annual meeting of the American Association of Suicidology, Washington, DC.

Brent, D. A. (1987). Correlates of medical lethality of suicide attempts in children and adolescents. *Journal of the American Academy of Child and Adolescent Psychiatry, 26,* 87–91.

Brent, D. A., Perper, J. A., Goldstein, C. E., Kolko, D. J., Allan, M. J., Allman, C. J., & Zelenak, J. P. (1988). Risk factors for adolescent suicide. *Archives of General Psychiatry, 45,* 581–588.

Cairns, R. B., Peterson, G., & Neckerman, H. J. (1988). Suicidal behavior in aggressive adolescents. *Journal of Clinical Child Psychology, 17,* 298–309.

Carlson, G. A., & Cantwell, D. P. (1980). Suicidal behavior and depression in children and adolescents. *Journal of the American Academy of Child and Adolescent Psychiatry, 21*, 361–368.

Casat, C. D., & Powell, K. (1988). The dexamethasone suppression test in children and adolescents with major depressive disorder: A review. *Journal of Clinical Psychiatry, 49*, 390–393.

Cohen-Sandler, R., & Berman, A. L. (1980). Diagnosis and treatment of childhood depression and self-destructive behavior. *Journal of Family Practice, 11*, 51–58.

Comstock, B. S. (1977). Suicide events and indications for hospitalization. In P. Cantor (Ed.), *Proceedings of the Tenth Annual Meeting of the American Association of Suicidology.* (pp. 75–77). Denver, CO: American Association of Suicidology.

Costello, E. J., & Angold, A. (1988). Scales to assess child and adolescent depression: Checklists, screens, and nets. *Journal of the American Academy of Child and Adolescent Psychiatry, 27*, 726–737.

Eddy, D. M., Wolpert, R. L., & Rosenberg, M. L. (1989). Estimating the effectiveness of interventions to prevent youth suicides: A report to the Secretary's Task Force on Youth Suicide. In Alcohol, Drug Abuse, and Mental Health Administration, *Report of the Secretary's Task Force on Youth Suicide: Volume 4. Strategies for the prevention of youth suicide* (pp. 37–81). (DHHS Publication No. ADM 89–1624). Washington, DC: U.S. Government Printing Office.

Eyman, J. R., Mikawa, J. K., & Eyman, S. K. (1990). The problem of adolescent suicide: Issues and assessment. In P. McReynolds, J. C. Rosen, & G. Chelune (Eds.), *Advances in psychological assessment.* (Vol. VII; pp. 165–202). New York: Plenum Press.

Garmezy, N. (1985). Stress-resistant children: The search for protective factors. In J. E. Stevenson (Ed.), *Recent research in developmental psychopathology: Journal of Child Psychology and Psychiatry Book Supplement No. 4* (pp. 213–233). Oxford: Pergamon Press.

Garmezy, N., & Masten, A. S. (1986). Stress, competence, and resilience: Common factors for therapist and psychologist. *Behavior Therapy, 17*, 500–521.

Hawton, K. (1987). *Attempted suicide.* New York: Oxford Press.

Hoberman, H. M., & Garfinkel, B. D. (1988). Completed suicide in youth. *Canadian Journal of Psychiatry, 33*, 494–502.

Kaplan, R. D., Kottler, D. B., & Frances, A. J. (1982). Reliability and rationality in the prediction of suicide. *Hospital & Community Psychiatry, 33*, 212–215.

Landau-Stanton, J. L., & Stanton, M. D. (1985). Treating suicidal adolescents and their families: In M. P. Mirkin & S. L. Koman (Eds.), *Handbook of adolescents and family therapy* (pp. 309–328). New York: Gardner Press.

Lewinsohn, P. M., Garrison, C. Z., Langhinrichsen, J., & Marsteller, F. (1989). *The assessment of suicidal behavior in adolescents: A review of scales suitable for epidemiologic and clinical research* (Contract Nos. 316774 and 316776). Rockville, MD: National Institute of Mental Health.

Linehan, M. M., Goodstein, J. L., Nielsen, S. L., & Chiles, J. A. (1983). Reasons for staying alive when you are thinking of killing yourself: The reasons for living inventory. *Journal of Consulting and Clinical Psychology, 51,* 276–286.

Maltsberger, J. T. (1986). *Suicide risk: The formulation of clinical judgment.* New York: New York University Press.

Marks, P. A., & Haller, D. L. (1977). Now I lay me down for keeps: A study of adolescent suicide attempts. *Journal of Clinical Psychology, 33,* 390–400.

Mattison, R. E. (1988). Suicide and other consequences of childhood and adolescent anxiety disorders. *Journal of Clinical Psychiatry, 49* (Suppl. 10), 9–11.

Motto, J. A. (1984). Suicide in male adolescents. In H. S. Sudak, A. B. Ford, & N. B. Rushforth (Eds.), *Suicide in the young* (pp. 227–244). Boston, MA: John Wright, PSG Inc.

Reynolds, W. M. (1987). Treatment of major depression in children and adolescents. In M. Hersen & C. G. Last (Eds.), *Child behavior therapy casebook.* New York: Plenum Press.

Rich, C. L., Young, D., & Fowler, R. C. (1986). San Diego suicide study: I. Young vs. old subjects. *Archives of General Psychiatry, 43,* 577–582.

Richman, J. (1986). *Family therapy for suicidal people.* New York: Springer.

Rotheram, M. J. (1987). Evaluation of imminent danger for suicide among youth. *American Journal of Orthopsychiatry, 57,* 102–110.

Rotheram-Borus, M. J., & Trautman, P. (1988). Hopelessness, depression, and suicide intent among adolescent suicide attempters. *Journal of the American Academy of Child and Adolescent Psychiatry, 27,* 700–704.

Rubenstein, J. L., Heeren, T., Housman, D., Rubin, C., & Stechler, G. (1989). Suicidal behavior in "normal" adolescents: Risk and protective factors. *American Journal of Orthopsychiatry, 59,* 59–71.

Runeson, B. (1989). Mental disorder in youth suicide. *Acta Psychiatrica Scandanavica, 79,* 490–497.

Shaffer, D. (1988). The epidemiology of teen suicide: An examination of risk factors. *Journal of Clinical Psychiatry, 49*(Suppl. 9), 36–39.

Shaffer, D., Garland, A., Gould, M., Fisher, P., & Trautman, P. (1988). Preventing teenage suicide: A critical review. *Journal of the American Academy of Child and Adolescent Psychiatry, 27,* 675–687.

Shaffer, D., & Gould, M. (1987). *A study of completed and attempted suicide in adolescents* (Progress Report; Grant No. MH 38198). Rockville, MD: National Institute of Mental Health.

Shafii, M., Carrigan, S., Whittinghill, J. R., & Derrick, A. (1985). Psychological autopsy of completed suicide in children and adolescents. *American Journal of Psychiatry, 142,* 1061–1064.

Shafii, M., Steltz-Lenarsky, J., Derrick, A. M., Beckner, C., & Whittinghill, J. R. (1988). Co-morbidity of mental disorders in the post-mortem diagnosis of completed suicide in children and adolescents. *Journal of Affective Disorders, 15,* 227–233.

Smith, K., Conroy, R. W., & Ehler, B. D. (1984). Lethality of suicide attempt rating scale. *Suicide and Life-Threatening Behavior, 14*, 215–242.

Spirito, A., Brown, L., Overholser, J., & Fritz, G. (1989). Attempted suicide in adolescence: A review and critique of the literature. *Clinical Psychology Review, 9*, 335–363.

Spirito, A., Faust, D., Myers, B., & Bechtel, D. (1988). Clinical utility of the MMPI in the evaluation of adolescent suicide attempters. *Journal of Personality Assessment, 52*, 204–211.

5

The Treatment of
the Suicidal Adolescent

I t is axiomatic that the adolescent identified to be at risk for
suicide needs help. But adolescents are notoriously reluctant
to seek help, particularly from mental health professionals, who
are frequently viewed as helpers of "last resort" (Aaronson,
Underwood, Gaffney, & Rotheram-Borus, 1989). Much of this
resistance is borne out of any of a number of irrational but well-
defended beliefs. Some adolescents believe that others will find
out they are seeing a "shrink," either through some breach in
confidentiality (the possibility of which is defined by any number of illustrative examples all too readily offered) or by the
adolescent's projected introspection, which gives rise to the
notion that "others are paying as much attention to me as I do
to myself," a process akin to the "imaginary audience" described by Elkind (1980). Elkind describes a corollary to this
belief, the "personal fable," which further reinforces the adolescent's rejection of the mental health care giver. The personal
fable refers to the adolescent's belief that his or her emotional
experiences are unique, a belief affirmed by the "fact" that
others (the imaginary audience) are so concerned with him or
her. This fable of uniqueness may then lead the adolescent to
believe that others, including and especially the therapist, could
not truly understand his or her problems.

Rinsley (1980) defines the "adolescent position" as predict-
ably resistant to engaging treatment structure. This position

may be operationalized by an attitude reflecting hostility toward being seen as mentally ill or sick. We should note that this attitude may reflect, as well, an adaptive function of the ego (i.e., a healthy concern for feeling humiliated or being labeled by peers, before whom one's dignity must be maintained).

Some resistance is due to the simple but unfortunate reality that therapists are adults, members of the same group from whom the youngster has been striving to gain autonomy. It is no wonder, then, that adults "cannot" understand the adolescent.

For more seriously disturbed adolescents, Rinsley (1980) argues that adult treatment figures will be readily seen as transference objects. The suicidal adolescent positions himself or herself to neutralize or avoid an expected recurrence of early trauma and narcissistic injury (e.g., punishment, rejection, abandonment) suffered at the hands of parents or significant other adults.

Issues of autonomy underlie another and perhaps much more distressing observation regarding the adolescent's reluctance to seek help, once that help, in the form of medical intervention, is required to avoid the consequences of parasuicidal behavior. Of those adolescents seen in the hospital emergency room for medical and psychological intervention after self-harm behavior, only a minority have been observed to comply with recommended follow-up appointments (Litt, Cuskey, & Rudd, 1983; Taylor & Stansfeld, 1984). This high rate of noncompliance with treatment referrals may simply validate the fact that a number of these parasuicidal behaviors are interpersonal and coercive in intent. Therefore, once an event has been medically treated, the behavior has served its intended purpose to alter the existing contingencies in the adolescent's interpersonal world. In the adolescent parasuicide's mind, nothing more is to be gained by further involvement with the mental health treatment system (see case of Angela to follow). Alternatively, adolescents are quick to feign a restored equilibrium after an acute emotional upset out of fear of having more permanently changed a family system's dynamics. The same dynamics that serve to keep a battered spouse in an abusive relationship may apply in such a case, as the adolescent may quickly collude to restore the unacceptable but familiar homeostasis that existed prior to their parasuicidal behavior. This enmeshment and felt responsibility for the family as a whole is the very opposite of the drive toward autonomy that may promote some parasuicidal behavior.

Case Illustration

> Angela, age 14, was treated in the emergency room after ingesting a "handful" of Aldomet and ampicillin in front of her mother and younger sister. This she did in retribution for being reprimanded and hit by her mother for staying out late. In the intake interview, she denied current suicidal ideation and stated that she was "glad" that her mother was worried. Once medically cleared, she was given an appointment with the outpatient psychiatry clinic for 9 days later, an appointment that was never kept. The nurse who attempted to contact the family by phone to follow up learned that the phone number given at intake had been disconnected for over 2 months.

Adolescents, like children, are rarely self-referred for therapy. Most are brought to therapy by adults. This is true particularly in cases of parasuicidal behavior, which acutely signals the family system to act in the adolescent's behalf. Therefore, most referrals for follow-up care are made with the awareness of the parent or parent-surrogate who brought the adolescent into the emergency room and was present during the emergency intervention. The high rate of no-shows at follow-up, then, more probably reflects the more serious denial or collusion of the family. With the literal wound repaired, the family acts as if the emotional wound had healed and the system's reparation were remarkably complete without any further observation or treatment.

Sometimes, as in the case of Brenda, the family's denial persists in spite of overwhelming evidence of the need for treatment.

Case Illustration

Brenda, age 15, was accompanied to the emergency room by her aunt after ingesting approximately 20 aspirin and 15 Chlortrimetron. Her ingestion came at the end point of a rageful loss of control in response to her mother's refusal to allow her to sleep in the basement. Brenda became enraged, assaulted her younger sister, broke several pieces of furniture, and tore the sheets off all the beds. She then locked herself in the bathroom, threatening to kill herself while ingesting what she could find in the medicine chest. Her mother eventually called the fire department to intercede and break down the door to the bathroom. Brenda was not brought for treatment until 6 hours later, when she complained to her aunt of abdominal discomfort. Although her attempt was seen as impulsive, she was evaluated to remain at high risk at intake. She was unable to assure the staff that she would not overdose again, she spoke of feeling hopeless, her affect remained depressed and shallow, and she was confused and alluded to hearing voices while in the bathroom urging her to "Do it, Do it!" Additionally, she described a long history of explosive rage and assaultive behavior toward her sister. In spite of Brenda's mental status, her mother refused to allow a voluntary admission into an inpatient psychiatry unit.

Rinsley (1980) has identified a number of reasons why the parents may wish to deflect attention away from the child (and the family), thereby precluding any significant involvement in treatment. Among these are: (a) feared exposure of the parent as a failure, as bad or "sick" ("regressive identification"); (b) feared punishment, including having the child taken away from the parent; and (c) the need to maintain control, to keep the child enmeshed and triangulated.

As in the case of Marcie, the consequence of such parental denial and noncompliance is the maintenance of the adolescent as the "bad seed" and as the identified patient.

Case Illustration

Marcie, age 13, was brought to the emergency room by her cousin after overdosing on an unknown quantity of unknown pills. The precipitating event for the ingestion was a dispute with her mother that included being hit in her face and threatened with being put into foster care. When Marcie's mother was contacted by phone, she denied the alleged beating, stating instead that Marcie was an unmanageable child who stayed out all night with unknown boys with whom she was sexually promiscuous. She refused to come to the hospital to meet with the treatment team.

One significant consequence of parental noncompliance is a maintained probability of further suicidal behavior on the part of the adolescent, perhaps in an increasingly lethal cycle of cause and effect behavior among family members. In Litt, Cuskey, and Rudd's (1983) study, 60% of noncompliant adolescents had made a prior suicide attempt; *none* of the compliant adolescent patients had made a prior attempt! This cycle, then, appears to underlie repetitive suicide attempts and defines a major task of therapy if and when a therapeutic alliance can be secured. This task is to help the family of the adolescent interpret their child's behavior as a family event and (particularly for the older adolescent or where family pathology is significant) help the adolescent truly gain autonomy from the family.

Perhaps it is tautological to suggest that one way to accomplish this end is to offer the adolescent individual psychotherapy in addition to or, if necessary, instead of family therapy. More to the point and irrespective of modality, the success of any treatment effort is dependent upon securing the initial compliance of the adolescent and his or her family and then establishing an effective working relationship with the adolescent (a "therapeutic alliance") that strives to accomplish mutually agreed-upon, nonsuicidal goals. Among several suggested approaches, those that follow appear to promise some measure of success.

Macrotherapeutic Issues: Developing a Working Relationship

Methods for Increasing Compliance

Assessment and treatment need to be inextricably linked at first contact. The adolescent patient and adult family members need to be given objective feedback regarding diagnosis and treatability, including a layman's understanding of what stimulates and reinforces the adolescent's suicidal behavior. It should also be made clear that, absent treatment of predisposing risk factors, the suicidal urge is likely to return, leading to consequences no one truly wishes. Clinicians are more likely to effect referrals if the topic of follow-up care is introduced early in the first contact or evaluation and given opportunity for discussion than if it is introduced without warning at the end of the assessment (Knesper, 1982).

As part of the assessment process, the attributions of the patient and his or her family regarding both the problems and their solutions need to be identified and, if necessary, redefined in a nonmoralistic manner. The patient is neither a bad child nor a lazy one, for instance, but one whose symptoms and behavior signal a problem out of control and in need of attention to solve. When patients are not held responsible for their problems (i.e., etiologies are described in terms of diagnoses, stressors, skill deficits, etc.) but are seen as important collaborators with the therapist in seeking solutions (the "compensatory model" described by Brickman, et al., 1982), help-seeking (and help-giving) behavior is optimized (Tessler & Schwartz, 1972). Similarly, if it is possible to make seeking help more normative to the adolescent, help-seeking behavior will be reinforced (Gross, Piliavin, Wallston, & Broll, 1972).

At the time of first contact, an appointment, at a definite time in the near future (never more than one week later and preferably within a few days) and with a specified therapist, needs to be made in the presence of the patient and his or her family. If possible, direct contact (e.g., by telephone) between the patient and therapist should occur in order to defuse the anxiety attendant to the unknown. Such active procedures generally have been found to be more successful at effecting compliance when compared to more passive procedures, such as merely giving the patient the name and number of a referral to contact (Kogan, 1957; Rogawski & Edmundson, 1971).

In support of the adolescent's autonomy, the adolescent should be involved in initial treatment decisions and, if possible, in selecting a therapist (including issues of gender, office location, etc.) acceptable to him or her. Being involved in treatment decisions has been found to influence the adolescent's subsequent motivation for and response to treatment (Adelman, Kaser-Boyd, & Taylor, 1984).

The adolescent and his or her family should be contacted by phone as a reminder of their first session's appointment and as a continuing expression of interest on the part of the initial evaluator. If staffing allows the luxury of a home visit prior to the first postcrisis appointment, the likelihood of compliance may increase (Deykin, Hsieh, Joshi, & McNamara, 1986).

Where evidence or suggestion exists that the adolescent lacks the capacity to trust and to tolerate frustration sufficiently to respond to an offer of outpatient treatment (Miller, 1986), or where the family appears unable to monitor the adolescent at home or to comply with follow-up recommendations, short-term inpatient care should be considered (see the section on Hospitalization in chapter 4).

The therapeutic alliance and countertransference. The quality of the therapist–patient relationship, or therapeutic alliance, has been cited as the most critical factor determining whether or not the process of psychotherapy is successful (Goldfried, 1980). Psychotherapy outcome studies have shown that more than 60% of the total treatment outcome variance may be attributable to the compatibility of the therapist–patient match (Beutler & Mitchell, 1981).

A good working alliance is crucial, as well, in the treatment of the suicidal adolescent. However, suicidal patients, particularly suicidal adolescents, have difficulty forming good therapeutic alliances. They often have histories of disturbed early relationships that are prototypical of difficulties in future, including therapeutic, relationships (Strupp, 1980). Early in treatment they are likely to exhibit feelings of hopelessness, helplessness, and despair about both themselves and treatment. They tend to predict more internal attributions for failure than do nondepressed patients (Zuroff, 1981), have expectations of continuing helplessness, and are pessimistic about controlling their futures (Beck, 1972). At best, they will express ambivalence about potential change for the better and, more often, expectations of further disappointment. Common to their dynamics, these patients are likely to behave regressively and with a demanding dependency on the therapist. Furthermore, they are prone to express anger and aggression, as well as passivity, behaviors destined to test the tolerance of the best of therapists if not merely validate their own sense of unlovability. For some, like Sam, their identity is rooted fragilely in their reactive autonomy, an oxymoronic dynamic reflecting a sense of personal control stimulated by a fear of being controlled by a transferential object.

Case Illustration (continued)

> Sam (see pp. 138, 148) by age 19 had a history of chronic depression, including multiple suicide attempts of low intentionality but high lethality. These attempts were typically coercive in response to a girlfriend's termination of a short but intense relationship in which Sam's lovability was demanded rather than earned. He entered outpatient therapy on the appeal of his latest girlfriend, who stated that Sam had been threatening to kill himself with a gun in his possession if she would not "give him a chance."
>
> Sam had left home at the age of 16, living in a succession of group homes while living off the streets and involving himself in peer groups defined by drug use and experimentation. The stimulus for his leaving home was his antagonistic relationship with his father, whom he described as punitive, rejecting, controlling, and contentious. Sam both rebelled against and identified with his father, describing himself as both stubborn and controlling. When the therapist, an older male, tested Sam's willingness to agree to an initial contract, Sam responded that he would make no commitments, that he would reject any attempt to control him, including any contract about his gun, his drinking or pot use, and so forth. He refused to consider a voluntary hospitalization. Furthermore, he stated that the therapist would have to take time to get to know him, that "you'll just have to accept me on my terms," and lastly that "we'll take this thing just one session at a time."

As therapists, we typically expect patients to be motivated to use offered help, to follow therapeutic advice, and to actively engage in the therapeutic process on their own behalf. Suicidal patients generally do not fit this "good patient" role (Vlasak, 1975). The therapist confronted with such a patient is likely to respond with similarly negative attitudes and feelings (Ansell & McGee, 1971). It is commonly observed that suicidal patients engender in therapists feelings ranging from those of irritation and inconvenience (Frederick, 1978; Reubin, 1973) to those of "countertransferential hate" (Maltsburger & Buie, 1974) and wishes to be rid of the patient (Bloom, 1970).

Such negative attitudes may have iatrogenic effects when countertransference reactions are not effectively controlled. One result is the loss of a help-giving therapeutic posture. For example, as the potential suicide's intentionality increases, the therapist's feelings become more anxious and negative and the less help is offered (Schopler & Matthews, 1965). The persistently suicidal patient—as we have noted a high risk for ultimate completion—is another example of the "bad patient" who stimulates an iatrogenic response. These patients, such as Sue Ellen, often are pejoratively referred to as "pseudocides," reflecting the staff's conditioning not to take seriously the significance of these behaviors. Unfortunately, the most serious consequence of such iatrogenesis is that of a completed suicide.

Case Illustration

> Sue Ellen, age 16, is well known by the emergency room staff, who invariably are called upon to treat her for an overdose or wrist-cutting attempt on a Saturday night busy with the usual trauma patients common to a city hospital. When she arrives for the sixth time, for a low-lethality attempt, the staff, impatient with and frustrated by her for manipulating their attention away from patients "really" in need, treat her with disdain. One overtaxed member of the treatment team says within Sue Ellen's earshot, "If she really wants to do it, she should get it over with already!" Two months later, after learning of her suicidal death, this same staff member responded with surprise.

Examples of therapeutic distancing are most evident in the labeling processes commonly observed in working with suicidal patients. Two that are most notable are the use of the labels "resistant" and "manipulative" to describe the suicidal patient. Both labels are attributions that hold the patient to blame for behaviors that are seen as obstacles to treatment rather than which, more appropriately, define reasons for the patient needing treatment. We will say more about these labels shortly; but suffice it to say for the moment that therapists' use of these labels is not likely to promote increased involvement with their patients. The most serious iatrogenic consequence attributed to the therapist's discouragement and intolerance of the suicidal patient's negative affect and behavior has been that of the patient's suicide (Modestin, 1987; Wheat, 1960).

It must therefore be the therapist's responsibility to manage his or her countertransference reactions and to skillfully foster the development of the therapeutic alliance.

Methods for Managing Countertransference Reactions

It is axiomatic among suicidologist–clinicians that, if possible, no more than two seriously at-risk suicidal patients be carried in treatment at any one time (Mintz, 1971). As this often is difficult to accomplish, or as clinicians are fallible enough to be caught by surprise by a previously nonsuicidal patient in an acute suicidal crisis, it is secondarily axiomatic that clinicians have available a trusted colleague for consultation, advice, and support, and that consultations with that colleague be scheduled with some regularity during periods of patient (and clinician?) crisis. Therapists working in agencies or hospitals should be aware of and attend to the structure of the institution's policies and procedures manual outlining both the structure and supports available within the organizational system.

Modestin (1987) argues that "the best protection . . . is constant self-monitoring . . . along with the ability to allow negative impulses to become conscious and to keep them in consciousness without excessive shame or guilt" (p. 384). Not all countertransference responses are negative. Some reactions, when both tolerated and understood, can be effective tools in understanding both the patient and others' reactions to the patient.

Paralleling the therapist's tolerance of his own negative affect (e.g., anxiety, anger, despair), the therapist must give clear and consistent messages that he or she can tolerate the patient's painful affect, a stance typically in stark contrast to that of the patient's parents (Hynes, 1989). This position, as well, fosters the therapeutic alliance.

One significant way to accomplish this tolerance is to keep in mind what we know about both adolescence and suicidality (i.e., that neither is constant) and therefore not to set false expectations and suffer ultimate disappointment when these are dashed. For example, a therapist cannot afford to be lulled into comfort and self-congratulations by the first report of improvement from a suicidal adolescent. Because the suicidal urge is state-dependent and therefore tends to wax and wane contingent on the adolescent's environmental context, mental status, and so on, this patient is quite likely to again express suicidal feelings. Accordingly, a continuous focus by the therapist on risk assessment should help to reduce the potential for disappointment.

It is our contention that the therapist's expectations also need to include a clear and consistent awareness that the suicidal adolescent enters treatment with a transferential relationship already in hand. The patient, irrespective of age, is like a helpless child, lacking in skills or resources to effectively cope with the exigencies of everyday life. These deficits exist either because the adolescent has yet to learn adaptive problem-solving skills or because the adolescent is temporarily out of control (due to overwhelming stress or psychopathology). This patient typically will be demanding and dependent on the therapist or, as noted before, will replicate earlier disturbed relationships, harboring and acting out fantasies the therapist cannot, in reality, fulfill.

On one level, it is imperative that the therapist not share the patient's delusions, (e.g., of the therapist's omnipotence). On another level, it is important that the therapist accept the transferential relationship and play the part of a good parent. Good parents do not expect behavior beyond the level of the patient's emotional maturity. Adolescents, in general, develop asynchronously; physical, emotional, and cognitive development do not keep equally apace. Suicidal adolescents have the added problems of dependency and helplessness, which need to be accepted as givens and tolerated by the therapist. Good parents nurture and gratify needs, but always within limits. Thus, limit setting both in the interest of the adolescent patient and in order not to negatively affect the therapist are essential to the management of negative countertransferential reactions.

In a similar vein, it is essential that the therapist examine his or her attributions regarding the cause of the patient's difficulties. There is an important distinction, for example, between (a) viewing suicidal patients as ill and therefore entitled to treatment by an expert and (b) seeing suicidal behavior as an attempt to solve the problem of pain stemming from skill deficits or psychopathology that are treatable. From the latter perspective, the patient can receive help without a label of weakness or culpability and can participate in using that help in a manner that enhances autonomy and self-esteem (Berman & Cohen-Sandler, 1983).

As a corollary, the tendency of some therapists to use pejorative labels to describe therapeutic impasses and undesirable patient behavior, as noted earlier, serves only to distance the therapist and create transferential and countertransferential problems. When the patient displays distancing, help-rejecting behavior, he or she is expressing dynamics learned and inherent in relationships in existence long before the establishment of the therapeutic relationship. "Resistance" identifies a primary reason for the patient to be in treatment rather than an obstacle to treatment. To blame the patient for displaying behavior that illustrates why he or she is in the mess precipitating therapy clearly displays the therapist's problem more than the patient's. Resistance is a learned defense. It serves a protective function (Lerner & Lerner, 1983). It is a reflection of the patient's pathological yet potentially understandable adaptation to his or her interpersonal environment, and as such, should be expected by the therapist.

To label the suicidal patient's behavior as "manipulative" similarly reduces therapeutic contact when it should provide reason for therapeutic involvement. In the same vein, we note how much in vogue it has become to label (inappropriately) nearly all difficult and manipulative patients as "borderlines". Some observers have astutely remarked that "it is noteworthy . . . that only patients are called manipulative" (Hamilton, Decker, & Rumbaut, 1986). By definition, to manipulate means to influence, manage, operate, or control "shrewdly or deviously" (Morris, 1973). Obviously, it is the deviousness of the adolescent's attempt to control another's (the therapist's) behavior that gives rise to the negative response to this behavior, particularly when suicidal behavior is used to accomplish that control. Yet, were adolescents capable of accomplishing their goals "shrewdly," they would, again, have little reason to need therapy. The suicidal adolescent should be expected to manipulate others. The therapist should establish as an objective of treatment helping the adolescent accomplish a more effective and more direct control over his or her interpersonal world as well as an acceptance and appreciation of those situations in which such control is unlikely to be exercised successfully. This reframing demands greater rather than less involvement in the treatment of the suicidal adolescent. With particular reference to the patient using suicidal behavior as a method of influence and control, clear and consistent limit setting by the therapist, including a matter-of-fact, nonreinforcing response to any suicidal behavior by the patient, needs to be emphasized. More will be said of this later.

Methods for Fostering the Therapeutic Alliance

Adolescents, particularly those in suicidal crisis, are more like children than adults. At one and the same time, they paradoxically ask permission to act like adults and seek excuse from responsibility when they have acted like children. Yet, like adults, they wish to have their independent thoughts respected, their feelings validated, and their personhood affirmed—all reasonable and appropriate needs. The therapeutic alliance is initially fostered by the therapist's attention to these human needs. In that vein, empathic pairing and listening and active, verbal validations of the adolescent's perspectives and feelings promote the initial connection necessary to move ahead on significant behavior change.

It is essential that the clinician remember (a) that he or she is generically a member of that same generation from which the adolescent is seeking autonomy, (b) that the adolescent's associations to seeing the "doctor" will have a long history that, more than likely, is antagonistic to the type of relationship both necessary to and sought by the clinician, and (c) that the doctor's office is a foreign, often formal place connoting role distantiation and pomposity, to which the adolescent may not be coming willingly. At the same time, it is important that the clinician's role be clearly differentiated as that of the authority and helper, one capable of being the "good parent." Thus the clinician must maintain the authority of the doctor's role while bridging the distance to the adolescent created by that role and its associated context. Walking the proverbial tightrope between these roles is often difficult and perhaps can best be accomplished with idiosyncratic style. Although we have little reason to suggest how individual therapists should decorate their office or present themselves to their patients, there are some generic considerations we would like to propose:

1. Doctor's white lab coats belong only in hospital settings, and only then when appropriate to role and function.

2. Doctors should be introduced as "Doctor . . ." and not by first name. Role expertise should be fostered while interpersonal distance reduced. For example, face-to-face seating is greatly preferable to that which places an office desk between patient and doctor.

3. Sessions should be limited to 45 minutes in length, but with flexibility to go longer when necessary or when the adolescent gives evidence of tolerating more time, or shorter if the adolescent's tolerance has been reached.

4. Adolescent patients should be encouraged to come to treatment, if they wish, with a friend who will wait for them and with whom they can leave at the end of the session. There may be virtue in considering having the friend join the session, if seen as appropriate by both patient and therapist (Bernstein, 1989).

5. Warmth and comfort in the office setting are important. This implies flexibility on the clinician's part regarding rules for such things as snacking and drinking soft drinks during sessions.

6. Warmth within the limits of the clinical role likewise is important. It is helpful for the therapist to self-disclose where relevant, to use humor where appropriate, and to appreciate and reinforce the adolescent's humor, even as more often cynically expressed.

In the initial session, an overview of therapy should be provided. At a minimum, this should include statements about frequency of meetings, the expected course of treatment with a particular focus on early goals, and some statement about termination of treatment. The adolescent needs to be presented with a clear statement about the therapist's rules for confidentiality and under what conditions significant adults (particularly parents) will or will not be involved or communicated with. (Confidentiality issues will be discussed later in this chapter.) We have found it helpful to anticipate the adolescent's distrust of these statements and to acknowledge that time together will have to prove the measure of the therapist's trustworthiness with regard to these issues. Similarly, the therapist's criteria for considering hospitalization may be presented while paradoxically siding with the adolescent's wish not to be hospitalized. That is, this choice can be presented as one of "last resort" in order to maximize the adolescent's alliance and compliance with an outpatient contract. The therapist's availability and accessibility should be discussed explicitly, as should the expected use of the telephone as an adjunct to the time spent in the office (see section on Availability and Accessibility, in this chapter).

The adolescent should be oriented toward thinking that therapy can help; that, thus far, the adolescent's attempted solutions to deal with the presenting problems have not been as effective as he or she would wish and that, at a minimum, "two heads are better than one" in arriving at more effective solutions, and that once the patient and therapist have agreed upon what the problems are, that the therapist has a variety of tools to lend and techniques to suggest that might be useful in producing change.

Together, the therapist and patient should define a common goal, ideally one simply worded in clear and measurable terms and related to the patient's central complaint. Short-term goals allow for accessible targets for change. The consensually measured accomplishment of small-step movement toward accomplishable goals allows for rewardable effort and hope, two conditions typically absent in the lives of suicidal teenagers. Motivation for treatment, also, is more likely to be maintained under conditions of perceived control and enhanced competence. Often, the therapist must reframe the presenting problem to allow for the establishment of such a short-term goal, one simply defined by what the therapist believes he or she can most readily accomplish, and not necessarily the one most relevant to the long-term goals. That change is possible is the overriding motto of early interventions.

Where "resistance" needs to be "outmanipulated" by the therapist in order to promote the therapeutic alliance, any of several sources of strategies might be recommended (cf. Bernstein, 1989; Hamilton et al., 1986; Lerner & Lerner, 1983).

The Treatment Plan

Comparatively little has been written in the professional literature on the treatment of the suicidal adolescent. In truth, treatment is not a frequent topic in the literature on suicide in general and more often is referred to as "management" (cf. Goldney & Burvill, 1980; Kreitman, 1986), a focus about which Hendin (1982) has written most critically. Treatment studies, where reported, typically focus on aftercare (postattempt) management and prevention of completions or repeat attempts and, to date, have not focused on the adolescent patient. In truth, little psychotherapy outcome research has been conducted on this population. If it is fair to assume that adolescence is a separate developmental period, then, as noted by Kendall and Williams (1986), "the utility of treatments designed for children or adults must be empirically verified when applied with adolescents, rather than tacitly assumed" (p. 533).

Trautman and Shaffer (1984) have reviewed and summarized the treatment outcome literature. Their conclusions suggest that there is at least evidence that contact is better than no contact with the suicidal patient and that perhaps psychosocial treatment "can lower the rates of completed and attempted suicide and suicide ideation and improve mental state and social adjustment" (p. 319). Liberman and Eckman's (1981) comparative treatment study further suggests that behavior therapy may have more significant effects with this population of patients than does insight-oriented therapy, at least in affecting mood; however, outcome measures of repeated suicide attempts did not differ by virtue of therapy interventions.

Without research-based guidelines for effective treatment models, clinicians must decide for themselves on a logical treatment plan based both on a theory of intervention and a thorough understanding of the suicidal adolescent, both generic and specific to the presenting case. Most therapists provide a type of therapy to their patients that is independent of patient diagnosis; rather, patients are most likely to get the type and format of psychotherapy in which the therapist is most experienced, trained, or devoted (Beutler, 1989). Additionally, it appears that much of the treatment outcome variance may be attributable more to the therapist–patient compatibility than to specific therapeutic techniques (Beutler & Mitchell, 1981).

Nevertheless, when treating suicidal adolescents, the therapist needs a therapeutic plan, specific to the goals of intervention and designed to provide short- and long-term antidotes to the problems of the suicidal adolescent. The therapeutic plan needs to address the site of treatment (inpatient or outpatient) and, consequently, the available therapeutic agents (primary and adjunct therapists and therapies); the multimodality of treatment (primarily individual, group or family therapy, as well as pharmacotherapy); and the therapeutic strategies to be used to attain specific treatment and patient goals.

The Site of Treatment

The need for emergency medical care, the presence of significant psychopathology, or the assessed imminent and unabated risk of suicide are the primary indicators for hospital admission and the inpatient treatment of the suicidal adolescent (see the section on Hospitalization in chapter 4). Once stabilized and out of crisis, the adolescent can and—we believe—should be treated on an outpatient basis. Additionally, the shorter the hospital stay, the less the possibility of reinforcing regression through an institutional dependency and the intrusive depersonalization and stigmata attendant to the need to be hospitalized and removed from one's everyday social milieu.

As a controlled environment, the adolescent psychiatric unit clearly has many distinct advantages over outpatient settings. Foremost among these is the fact that inpatient psychiatric care allows for complete medical management of any injuries sustained from an attempt. In addition, inpatient care provides for: (a) the removal of the adolescent from sources of environmental stress and the immediate change in patient–systems (family, peer, etc.) dynamics; (b) maximum control over the possibility of unresisted self-harm behavior; (c) multiple sources of observation and assessment; (d) 24-hour support; (e) decreased interpersonal isolation and increased behavioral activity through multimodal treatments and required participant interactions (e.g., milieu therapy; formal and informal peer group meetings; ward government; point-system–contingent reward programs; art, music, and recreational therapies; and intensive psychotherapy; [individual and family] and pharmacotherapies); and (f) a step-wise attainment of goals leading to a planned discharge to follow up outpatient care. It should be noted that one likely outcome of extended psychiatric hospitalization is discharge to a setting other than the familial home. In one follow-up study of hospitalized child and early adolescent suicide attempters, less than half were living at home at the time of follow-up, which was, on average, 18 months postdischarge (Cohen-Sandler, Berman, & King, 1982).

Outpatient psychotherapy allows for an in-vivo maintenance and observed test of the adolescent's everyday functioning and interactions. Additionally, outpatient treatment provides: (a) support for the adolescent's autonomy and self-esteem to endure under difficult conditions and to function successfully, (b) the long-term involvement of both a consistent therapist and available community services, and (c) coordination with the adolescent's school (e.g., teachers and counselors) and other professionals in the resource network available to the adolescent.

Treatment Modalities

Individual psychotherapy is the mainstay of the suicidal adolescent. However, family therapy may be considered the treatment of choice, particularly where family conflict or pathology is central to the adolescent's continued suicidality or where family enmeshment of the adolescent is central to the adolescent's struggle toward autonomy. Thus, even with the older adolescent, family therapy should be considered and implemented, if possible, in order to help the adolescent free himself or herself from the family system. Group psychotherapy, with its emphasis on verbal versus physical expression and ventilation of affect, communication and listening skill development, peer support, and role modeling is also a significant modality of choice, where available and led by a competent and trained group therapist. As most of the remainder of this chapter will focus on strategies of intervention primarily based on an individual psychotherapy model, brief mention of these two procedures is in order.

Group psychotherapy. In contrast to a variety of group-based, skill enhancement programs (to be described later), homogeneous group psychotherapy with at-risk adolescents is a relatively underreported treatment modality, given the numbers of patients necessary, and one most easily accomplished on and specific to the psychiatric ward. Ross and Motto (1984) have described their experiences with an open-ended, mixed-sex outpatient group with eight high-risk adolescents, six of whom had made prior suicide attempts. The primary themes that emerged in the group were those relating to family relationships, peer relationships, and the control of potentially overwhelming affects and impulses. Through group support and befriending, group members learned alternative strategies for stress and affect management and improved both self-control and self-esteem. Although no operational measures of outcome were presented, the authors were encouraged by their experience with this model and suggested its use as a supplemental modality and of particular benefit where family therapy is not feasible. Similarly, Glaser (1978) has argued that group therapy is a useful alternative when the adolescent attempter is in florid rebellion against his or her parents.

Family therapy. Brown (1985) has asserted that an adolescent's suicidal behavior frequently is reflective of a "profound deficit in [the] family system" causing the ultimately suicidal child "to be devoid of a deeply felt sense of being a lovable and valued person." His observation is supported by the plethora of research findings related to disturbed familial and parental systems within which the suicidal adolescent lives and from which he or she struggles for independence (see chapter 3) and the high frequency with which a conflict or argument between the adolescent and parent precipitates suicidal behavior. The importance of the family to the etiology of the suicidal condition bespeaks its importance in the therapeutic process. Fishman (1988) goes so far as to label as "absurd" the idea of treating the troubled adolescent apart from his or her ongoing social context. Thus, it is imperative that therapists who treat adolescents at risk for suicidal behavior have knowledge of family processes and the characteristics of suicidal families in particular, *and* the skill to work with the family in (or alternatively, to refer the family for) family therapy.

The principal goals of family therapy with suicidal adolescents are the modification of communication patterns and pathological interactions among family members, increasing support for the adolescent's attempts at self-care and tolerance for separation, and improving the family's problem-solving behavior. Subsidiary to these goals are those of increasing flexibility and decreasing patterns of rigidity, reinforcing family strengths and teaching reinforcement strategies for use among family members, and reframing the family's understanding of the communication and interactive patterns of the adolescent (as well as those of the parents and siblings to the adolescent). Perhaps most importantly, a central goal is to develop an understanding within the family of the meaning of the adolescent's suicidal behavior and the possible death wishes held by family members toward the suicidal adolescent. In this vein, Richman's (1986) psychoanalytically oriented theory of family therapy approach seeks to help suicidal families differentiate and accept what he terms "the terror of change," as well as opening an otherwise closed system.

In contrast, Bond and Steinberg (1988) present a case study of a suicidal adolescent and family from the perspective of the strategic family therapist. This approach is central to the structural–strategic model proposed by Landau-Stanton and Stanton (1985). In this model, a number of strategies are used to reframe the meaning of the adolescent's suicide attempt within the family (e.g., as a noble self-sacrifice or as a deflection away from other family conflict or distress), to unite and empower the parents, and to expose family secrets. Parents and extended family members participate, as well, in any inpatient "suicide watch" of the adolescent.

Clearly, where parental pathology is intrinsic to the adolescent's suicidality, an appropriately therapeutic focus on these suicidogenic conditions is called for. The therapist should keep in mind that the lack of observed motivation or the noncompliance of families to be involved in recommended psychotherapeutic interventions (referred to earlier) is contraindicative of family therapy. Individual psychotherapy is indicated instead of family therapy where the adolescent is older and where therapeutic issues relate primarily to the adolescent's peer system (see section on Individual Psychotherapy).

In some instances, parents who are noncompliant with a recommendation for family therapy will force their child (the "identified patient") into individual therapy. In such a case, it is incumbent on the psychotherapist not to collude with the parents. The potential for life-threatening, iatrogenic effects is too great. In the case example that follows, the therapist's position and understanding of his patient was not one of empathy.

Case Illustration

> Sally, age 15, was sent to analytic psychotherapy by her divorced mother. Sally had a history of depression and rageful acting out that included the destruction of her bedroom and one suicide attempt by overdose. Her parents, neither of whom would agree to enter either individual or family

therapy themselves, were appropriately described by Sally (and others) as "intrusive, invading, overcontrolling, manipulative, narcissistic, erratic, and megalomanic." After several months of frustrating thrice-weekly sessions, Sally vehemently refused to come to treatment, stating both that she had no after-school time for herself and that it was her parents who needed treatment, not her. Her analyst maintained an analytic posture, interpreting her treatment resistance and "transferential rage"; he did not see her behavior as appropriate to either her view or her entrapment.

As noted, teaching reinforcement strategies to parents is an important aspect of family therapy. Parents can be taught to provide contingent reinforcement to the adolescent's behavior, particularly to reinforce appropriate behaviors and not to reward, primarily through attention, noncompliant and provocative behaviors. As noted by Egan (1988), behavioral and psychoanalytical approaches to family work can be routinely used *concurrently* by clinicians skilled in these techniques.

Pharmacotherapy. Drug treatment plays a small but not inconsiderable role in the therapy of suicidal adolescents. There is no drug that serves as an "antisuicide pill." However, where the underlying pathology (diagnostic condition, symptoms) may be appropriately treated by medication—particularly when a hoped-for symptom reduction allows for greater accessibility of the patient to verbal modes of intervention—drugs should be considered. For example, antidepressants, or more specifically, tricyclic antidepressants (e.g., imipramine, amitriptyline) may be indicated should a major depressive disorder be diagnosed, and major tranquilizers if there is evidence of schizophrenia. Should neuroleptics be called for, intramuscular injections of prolixin decanoate (or halperidol) might be considered to be preferable to pills, particularly to ensure compliance.

It should be noted, however, that only a few well-controlled drug studies with adolescent patient–subjects have appeared to date in the literature, without much support for effectiveness (Trautman, 1989). One reason for this outcome is that adolescents tend to respond well to placebo treatment, thereby masking differences between drug and placebo treatments. This should not be taken as evidence that pharmacological treatment is useless. Nonmedically oriented therapists need to be cautious in taking an antimedication stance a priori, because the standard of care in the treatment of the suicidal condition demands some respect for consideration of possible beneficial effects.

When medications are prescribed, careful monitoring of their administration to the suicidal adolescent is essential. Dosage levels must be considered carefully and hoarding of pills by the patient prevented. In a similar sense, access to medications by a suicidal adolescent must be severely limited. Pills should be administered by a trusted and available significant other, with specific instructions given to carefully guard against the easy availability of these medications to the adolescent at risk. When no trustworthy significant other is available—for example, in the case where parental pathology is evident—physicians should be warned to maintain control over available supplies of medications through scheduled weekly office visits and weekly control over the quantity of medications made available to the adolescent. When the therapist is not a physician but rather works with a physician who prescribes medication for referred patients, it is essential that interactive lines of communication remain open. The therapist should familiarize himself or herself with the common dosages, properties, and effects, particularly side effects, of prescribed medications. The therapist must be on top of the case and cognizant of *all* treatments provided to his or her patient, making sure as well that those who provide concurrent treatments are informed of significant changes in the patient's behavior, significant events threatening behavioral response, and any observed responses to medication (lack of compliance, side effects, etc.) perhaps not reported directly to the psychopharmacologist.

Individual psychotherapy. The modal treatment approach to working with the suicidal adolescent is that of individual therapy on an outpatient basis. In general, the length of treatment will depend on the severity of pathology and the response of the patient to treatment interventions; however, brief crisis intervention treatment is invariably called for initially to deal with the suicidal crisis. Additionally, Trautman (1989) references the work of others to provide support for those therapist qualities found more effective for youth: active, assertive, explanatory, and responsive, attributes common to those demanded in brief, problem-solving therapies. Moreover, it is our experience that adolescent suicidal patients tend to respond best to structured forms of therapy, particularly cognitive–behavioral and instrumental skill-enhancement interventions. As will be apparent, however, there remains considerable room for more interpretive treatments in the design of effective interventions in dealing with suicidal adolescents.

Case Illustration: The Treatment Plan

Rhonda, age 17, ingested the contents of her family medicine chest (primarily antihistamines and analgesics) at 3 a.m. She was brought to the emergency room by her father, who found her confused and difficult to awaken for school in the morning.

On intake, Rhonda stated that she had wanted "to drown out the pain" and that she had been preoccupied for several days with ending bad feelings she had about herself, ever since her "boyfriend" tried to drown himself. This relationship not only served to precipitate her suicide attempt but was prototypical of the predisposing condition to her suicidality. Rhonda was enmeshed with this friend, Tommy, who was either an asexual or bisexual classmate and who was described as both confused and mesmerizing, like a cult leader. Each of them, in turn, had triangulated this relationship with a 15-year-old male who appeared to be of sexual interest more to Tommy than to Rhonda. Rhonda's bad feelings about herself were in part stimulated by Tommy's competitive strivings and attempts to control Rhonda's involvement with this younger male.

Underlying this enmeshment was Rhonda's fusion with her father, to whom she told all, including sexual secrets and behaviors. In turn, her father related his extramarital affairs to Rhonda. Without discomfort, Rhonda shared that both she and her father were "perpetually horny." Although there was no intimation of more overt incestuous behavior, Rhonda clearly had displaced her mother, who was described as meek, naive, and socially unskilled.

Treatment goals were established through individual and family outpatient therapy and included concurrent individual therapy for her father and marital therapy. Family therapy focused on the establishment of appropriate boundaries and role responsibilities. Marital therapy attempted to increase the parental union and develop an appropriate sexual relationship.

Rhonda's individual work focused on increasingly differentiating from her father and from Tommy while increasing her involvements with healthy peer supports and youth groups. Definitions of self-worth were established to be dependent not on pleasing a dominant male (either father or Tommy) but on aspects of self-control and self-determination.

Crisis Intervention

Protecting the Adolescent From Self-Harm

The initial target goal in any therapeutic plan must be that of protecting the adolescent from self-harm behavior. Thus, decreasing lethality and perturbation, or "upsetness" (Shneidman, 1985) must precede therapeutic work on those conditions (e.g., intrapsychic, interpersonal, and environmental) that predispose the patient to be at risk. Sometimes, as noted earlier, this may require removal from a stressful to a nonstressful environment (e.g., hospitalization). More often, it involves an active, mutual problem-solving strategy that concurrently offers the interpersonal support and caring warmth otherwise felt to be absent in the adolescent's network of significant others. It is for this reason that in the midst of crisis intervention treatment, brief psychoanalytic strategies, as proposed by Mintz (1971), have their appropriate place.

Decreasing Perturbation and Lethality

The treatment of the suicidal adolescent often begins with the patient in a state of crisis. External stressors may overwhelm the patient's resources and coping skills, or predisposing conditions may make the patient highly vulnerable to otherwise minor events, not unlike the acute pain experienced when clothing brushes against an open wound on the skin. The level of upset and reactivity severely constrict the adolescent's ability to process information and use cognitive resources to solve problems. Also, the painful affect experienced by the patient may heighten the attractiveness of suicidal behavior as a perceived antidote; the opposite of pain is no pain.

The immediate therapeutic task is to prevent self-harm behavior, that is, to block suicidal action as an available solution and possible lethality as its outcome. Even if a state of nonbeing is not sought by the suicidal adolescent, suicidal action may reinforce continued use of such behavior because it often translates psychological pain into physical pain and achieves desired instrumental outcomes of altering family dynamics and shifting the attention and behavior of significant others.

Several excellent crisis intervention treatment guides and approaches are available to the reader (Aguilera & Messick, 1978; Hatton, Valente & Rink, 1977; Hoff, 1984; Jobes & Berman, 1991) and need not be replicated here. As described by these authors, and in accordance with our experience, a series of strategic steps needs to be considered and implemented to ensure the adolescent's immediate safety, diffuse the lethality of the situation, and prepare the patient for treatment of the problems giving rise to the crisis.

Restricting access to available means. As noted in chapter 1, suicidal action requires access to, the availability of, and often knowledge of a potentially lethal method. Additionally, readily available methods of self-destruction are those overwhelmingly chosen to be used by suicidal people either on impulse or by design. The potential for significant self-harm is severely reduced when these means are either unavailable or inaccessible to the suicidal patient (cf. Lester, 1989). Such a patient is immediately confronted with a new problem at a time of cognitive constriction and inflexibility, thereby limiting the application of good problem-solving skills. Therefore, the clinician, personally or through available significant others, should ask about and subsequently take the necessary steps to remove available means (e.g., firearms, pills) from the patient's access or, at a minimum, arrange for significant delay in their ready access to the patient. Ideally, the patient himself or herself should be contracted with, under the watchful eyes of significant others, to remove these means. Firearms kept in the home can be removed from the house and handed over to significant others for safekeeping, literally placed in a safe-deposit box or car trunk (with the key under another's control), or brought to the therapist for control. Medicine chests need to be purged of old and unneccessary prescriptions and over-the-counter remedies, and all pills placed in the care of a significant other. Where significant others are involved in control over means availability, they need to be educated in the significance of this responsibility and to be guided by the therapist's directives only. Where the patient is asked to take responsible steps toward control, it often is helpful to place this directive in a self-disclosing frame, such as "It makes me uncomfortable . . . ," with statements to the patient that such anxiety on the therapist's part would undesirably interfere with the therapist's helpfulness. In some cases, such as Ray's, there is almost a literal scream for protection from self-destructive urges, only to have that communication remain apparently unheard by others in a position to act on behalf of the adolescent.

Case Illustration

> Ray, age 14, had made three suicide attempts prior to completing his suicide. Each time there had been someone there to stop him. He communicated often about his intent, remarking that "Life's a bitch" and asking others about which way they thought it would be better to kill oneself. The day before his death, he asked his mother whether it would be better to stick a gun "in your mouth or in your temple?" He chose the latter, using a .357 Magnum that had been kept, fully loaded, in his mother's nightstand.

"No-suicide agreement." The use of contracts or, better, "agreements" with adolescents has both a structuring and linking function and may provide additional, valuable assessment data. The adolescent is asked, typically verbally, to agree not to hurt himself or herself for an explicit, time-limited period, typically until the next therapy session. Instead, the adolescent is asked to contact the therapist, or recommended others, as a therapeutic detour behavior when and if but *before* the suicidal urge impels action. Such agreements serve to build a switching mechanism into the adolescent's behavioral and problem-solving repertoire. These agreements furthermore provide needed parameters and controls and reinforce the therapist's intent to forge a linkage with the patient. Where the patient's response is of the "I'll try" or "Maybe" variety, the therapist has significant information regarding the patient's relative reluctance to align himself or herself with treatment, and appropriate consideration of more restrictive, but protective treatment alternatives (e.g., hospitalization) need to be considered. The therapist also needs to keep in mind that agreements are time-limited because of the patient's limited time perspective and therefore must be renewed. In hospital settings, behavioral contracting is necessarily more complex (O'Farrell, Goodenough, & Cutter, 1981).

Decreasing isolation. During the suicidal crisis, it is imperative that the adolescent not be left alone. The patient should effectively be under "suicide watch" by a significant other. Significant others must be explicitly told not to leave the patient alone during the crisis phase. In cases where family or friends are unavailable, hospitalization must be considered.

Decreasing symptom-caused perturbation. Particularly where symptoms of acute anxiety and insomnia are concerned, immediate attention must be given to settling down the patient's level of upset. Consideration of well-monitored medication, removal from external sources of perturbation, or immediate cognitive–behavioral attention to anxiety-provoking cognitions, such as those that lead to anticipatory fears of impending decompensation, can be dramatically helpful.

Treatment structuring. The adolescent in crisis needs handles onto which he or she may grab for security and stabilization. Linkage with the therapist begins to accomplish that goal. Linkage with treatment represents a sustaining alliance with both the therapist and the future, of which the adolescent's perspective may be severely limited by both overwhelming affect and cognitive constriction.

Treatment structuring, or therapy pretraining, can occur in a number of significant ways. The initial contact is just that—the first of an indefinite number in a sequence of further contacts. The goal of the initial contact must clearly be stated between therapist and patient: to formulate and define the problem in order to intervene with a successful solution. The long-term goal may also be stated: to achieve significant change where deemed necessary to improve the adolescent's sense of self and relationship to others. To accomplish these ends, the therapist structures for the adolescent their mutual responsibilities (the patient to stay alive and come to therapy; the therapist to provide therapy); the structure of sessions (e.g., the when, where, frequency, time limits); and the process of therapy (e.g., in the beginning, mutual problem solving to reduce the patient's suicidality; issues of confidentiality). Together, the dyad must establish the therapeutic goals, with the therapist carefully attending to make sure that these goals are within the patient's capability to achieve.

To reinforce the no-suicide agreement, the adolescent needs to understand what the therapist will and will not do if the adolescent calls after rather than before initiating a suicide attempt. If an attempt is in process, the therapist has the responsibility to do what is necessary to help the adolescent get emergency treatment. This is not the time for talk. The rules of confidentiality no longer apply. To this end, a clear statement about confidentiality and the therapist's responsibility to place concerns for life and limb ahead of confidentiality should be given to the adolescent in language free from professional jargon.

Where necessary, the therapist should provide factual information to the adolescent, replacing confusing experiences with clarity and labels. Symptoms need to be named and syndromes described as clusters of symptoms and experiences with which the adolescent can identify. It is helpful to place such diagnostic structures in the frame of hope, that is, that we *can* treat this disorder (analogies to physical illness may be helpful in this regard); that some symptoms or diagnostic conditions are due to biochemistry, which can be regulated, others to negative learnings and nonnurturant environments, which are changeable, and still others to the effects of skill deficits, which are remediable. None of these frames convey the typical suicidal adolescent belief that what is at the core of his or her experience is an awful, very bad, no-good person!

The therapist needs to play soothsayer as well, providing some statements about what the adolescent can expect. These include a longer term statement about the termination of therapy and, more immediately, an understanding that the suicidal urge waxes, wanes, and returns. This understanding prepares the adolescent not to be disappointed following inappropriate expectations early in treatment.

Problem-solving intervention. The crux of crisis intervention work is that of problem-solving therapy. This involves a brief course of sessions designed to reduce suicidality. It is accomplished through collaborative effort ("two heads are better than one") following a relatively standardized procedure of problem exploration, problem definition, generating alternative solutions, hypothesis testing, and resolution.

The exploration phase of problem solving involves understanding the pertinent aspects of the precipitating event and the adolescent's response (emotional, cognitive, and behavioral). Through structured and semistructured questions, the therapist must carefully explore the pervasiveness, duration, and frequency of events that set off the current crisis response and threaten a loss of control. Most importantly, the antecedent and reinforcing conditions for suicidal ideation or behavior must be developed as framed from the patient's perspective. It is essential during this phase that reflective comments ("mirroring") be made to the adolescent to convey that a common frame of reference is being established and that his or her emotional responses are understandable and therefore valid.

For the adolescent patient, this is an opportunity for ventilation and catharsis, for narcissistic gratification for both what one has to say and how one feels. For the therapist, this is an opportunity to forge an alliance and to *selectively* listen. Most patients "spill" their problems, prompting some of our colleagues to refer to this stage of intervention as "mess solving." It is the therapist's task to skillfully identify the essential and manageable elements of the crisis situation in order to identify and define what is within the patient's and the therapist's capacity to modify quickly.

Defining the problem should be a natural outgrowth of the foregoing exploration. The goal of exploration is to identify and clarify the problem and to describe the problem in terms that the adolescent can accept. Such a description needs to focus on the role the adolescent's suicidality has played as one of many possible solutions. Note that the adolescent's suicidality is not presented to the patient as the problem but as a potential solution—it is the goal of problem solving to arrive at a more effective solution to the problem being defined.

The therapist's role in the problem-solving intervention is to actively lend an ego to the patient. The adolescent is confused, overwhelmed, frightened, and dysfunctional. Inappropriate solutions are grasped at as futile attempts to change a situation causing intense pain. The therapist offers a third eye and a second brain to better perceive and abstract the essential elements of the situation causing pain. Once defined within manageable terms, the task then shifts to a thoughtful (versus an impulsive) consideration of various alternative solutions to the problem. It is helpful therefore to present the problem in terms of separate but integrated parts, and solutions in terms of achievable steps toward an agreed-upon goal.

By understanding the goal or instrumental purpose of the suicidal behavior (the "functional analysis of motive"), the therapist can steer the patient toward available, alternative behaviors. Typically, the goal of suicidal behavior is reasonable. It is designed to satisfy some unmet need, to change some intolerable situation, to effect change in others, or to reduce painful affect. The adolescent needs to appreciate that his or her suicidal behavior has not accomplished a change and does not change problems for the better; in fact, it typically perpetuates problems. The therapeutic task is to arrive at more effective solutions, a task that first requires not acting on the suicidal urge.

One model for problem definition we have found readily understandable to adolescents is a simplified and debased psychodynamic explanation: *Stress* (antecedent and precipitating events) leads to *pain* (feelings of hurt and fear) leads to *defense* (attempts to escape pain). It is often useful to schematize this on paper with the adolescent to illustrate clearly that, for example, suicidal behavior has been the adolescent's attempted solution (defense) to change another's unwanted behavior (stress) which has made the adolescent feel unloved, humiliated, or rejected (pain).

With this explanation and a reasonable assessment of the function of suicidal behavior, consensual goal setting can be achieved. For example, where a suicide attempt has been instituted to decrease affective distress, the short-term goal might be to seek ways to remove the adolescent from the stress-provoking situation and to decrease the intrusiveness of anxiety symptoms. The longer term goals might involve teaching stress inoculation techniques, anger management skills, or tension reduction skills.

Generating alternative strategies of problem resolution should be presented as a joint enterprise between patient and therapist, but in truth, this stage of intervention involves considerable and careful direction by the therapist. The therapist has clearer perceptions and more rational perspectives. He or she has tools to lend to the adolescent. Advice should be given. Directives and suggestions are warranted. This phase of problem-solving treatment is not the time for more passive or inactive therapeutic postures. The adolescent needs to arrive at a relatively immediate structure both with which to understand what has happened and to make some change occur.

Alternatives generated under the guidance of the therapist should involve consideration of the availability of significant others who are not part of the matrix of factors making the patient suicidal; available community resources; and the adolescent's history of and currently available coping skills. The adolescent should be exhorted to generate possible alternative solutions first, without regard to evaluating their effectiveness. The cognitive rigidity common to the suicidal mind needs to be pushed toward flexibility. The therapist should sell the model that it is better to discard choices in hand than to limit oneself to only one alternative. The therapist needs to be prepared to counter the adolescent's attempts to reject the therapist as "not understanding" when the adolescent presents merely one mal-adaptive choice by iterating the problem defined earlier. The therapist should maintain a focus on generating, together with the patient, as many alternatives as possible. In contrast, it should go without saying that any appropriate and creative responses should be reinforced with praise and encourage-ment.

Cognitive rehearsal and role playing of alternatives often helps clarify the pros and cons of, and foreseeable roadblocks to, the various ideas generated. What is sought is a hierarchy of choices available to the adolescent for hypothesis testing. Suicide should be affirmed as one of these choices although it is hoped that this choice is seen as one of relative ineffectiveness.

Hypothesis testing simply is a directed and structured sci-entific technique of trying alternative approaches to accomplish a short-term goal. Small, accomplishable homework assign-ments can be structured to try this or observe that. Revisions and modifications to initial hypotheses often occur as infor-mation is collected and observations analyzed. New informa-tion should lead to modified approaches. The most important point is that once at this stage of problem-solving intervention, the adolescent has joined with the therapist in *working* on the defined problems and is, by definition, no longer acutely and impulsively trying to end the problems with suicidal behavior. In other words, the initial problems of heightened lethality and perturbation are essentially resolved as long as continued treat-ment can occur. It is at this point that the broader perspectives and goals of individual therapy can be approached.

Availability and accessibility. As noted before, individual sessions need to be scheduled as often as possible and as deemed necessary, particularly in the early stages of treatment. Contact with the therapist should be encouraged and reinforced to occur between sessions and particularly during periods of heightened affect and reactivity. We strongly believe that therapists antag-onistic to being contacted between office sessions not work with suicidal adolescents and immediately refer these patients to others.

Accessibility means the possibility of contact at any time of the day. Obviously, this means that the telephone is an ad-junctive means of contact between therapist and patient. This does not mean that the therapist should feel constrained to be available 24 hours a day nor that demands for contact, no matter how unreasonable, will be met. Following are some guidelines for maximizing the appropriate use of this means of contact:

1. Give your phone number and those of at least two others of use should you be unreachable. One of these should be that of a 24-hour telephone service (suicide prevention center, hot-line, crisis center) that you have screened as well administered. Make sure your patient retains these numbers, for example, on a wallet card.

2. Teach your patient how, when, and where to reach you. For example, providing on paper a picture of your typical weekly schedule helps the adolescent understand that you may be teaching on one day, typically at home writing on another, and so on.

3. Educate your patient as to what to expect when and if he or she calls. For example, an answering machine (or service) at the office or at home may answer when you are unavailable, or if you are reached at 2 a.m., you may be groggy, speak unintelligibly for the first few moments, and so forth. These directives should include contingency instructions, that is, "If this happens, then do the following . . . ."

4. Educate your patient as to what to expect should they call a crisis service. It may be helpful to explore his or her attitudes toward and history of using a hotline. It may be helpful to role play or, better yet, to have an in vivo phone call to a hotline in order to desensitize any discomfort with this resource and to dispel concerns about flashing red lights suddenly appearing and sirens sounding at the door.

5. Remind the adolescent that he or she is to call *before* acting on any suicidal wish and that he or she does not have to feel suicidal to call.

6. Encourage noncrisis phone contacts, such as immediate follow-ups to homework assignments, or brief between-session check-ins. These contacts should be kept brief, less than 5 minutes, and can be scheduled if necessary to occur at defined times of mutual convenience. Over time, these calls can be channeled into prearranged contacts, thereby reinforcing the adolescent's tolerance for distress until the appointed hour of contact.

7. Do not assume a priori that this telephone accessibility will be abused. Interpret for your patient, at the appropriate time, that too frequent late-night or early-morning telephone calls indicates to you that the therapy has yet to sufficiently help the patient get needed rest and sleep; that what has prompted calls overnight could have been handled perhaps even better in the morning (again, "tolerating" some distress); and that such frequent need to connect may indicate that office sessions are currently scheduled too infrequently and that therefore either more sessions must be scheduled or, if at the limit of what is feasible to schedule, hospitalization needs to be considered.

8. Use the telephone proactively. With perhaps no more of an agenda than "I was thinking about how what we talked about in our last session went . . . ," find reason to reinforce a message of your constancy and care for your patient as a nonsuicidal person. These calls also should be kept quite brief and used as a link between in-office contacts.

9. Lastly, as insurance, be sure that you have available and accessible names and addresses of significant others (family and friends) should, in the midst of suicidal crisis, you need to contact the adolescent's supports to help effect a rescue. Nothing can feel more agonizing, short of news of a completed suicide, than to attempt to deal with such an event without any way to help emergency medical personnel locate an uncooperative patient.

Beyond Crisis Intervention

Four major goals of outpatient intervention have been addressed thus far: (a) developing a working relationship, (b) having a treatment plan, (c) protecting the adolescent from self-harm through crisis intervention, and (d) decreasing perturbation and lethality through crisis intervention. With these reasonably accomplished, the work of psychotherapy then can focus on broadening the adolescent's linkages beyond the here and now crisis (temporal linkages) to a wider network of interpersonal and group resources (support linkages), and on those predisposing conditions that make the adolescent vulnerable to becoming suicidal. Goals related to this latter focus typically include reducing the effect of psychopathology and maladaptive cognitions and behaviors and increasing self-esteem, enhancing instrumental skills, and improving object relations.

These goals may be achieved through any of a variety of therapeutic strategies, the choice of which is more dependent on therapist orientation, temperament, and training than anything else. As noted in the introduction to this book, however, few therapists have received specific training other than that accomplished "by the seat of one's pants" in working with suicidal patients. Therefore, it may be helpful to briefly acquaint the reader with a few of the several models for accomplishing these longer term therapeutic goals. Many of these approaches are available in much greater depth in well-developed treatment manuals (cf. Beck, Rush, Shaw, & Emery, 1978; Linehan, 1984), which in toto or through abstraction contain techniques easily assimilated into the therapist's everyday treatment armamentaria.

Temporal Linkages

Insight-oriented therapies are constructed upon a foundation of the past—in fact, the distant past, rooted in the influences of early childhood. Irrespective of the type of therapy, it is important that the suicidal adolescent, whose perspectives are severely constricted by the pain of the immediate precipitant and the demands of a suicidal urge, have the proverbial blinders removed in order to appreciate that the current intense moment is but a moment in time. Time stretches from early childhood through the present and into the future.

There are a number of orientation techniques that reinforce the idea of temporality to the adolescent. One has already been discussed, the no-suicide agreement. In a similar sense, wherever impulse can be thwarted by delay, time—perhaps the most powerful of therapeutics—can work to provide a lessened urgency, a surprise change in environmental circumstances, and even therapy a chance to take place. The adage to be sold to the adolescent is simply, "What can be done in May can be done in December." Future time perspective is reinforced by discussions about the course or process of treatment and by rehearsal strategies to deal with the recurrence of suicidal urges as well as any of a multitude of situations one might foresee and for which responses might be predeveloped.

As noted, continuity with the past is the hallmark of classical therapies and is also appropriate to the newer, more behavioral treatments, which still must allow for the role of prior learnings and patterns developed over time. These should be shared with the adolescent patient, particularly as they help explain the problems presented and help attribute causes to something other that the adolescent's inadequacy. The fact that the adolescent has weathered past crises and depressions also needs to be affirmed, although one has to be careful not to stimulate the adolescent's tendency to interpret such feedback as evidence of how long he or she has struggled to no avail and therefore as evidence of ultimate failure.

Of note in this context is the importance of interpretation. Interpretations, particularly those relating to the transference relationship, provide essential links between current observation and early childhood referents. Borderline patients, especially, will both attack and idealize the therapist, often rapidly shifting these projections. Interpreted connections to early parental introjections and their resulting masochistic and destructive transference reactions help the patient come to give up unrealistic expectations of both himself or herself and others. As a result, we might expect less idealization and need to attack, as self and therapist are viewed more realistically.

The relationship between the "now" and future time can be reinforced between sessions by the assignment of concrete, accomplishable homework assignments that link session X to session X + 1 and by between-session telephone contacts. Anxiety about the short-term future can be diffused by such "connectors" or bridging maneuvers. Another example is a long-held technique designed to stimulate curiosity and to bridge sessions, in which patient-initiated content, introduced toward the end of a session, is held for discussion at the start of the next session, as suggested by the therapist's statement, "That's really worth spending some time talking about. But we have so little time left today, let's make sure we start Tuesday's session on that note. I've got some thoughts about that I'd really like to share with you then."

Support Linkages

The therapist is the primary support in the suicidal patient's life. Too often, we learn just how significant this bond is through the unfortunate consequence of suicide. For example, Roy and Glaister (1984) reported that 90% of psychiatric patients in their study of adult completers had seen their psychiatrist in the last 30 days of their life. They found that in general, those who committed suicide had "less frequent appointments than [did] controls."

It is one of the therapist's primary responsibilities to recognize the power of his or her role and function for patients, and to use that power to broaden the patient's attachments beyond the therapeutic office. For example, it is hoped that with the therapist as an ally, the adolescent can realign with one's family, if appropriate, or separate to the world of peer alliances. Increasingly, therapy should be directed toward the identification of available and healthy significant others and promotion of those linkages. As the support network develops and is trusted, the adolescent's interpersonal isolation is diffused, and adjunct therapists become available among whom the demands of the suicidal adolescent can be spread.

Where relevant in the adolescent's natural environment, cultural, interest, hobby, or religious group involvements may be available. Where they were once of value but decathected as the adolescent increasingly alienated himself or herself, they may be reattached as emotional energy becomes freed up and available.

In some settings, such as high schools or colleges, supports may be created as adjunctive lay therapists. For example, trained volunteers may serve as "companions" (McCarthy, Wasserman, & Ferree, 1975) or befrienders, surrogate siblings who provide both basic support functions and social skills training to the adolescent patient. Lastly, various therapy modalities are built on a premise of broadened support. For example, group therapy and inpatient ward meetings serve similar support functions, as do telephone hotlines.

Social Skills Training

The lack of available social supports and resources and the difficulties in allying with available resources have been noted frequently as areas of deficit among suicidal adolescents. These deficits often underlie those adolescent parasuicidal behaviors that are intended to control others or gain control over the responses of others. However, these behaviors, designed to accomplish a worthwhile goal, are often counterproductive (e.g., they only alienate others more) and unnecessarily destructive. It is therefore appropriate to consider and incorporate into treatment structured models to ameliorate these deficits in interpersonal and social skills.

Social skills training procedures have been developed by a number of researcher–clinicians (cf. Lindsay, 1987). Through modeling, role playing, role reversal, reinforcements (both tangible and social), and practice, skills can be developed and enhanced to give the adolescent the tools to manage and accomplish relationships with others more effectively and rewardingly. Typically, specific behaviors are targeted: assertiveness, conversational skills, and problem-solving skills. Situation-specific social skills, for example—those relevant to entry to a new social system such as a college campus or high school—can be taught by trained peer–companions, as noted before.

Hansen, Watson-Perczel, and Christopher (1989) have provided an overview of social skills training with adolescents, finding general support for the effectiveness of these interventions. In addition, they discuss a number of clinical issues (e.g., dealing with compliance with and resistance to these procedures) of importance to implementing these procedures as components in a more comprehensive treatment model.

The Treatment of Loneliness

In a similar vein, interventions to alleviate loneliness serve to facilitate more rewarding social interactions and to teach skills of being alone when necessary, but without negative affect such as anxiety, panic, or sadness. Young (1982) has developed a treatment model, based in cognitive theory, that focuses on those cognitions (e.g., automatic thoughts such as "There's something wrong with me" and maladaptive assumptions such as "If someone leaves me, there must be something wrong with me"); behaviors (e.g., avoidance, lack of assertiveness); and emotions (e.g., boredom, sadness, hopelessness) that predispose the adolescent to feel lonely and maintain loneliness.

Cognitive–Behavioral Therapy

Particularly useful with younger patients, cognitive therapy (Beck et al., 1978) has gained repute as a primary treatment modality with depressed and suicidal patients. This is especially true when depressive symptoms make introspection difficult. These patients must first learn to alter their cognitions before thay can use more insight-oriented treatments. Beck's model of treatment is highly structured and collaborative. Although not touted as such, it makes maximum use of the relationship between patient and therapist, wherein the latter plays roles ranging from teacher to cheerleader. Most importantly, the cognitive therapist works to develop a "collaborative empiricism" (Beck, Hollon, Young, Bedrosian, & Budenz, 1985), a cooperative scientific–investigative relationship to identify those maladaptive cognitions and underlying assumptions maintaining the patient's negative mood, to test and analyze the validity of those assumptions, and to target, jointly, goals for changing those found invalid.

As noted in chapter 3, depressed and suicidal adolescents exhibit a number of cognitive deficits. The cognitive model of treatment strictly focuses on these and the distorted and negative cognitions that are used by the patient. Cognitive therapy postulates three primary areas of maladaptive thinking for attention: (a) the "cognitive triad," the idiosyncratic and negative view of self, experience, and future; (b) "schemas," stable patterns of molding data or events into cognitions; and (c) "systematic errors" in thinking that establish and maintain a depressed mood and the hopelessness that Beck believes is "at the core of the suicidal wishes" (Beck et al., 1978, p. 151).

In the cognitive–behavioral model of treatment, the adolescent is taught to monitor his or her own behavior and thoughts through a diary of daily activies and pleasurable thoughts. From these observations might be constructed activity schedules, or systematic plans for decreasing negative and increasing positive thoughts and activities. Through graded homework tasks, the patient is taught mastery (the opposite of helplessness) through small-step goal attainment experiences and pleasure (the opposite of dysphoria) by engaging in reinforcing experiences. Dysfunctional cognitions are restructured, attributions are appropriately refocused, and self-evaluations are modified as appropriate to more rational beliefs and interpretations of more scientifically observed data.

Teaching the adolescent to observe the immediate social environment, collect data through accomplishable homework assignments, and bring those observations into the therapy session for collaborative interpretation is akin to teaching college students the scientific method: Establish a research hypothesis, pose a way to test and measure that hypothesis, collect data in an *unbiased* manner, and then analyze and interpret results to prove the hypothesis (or if the null hypothesis is accepted, establish a new research hypothesis). By teaching the scientific method to suicidal adolescents, the therapist is proposing both a model of rational thinking and participant observation in one's personal–social world and that control in that world is possible. For example, a suicidal adolescent who reports that her parents singularly ignore her during the family dinner might be instructed to closely observe in one-minute units who initiates conversation, who responds to whom, and so on over several mealtime gatherings and to bring her "data" to the next session. With these "baseline observations" in hand and interpreted with the therapist's guidance, any of several "experiments" might be constucted to see what stimuli produce what responses from whom. With these new data in hand, specific behaviors might be targeted by the adolescent as more or less effective in accomplishing desired goals in her relationship with her parents.

Some researchers report that the effectiveness of the cognitive model has been demonstrated with adults to be at least the equal of tricyclic antidepressants in modifying depressed mood (Beck et al., 1985); but these same authors caution that it is not for use with patients diagnosed as having a schizoaffective disorder or a borderline personality disorder. Reynolds and Coats (1986) reported on a 5-week, 10-session cognitive behavior therapy program with 30 high-school-aged depressives. Their self-control skill training model produced significant improvements as rated on a number of measures of depression, as compared to a no-treatment control group. A similar approach has been tested by Rehm (1987), whose treatment model focuses on self-evaluation and self-reinforcement as essential aspects of self-control training.

Other Behavioral Approaches

Lewinsohn, Antonuccio, Steinmetz, and Teri (1984) have a behavioral treatment program, teachable in groups, to modify depression. Their model relies on activity schedules, the identification of reinforcing contingencies (pleasant events), desensitization to anxiety-provoking stimuli, and the development of social and assertiveness skills in the depressed adolescent.

Desensitization, or anxiety management training, consists of helpful adjunctive techniques when anxiety or panic characterize the adolescent's suicidality. Both relaxation training and cognitive training to use pleasant or mastery imagery in response to anxiety-provoking stimuli translate into self-control skills for the adolescent.

Linehan (1984) has further refined cognitive–behavioral strategies into a "dialectical behavior therapy" (DBT) for the treatment of parasuicidal women (men are not excluded from treatment, merely greatly underrepresented in this population). Drawing from social-behavioral theory, Linehan postulates that suicidal actions are due to aversive affective states caused by negative environmental events, self-generated dysfunctional behavior patterns, and deficiencies in both distress tolerance and in distress-reducing resources. Among these deficient resources are: emotion regulation skills, behavior management skills, interpersonal problem-solving skills (including communication and assertion skills), and competent social support networks. Correspondingly, her treatment protocol targets behaviors to modify in the areas of distress tolerance (e.g., refocusing on positive aspects of a negative situation, replacing catastrophic beliefs), affect regulation (e.g., cognitive restructuring, relaxation), self-management skills (contingency management skills, establishing reasonable standards of expected performance), and interpersonal problem-solving skills, among others.

Problem-Solving Skills Training

As noted in chapter 3, among a number of areas of cognitive deficit shown by suicidal adolescents, one consists of effective problem-solving skills, particularly those involving situations of emotionally laden interpersonal conflict. Parasuicidal behavior often is intended to affect and coerce significant others, given that more adaptive strategies are lacking and the resulting experience is one of powerlessness. Shure and Spivack (1978; Spivack & Shure, 1974) have developed models for training in interpersonal problem-solving skills, which through didactic exercises, modeling, and behavioral rehearsal are adaptable for use with suicidal adolescents. The primary focus of this training is that of *social* reasoning. Thus social and empathy skills are embedded in the teaching of cognitive problem-solving behaviors. These latter behaviors involve learning how to identify the problem; generate alternative solutions to the problem; anticipate obstacles and time factors and consider the likely consequences (including the likely reactions of others) to these possible solutions; make decisions; and plan the selected strategy to deal with situations of interpersonal conflict.

Studies with adolescents have documented improved problem-solving ability and decreases in measured levels of depression following training in these skills (Kolko & Brent, 1987). In one controlled test of the efficacy of these procedures with suicidal children and early adolescents, Cohen-Sandler (1982) was able to demonstrate that with only seven treatment sessions, suicidal subjects were significantly more efficient and flexible in their problem-solving thinking and that, even though training was entirely interpersonally oriented, such gains generalized to impersonal problems as well. However, one striking finding of this study was that suicidal subjects, unlike nonsuicidal controls, did not reduce significantly the amount of aggression in problem-solving strategies selected following treatment. The fact that aggression was resistant to modification may signal the need to particularly target the regulation of aggressive impulses as part of a comprehensive treatment program.

Anger and Aggression Management

Most of the behavioral treatments of suicidal adolescents derive from their focus on depression and its underlying cognitions and behaviors as a target symptom or diagnosis. Consistent with its central role in the psychodynamics of depression and self-destructive behavior, aggression (the behavioral expression of rage, anger, or hostility) often needs to be considered a primary target for intervention. This is true irrespective of whether aggression is seen as a primary or contributing factor to the adolescent's suicidality.

Novaco (1979) has developed a behavioral intervention to deal with anger and cope with provocation. Techniques of anger management, meaning the regulation rather than the suppression of anger, taught to the adolescent include: cognitive controls (understanding one's own and others' feelings, self-statements in preparation for and confronting arousal), emotional controls (relaxation, humor), and behavioral controls (effective communication, assertion training, task-oriented problem solving). Lochman and Curry (1986) and Feindler & Ecton (1986) have similar models, teachable to groups of aggressive, acting-out adolescents through discussion, role playing, and rehearsal (using also videotape feedback).

Aggression may also be controlled through medication, anxiety management procedures, and other approaches to improving impulse control problems common to the suicidal condition. Central to the control of aggression and to the observed risk for suicide is the involvement of drugs or alcohol.

Thus it is essential, where substance abuse is involved, that these be targeted as foci for self-management. Cognitive self-control procedures simply cannot succeed when the adolescent patient uses self-medication to alleviate distress, deaden emotional pain, or gain entry to a peer group. As such, changing the adolescent's social system might be required, including an intervening period of increased loneliness before new relationships are formed. Group psychotherapy and available forms of Alcoholics Anonymous and Narcotics Anonymous groups should be considered as networks of support while the focus of treatment addresses decreasing substance-use-related cues and substituting aversive consequences for positive reinforcers to substance use.

The regulation of intense affect, lastly, must include attention to the overinvolvement of everyday stimulants (e.g., caffeine, nicotine), effects of nutritional deficiencies, and intrusions in sleep regulation, the results of which invariably will be increased confusion, irrationality, and poor behavioral control. The increased use of exercise, even low-level physical activity, can do much to modulate arousal and increase adaptive energy. The judicious and modeled use of humor—where natural, appropriate to the situation, and not self-deprecatory—serves as a tension releaser, a healthy stimulant (particularly of affect incompatible with depression or anger), and a mechanism promoting the therapeutic alliance.

It is most difficult to convey the process and interactive dynamics of treatment in relatively brief case illustrations. The two cases of successful treatment that follow reflect multimodal interventions necessitated by the typical complexity of problems presented by suicidal youth.

Case Illustrations: Treatment

Ellen, age 15, was a sophomore in high school when she was referred for outpatient treatment 5 weeks after cutting her wrists at home. A tall, physically well-developed girl, she was cooperative in interview, fully oriented, but clearly depressed. She reported that she cut herself because she was "mad at [her]self" because she was "doing nothing right."

Few specific referents were given to explain what standards were not being met to her satisfaction.

Ellen described a long history of self-harm behavior, beginning in the fifth grade, when she first scratched hesitation marks into her wrist with the point of a school compass after being reprimanded by her parents. Her second episode occurred 2 years later, when she ingested a number of different medications from her parents' medicine chest. This was the only one of her several gestures and attempts that required medical attention and led to her first course of outpatient psychotherapy. She reported that this attempt was in response to her "wanting attention" at a time when her parents were involved with her older brother (age 19), who had been arrested for stealing a car. Two other low-lethality attempts occurred over the subsequent 2 years and prior to the latest, one by cutting and one by overdose. Both these attempts were in response to conflicts within her family, feelings of intense guilt, and an apparent need to punish herself. With regard to self-punishment, she stated that she often "craved pain" and that she accomplished this by digging her long nails deep into her skin or repeatedly scratching herself.

Ellen was the youngest of three children and the only girl. Her oldest brother was expelled from high school soon after his arrest for car theft. He currently lived in a halfway house for recovering drug abusers. He also had a history of self-harm behavior. Her 18-year-old brother quit high school and was currently in the Army.

Ellen's father had battled a 20-year history of depression, for which he had been treated with medication during most of that time. In her early childhood, he frequently physically abused Ellen, although no incidents were reported in the last 7 years. His father was reported to be depressed as well. Ellen's mother, who had become pregnant at 17, was the daughter of an alcoholic mother. Her father had died of cancer when she was 8. She was the oldest of three; her brother was a drug-addicted bisexual and her sister had been sexually abused by her stepfather.

Ellen, once a straight-A student, was currently performing at a C average. She was sexually active and, with her mother's permission, had begun taking the pill at age 12. In spite of this precaution, she had had two pregnancies and two miscarriages in the last 3 years. She was currently involved with and having daily sexual relations with a sometime employed, 21-year-old, Danny. Ellen had experimented with LSD, PCP, cocaine, and marijuana. She drank regularly on the weekends with her boyfriend and smoked a pack of cigarettes each day.

Ellen exemplified well Maltsberger's (1986) "unendurable affect states." As a child of abuse, her introjections were hostile. She was the bad child, worthless, guilty, and fearful. She had great difficulty trusting others and was convinced she was beyond lovability. She was contemptuous of herself and unable to express her rage externally. Only slight refuge came from her retreat into drugs or alcohol.

The following journal entry illustrated well Ellen's sense of painful entrapment in a world of confusion and guilt:

> Why does it have to be me with the problems, emotions so hard to handle? Why should he have to handle them, problems that I imagine? Because supposedly there are no problems. Why can't I see that and just be happy? No, I am not allowed . . . something will not allow me to be happy.
>
> They each have their own place to be put, but I can't figure out where they belong. It is like a puzzle and I have the wrong pieces. Or do I just not fit? I want to die. Why should they have to put up with my problems? Why do they have to, or do they? Do they know what's going on? Do I know?

The treatment plan outlined for Ellen consisted of individual and group outpatient psychotherapy, with goals of decreasing suicidal tendencies and depression, decreasing substance abuse, and enhancing self-worth and self-esteem. A cognitive approach was taken to decrease depressogenic thinking, inappropriate guilt, and self-blame. Group psychotherapy focused on establishing a peer support system, on defining ways Ellen could establish her sense of lovability other than through a sexual relationship with a "must-have" boyfriend, and on establishing greater self-respect in her relationships in general. Anticipatory problem-solving training allowed her to increasingly approach a number of difficult interactions with forethought rather than impulsivity. Inherent in her treatment was a greater appreciation of her father's and grandfather's depressions and her parents' unintended reinforcement of her early and active sexuality. This was accomplished through monthly family sessions that also allowed discussion of the effects of her brother's acting out on both her and her parents.

In the course of an 18-month treatment, prior to a 6-month termination and follow-up phase (see section on Termination Notes), Ellen was able to establish much of her self-worth on evidence of self-control—no further self-harm episodes occurred—and on her academic performance, which improved to consistent honor roll status. She got and maintained a part-time job, the earnings from which went primarily toward the purchase and support of a used car. She eventually felt strong enough to risk leaving her long-standing relationship with Danny, after first becoming pregnant and making a difficult decision to have an abortion; thereafter she chose a series of increasingly respectful boyfriends. In these relationships, sex was not the reason for contact. After several early episodes of drug experimentation, including one frightening experience of freebasing cocaine, she essentially had been drug-free during the last several months of therapy, except for occasional beer drinking at parties. Treatment ended at the end of her senior year, soon after her acceptance to college.

The initial goals of John's (see p. 154) outpatient treatment consisted of decreasing his suicidality, his depression, and his sensitivity or reactivity to perceived rejections. Concurrently, a primary focus was established on increasing interpersonal skills. Treatment was multimodal in focus, including both cognitive and behavioral approaches and much insight-oriented discussion of early wounds and disappointments by his parents. Because John's parents were several hundred miles away from his college and because of his age, no family therapy was offered. However, directives for dealing with and reframing his parents' involvement were given when home visits were to occur.

Six weeks after initiating outpatient therapy, John became increasingly agitated and took a low-lethality overdose of sleeping pills. He rejected the need for hospitalization. Instead, he implied through multiple references to a secret he was not ready to share, but which defined his self-hate and aloneness, that this attempt was meant to relieve the tension created by this withholding. Within a week, he shared that he was gay "at least in spirit." Over the next several months, he began experimenting sexually, acting with disregard for directives about safe sex and proclaiming relief that "the chains were off." He refused to use recommended resources to learn about the gay world and to enter a group composed of gay men his age who were "coming out." Instead, he increasingly behaved inappropriately, choosing as a liaison anyone who would approach him at a gay bar. He soon developed a preoccupation with a fellow student whom he began to idealize in spite of receiving clearly rejecting responses, including an off-putting suggestion, "Why don't you just kill yourself and leave me alone." After this, John ingested more than 50 Extra-Strength Tylenol and immediately called for an unscheduled therapy appointment in which he divulged his ingestion and accepted immediate hospitalization.

In spite of this, his sixth suicide attempt and second hospitalization, John's therapist viewed this as a pivotal period in his therapy. For the first time, John had opened the door to a long-held secret and reason for self-hate, and he no longer rejected hospital care. His ingestion was followed by an immediate seeking of help and intervention.

John's 2-week inpatient treatment involved intensive individual therapy, milieu therapy, including structured ward meetings, and the usual range of group therapies, including recreational, art, and occupational groups. His outpatient therapist, although not the primary treating therapist, continued to meet with John while hospitalized and consulted with the inpatient staff on treatment decisions. On discharge, John returned to outpatient care, now meeting twice weekly. After another 3 weeks of tenuous stabilization, John gradually accepted his therapist's recommendations to accept the several referrals to support groups in the gay community. With this involvement came increasing contact with gay friends who were not sexual partners, and within 4 months, a coming-out with his parents, who were suprisingly accepting, informing John that they had suspected he was gay for the past few years. Through this period of adjustment, John was able to accept the metaphor of "the ugly duckling" to explain his earlier social anxiety and self-hate. Two years after beginning therapy, John was involved in a healthy gay relationship of some 4 months' duration and began terminating ongoing treatment.

Termination Notes

Because attachment issues, and therefore separation and individuation issues, are primary in the genesis of suicidality, termination is a crucial phase of the treatment process. Therapists experienced in working with suicidal patients know well to be aware of the patient's increasing separation anxiety, and the patient's denial of same, as termination becomes a reality. Also, this is one of the causal explanations offered for suicides that occur soon after hospital discharge.

For this reason, termination perhaps ought to be labeled "weaning." Termination with a once-suicidal adolescent begins as the adolescent stabilizes, that is, as the risk of suicidal behavior abates, and continues through the end of formal, weekly in-office contacts over a long period of follow-up. It is the adolescent who ultimately leaves therapy, much as it is the adolescent who ultimately leaves home.

Sessions initially scheduled with greater frequency should be scheduled with greater infrequency, but with continued regularity, over time. Thus, as therapy goals are attained, twice weekly contacts may be reduced to weekly, then to twice monthly, and so forth.

Decisions to wean are based on an ongoing assessment of goals: (a) there has been no further imminent risk for self-harm over an extended period of observation and contact; (b) the probability of self-harm, assessed continuously throughout treatment, has reduced to a level of minimal or no risk, particularly as evidenced by no self-harm behavior over the term of treatment and during stressful times and situations; (c) skill enhancement has occurred as appropriate to treatment goals; and (d) the quality of life (e.g., mood, self-image, supports) has improved such that the adolescent is behaving unambivalently on the side of life versus death (e.g., hope has replaced hopelessness).

Particular attention must be paid to helping the adolescent cope with feelings of loss inherent in the developing separation from therapy. Issues of loss need to be framed within the context of gains in both therapeutic goals and specifically in strengthened bonds with others outside the therapy session.

It has been our experience that weaning extends well into the future. As appropriate, sessions can be scheduled on a monthly basis, then on a quarterly basis, and so on. In addition, and particularly should the adolescent leave home to attend school, for example, contactability can be maintained by infrequent postcards between the adolescent and the therapist. These contacts serve to provide a follow-up monitoring of treatment benefits, a continued link (therapist constancy) should the adolescent ever need to reconnect, or a basis for referral making in the adolescent's new environment should the need arise. Also, follow-up sessions are useful as "booster shots" to smooth rough edges or retrain specific skills if needed, or in anticipation of and to sustain through anniversary dates of importance in the history of the adolescent's suicidality.

From Good Practice to Malpractice

No discussion of treatment would be complete without brief mention of two additional themes: malpractice and ethics.

Malpractice

As will be described in chapter 6, suicide visits upon bereaved survivors some unique traumata. Among these is anger and an implicit, if not explicit, blameworthiness for: (a) not being good enough to have made the suicide value life sufficiently to hang around (an act of omission), or (b) having done something to have made the suicide wish to take his or her life (an act of commission).

For psychotherapists, a completed suicide visits quite the same sequelae, that is, feelings of loss, helplessness, anger, and guilt. Additionally, given their professional role, psychotherapists often fear being humiliated in some public way among their colleagues or among referral sources. The most feared sequela of a patient's suicide, however, is the threat of a malpractice action.

Modern legal considerations have shifted from viewing suicide as a punishable wrong (because the state was deprived of something or someone of value) to viewing suicide as a product of mental disorder requiring prevention, and to the recognition of pain and suffering among those bereaved by the loss (Litman, 1987). Those charged with the care and treatment of patients are, de facto, charged with the task of preventing the suicide of that patient. This responsibility makes psychotherapists ripe targets for the externalization of survivors' rage.

Litman (1982) has estimated that 1 in 3 suicides by patients in inpatient care results in a lawsuit. Although he further estimates that only about 1 in 10 of these ever makes it to the courtroom, even "nuisance" suits pose threats of considerable media exposure in addition to the costs in time and expense to the therapist in order to mount an effective defense. As noted in our Introduction, psychologist practitioners have more than a 1 in 5 chance (and psychiatrists a 1 in 2 chance) of having one or more patients commit suicide during the course of their professional career. Therefore there appears to be considerable reason for therapists to be alert to and protective against the possibility of such litigation.

As is apparent from the research-based findings describing characteristics of the suicidal adolescent, these patients generally do not fit the model of the ideal patient. By the time they are seen in therapy, typically not of their own volition, they have developed a character pathology or multiproblem presentations that make positive working relationships difficult at best. At the same time, the parent of the suicidal adolescent will indeed make and hold the therapist responsible for what they have not thus far been able to accomplish well. When that adolescent commits suicide, parental blame will understandably be denied and externalized to the therapist. Such claims are number one on the heirarchy of suits brought against psychiatrists (Gutheil, 1989) and, as of July 1988, the sixth most frequent type of claim (and the second most costly) filed against psychologists (Pope, 1989). More importantly, these actions are increasing in frequency and correspondingly, in legal costs (Berman, 1990a).

What does the court expect of the therapist? Foremost is the duty to attempt reasonably to prevent the suicide of the patient. If the court finds that this duty was breached through negligence, either through an omission or commission relative to the standard of care, a finding of malpractice may result.

The standard of care is established by judgment and opinion as to whether the care provided was *reasonable*, that is, not significantly and indefensibly deviant from that of reasonable professionals of similar training and experience. Opinions regarding the possible deviation from standard care are provided by expert witnesses, professionals purporting to have some expertise in treating and understanding suicidal patients, who are hired by opposing attorneys. And therein lies the rub. Even in nuisance suits, where the defendant psychotherapist is convinced that his or her behavior was reasonable, both the plaintiff and the defendant will have their experts, each testifying honestly to their opinion that the therapist did or did not practice negligently. For this reason, it behooves the clinician to understand well what the court, through case law, asks in addressing the question of reasonable care.

Essentially, there are two factors that determine liability in a suicidal death. First and foremost is *foreseeability*. Foreseeability has nothing to do with crystal-ball gazing or predicting suicide. It has everything to do with the assessment of risk. Failing to assess risk in all patients is an egregious professional failing on the part of the therapist. The assessment of risk involves, at a minimum, attention to the possibility of suicidal behavior through the asking of questions about risk factors and the making and documentation of judgments based on these observations. One cannot be held liable for incorrect judgment, defined operationally in this instance by the very fact of the suicide. However, judgments should be reasonable, based on the data observed, and the data observed should be reasonably sought. This would include attention to prior history and obtaining available records (in the absence of a thorough current history).

Inherent in this focus is a very important subtheme of documentation, the recording of observations and judgments. The failure to keep proper records is a common source of liability (Berman, 1990a; VandeCreek & Young, 1989) and makes any claims made in defense of one's practice simply indefensible.

The second factor determining liability is that of *reasonable care*, that is, that appropriate precautions should follow the assessment of suicide risk. Should an adolescent be judged to be at high risk, for example, then precautions against the adolescent acting in some self-harm manner must be considered and attempted. A high-risk adolescent cannot be sent home unmonitored or given medications in sufficient quantity to kill himself or herself. Where recommendations for follow-up behavior are not acted upon by the adolescent and the parents, documentations in the patient's record to that effect are self-protective. Calculated risks taken for presumed therapeutic gain are within the standard of care and also benefit the therapist if documented.

Lastly, a breach of duty to protect the patient ("abandonment") may be found if the therapist did not act to have ordered precautions carried out with *dependability*. Thus, for example, the therapist who orders a suicide watch of a patient on the inpatient ward will be held responsible if that watch is not carried out by the nursing staff responsible for its accomplishment.

The topic of malpractice is too important for a brief review such as this. The reader is directed to any of a number of reviews of case law (VandeCreek & Young, 1989) and recommended guidelines for good practice with regard to the treatment of the suicidal patient (Berman, 1990a; Berman & Cohen-Sandler, 1982, 1983; Pope, 1989). A good example of how two experts viewed a case of an adolescent suicide, judged by a jury for the plaintiff in spite of these experts' siding with the defense, can be found in Berman (1990b).

A Brief Note on Ethical Issues

Motto (1983) observes that philosophical views of suicide and those of the clinical practitioner, the potential healer of self-destructive individuals, are vastly different. One deals with suicide within the frame of rationality and the ideal, the other through the eyes of his or her patient—eyes clouded by confusion, mental disturbance, and a chaotic reality. The philosopher can establish criteria to determine whether a given suicide would be an ethical act, a morally defensible decision to maintain autonomy, have a rational choice, or free oneself from overwhelming pain. The clinician, on the other hand, establishes criteria to restrict autonomy (i.e., hospitalize, even involuntarily) on the basis of the patient's lack of rationality or inability to tolerate pain without intervention.

We substantially agree with Clements, Sider, and Perlmutter (1983) that the crucial question for clinicians is not whether suicide is justifiable, but rather whether suicide intervention is justifiable. These authors argue, correctly, that clinicians *must*, in fact as discussed above, are legally *expected to* have an affirmative stance toward intervention. A patient in therapy has entered a therapeutic value system which, in part, defines what are the best interests of that individual.

Suicide is rarely in the best interest of the individual, especially the young patient. Because the data presented in this book support the view that youth suicide is the consequence of a complex system of interacting forces, ranging from psychopathology to irrational cognitions to disturbed family systems and even biological dysfunction, it is difficult to defend the suicidal act as one of autonomous choice. An empathic understanding of the suicidal adolescent demands that those conditions making the adolescent suicidal be treated; and with that treatment it is reasonable to expect a decrease in that patient's suicidality.

Thus, the important clinical and ethical questions are those related to what kind of treatments or interventions will best accomplish that outcome. In this vein, the best intervention is not always coercive prevention or even hospitalization. The clinical goal is to reduce risk for suicide at an acceptable cost. We believe that the myopia of the suicidal adolescent demands whatever cost is necessary to establish time and treatment to help create a truly autonomous individual.

Confidentiality

A related question of ethics has to do with the issue of confidentiality. Each of the major mental health disciplines has specific guidelines of ethical priniciples that bear on a patient's right to confidentiality. For psychologists, the American Psychological Association's (APA, 1989) ethical principles describe the various circumstances and conditions in which a patient's right to confidentiality may be broken (no matter what their age). In essence, the patient's confidentiality is protected at all times except for circumstances in which there is clear and imminent danger to self or others (in some circumstances, substantial inability to care for oneself and cases of ongoing sexual abuse of a minor will warrant a break in confidentiality).

Generally speaking, evidence of clear and imminent danger to self (in the absence of a clear commitment to safety) requires the clinician to take whatever steps are necessary to ensure the physical safety of the patient. Necessary steps may include hospitalization, initiation of commitment procedures, or notification of law enforcement officials. As will be discussed in the following section, parents of a minor at clear and imminent risk must be informed as well.

Confidentiality and Minors

While the need to break confidence is evident in situations of clear and imminent danger, there may be somewhat less clarity about issues of confidentiality in ongoing clinical work with minors. Under current statutes, parents of a minor child (under 18 years of age) retain the legal authority to permit or refuse treatment of their child. As parents are legally responsible for the welfare of their children, they are in the position to grant informed consent and make key decisions about their child's treatment. In the eyes of the law, the parents technically have a right to any and all information obtained in an evaluation or treatment of their child. Therefore, while the child is the recipient of treatment, the parents in effect become the clients of the provider (Brewer & Faitak, 1989).

Counterbalancing the laws pertaining to minors and their lack of rights to informed consent and confidentiality is Principle 5D of the APA (1989) ethical priniciples, which states that clinicians must take special care to protect the overall welfare and best interests of the adolescent patient. To this end, clinicians who work with minors must find a balance between respecting the legal rights of the parents while ensuring the best possible care for their child. Parents should therefore be fully informed of their legal rights as well as the clinical issues that bear on the best interests (i.e., the treatment) of their child.

While parents may technically have a right to any information shared in treatment, successful therapy may be undermined if the adolescent believes that anything they say may be readily and inappropriately disclosed to their parents. For treatment to be effective, the adolescent must be able to trust the therapist with their most private thoughts and feelings and, conversely, parents must trust the therapist's good judgment to disclose relevant information in an amount and manner that best serves their child's treatment.

To address the inherent issues, thoughtful, thorough, and proactive treatment planning, ideally with both the parents and the adolescent, is essential to laying the foundation for successful treatment of a minor. All the potential legal and clinical issues pertaining to informed consent and confidentiality should be thoroughly discussed prior to the onset of treatment. The nature, timing, and extent of disclosure of clinical information to the parents should be specifically discussed and understood by all parties. Periodic meetings to update and modify the treatment should be planned as well. When working with a suicidal youth, it is sometimes valuable to discuss problem-solving strategies that might enlist the support of the parents should the adolescent become actively suicidal. The goal is to think through and plan around potential hurdles in advance and thereby begin to build a team approach to working through the inherent issues. In a similar vein, Taylor and Adelman (1989) describe reframing approaches to enable the patient's motivation to share information when considered to be in his or her best interest. It is with the adolescent's best interest in mind that these ethical and legal issues frame good clinical practice.

Conclusion

Two overriding themes emerge in consideration of the therapeutic process with the suicidal adolescent. First is the core role that attachment plays in both the problem and its resolution. We began our discussion with a focus on the issues posed by the help-seeking–giving–receiving process, describing the suicidal adolescent as unused to working alliances with significant adults and the therapist's task as that of gently forging a cooperative partnership. Furthermore, the ultimate goal of treatment was described as one of generalizing the developed therapeutic attachment to multiple attachments in the community at large. Thus, from beginning to end, treatment demands attention to issues of linkage and attachment and the success of treatment is largely dependent on these themes.

Second is the therapist's need for a protocol, a plan of treatment that takes into account the idiographic aspects of each presenting case, an understanding of potentially helpful strategies and techniques, and the therapeutic armamentarium from which the therapist may selectively cull and apply strategies deemed appropriate. Based on the functional analysis of the suicidal adolescent's motives and a complete assessment of the suicidal adolescent, these applied interventions translate treatment into prevention, a theme to be more broadly considered in our next chapter.

References

Aaronson, S. L., Underwood, M., Gaffney, D., & Rotheram-Borus, M. J. (1989, April). *Reluctance to help-seeking by adolescents*. Paper presented at the annual meeting of the American Association of Suicidology, San Diego, CA.

Adelman, H. S., Kaser-Boyd, N., & Taylor, L. (1984). Children's participation in consent for psychotherapy and their subsequent response to treatment. *Journal of Clinical Child Psychology, 13*, 170–178.

Aguilera, D. C., & Messick, J. M. (1978). *Crisis Intervention: Theory and Methodology,* St. Louis: C. V. Mosby.

American Psychological Association. (1989). Ethical principles of psychologists. *American Psychologist, 45*, 390–395.

Ansell, E. L., & McGee, R. K. (1971). Attitudes toward suicide attempters. *Bulletin of Suicidology, 8*, 22–28.

Beck, A. T. (1972). *Depression: Causes and treatment.* Philadelphia, PA: University of Pennsylvania Press.

Beck, A. T., Rush, A. J., Shaw, B. F., & Emery, G. (1978). *Cognitive therapy of depression: A treatment manual.* New York: Guilford Press.

Beck, A. T., Hollon, S. D., & Young, J. E., Bedrosian, R. C., & Budenz, D. (1985). Treatment of depression with cognitive therapy and amitriptyline. *Archive of General Psychiatry, 42*, 142–148.

Berman, A. L. (1990a). Standard of care in assessment of suicidal potential. *Psychotherapy in Private Practice, 8*, 35–41.

Berman, A. L. (Ed.). (1990b). Case consultation: Malpractice. *Suicide and Life-Threatening Behavior, 19*, 395–402.

Berman, A. L., & Cohen-Sandler, R. (1982). Suicide and the standard of care: Optimal vs. acceptable. *Suicide and Life-Threatening Behavior, 12*, 114–122.

Berman, A. L., & Cohen-Sandler, R. (1983). Suicide and malpractice: Expert testimony and the standard of care. *Professional Psychology: Research and Practice, 14*, 6–19.

Bernstein, N. I. (1989). Managing the difficult adolescent patient. *The Independent Practitioner, 9*, 30–33.

Beutler, L. E. (1989). Differential treatment selection: The role of diagnosis in psychotherapy. *Psychotherapy, 26*, 271–281.

Beutler, L. E., & Mitchell, R. (1981). Psychotherapy outcome in depressed and impulsive patients as a function of analytic and experiential treatment procedures. *Psychiatry, 44*, 297–306.

Bloom, V. (1970). Prevention of suicide. *Current Psychiatric Therapy, 10*, 105–109.

Bond, M., & Steinberg, M. (1988). Using psychodynamic concepts in strategic family therapy: A suicidal adolescent case. *Contemporary Family Therapy, 10*, 154–168.

Brewer T., & Faitak, M. T. (1989). Ethical guidelines for inpatient psychiatric care of children. *Professional Psychology: Research and Practice, 20*, 142–147.

Brickman, P., Rabinowitz, V. C., Karuza, J., Jr., Coates, D., Cohn, E., & Kidder, L. (1982). Models of helping and coping. *American Psychologist, 37*, 368–384.

Brown, S. (1985). Adolescents and family systems. In M. L. Peck, N. L Farberow, & R. E. Litman (Eds.), *Youth suicide* (pp. 71–79). New York: Springer Publishing.

Clements, C. D., Sider, R. C., & Perlmutter, R. (1983). Suicide: Bad act or good intervention. *Suicide and Life-Threatening Behavior, 13*, 28–41.

Cohen-Sandler, R. (1982). *Interpersonal problem-solving skills of suicidal and non-suicidal children: Assessment and treatment.* Unpublished manuscript, American University, Washington, DC.

Cohen-Sandler, R., Berman, A. L., & King, R. (1982). Life stress and symptomatology: Determinants of suicidal behavior in children. *Journal of the American Academy of Child Psychiatry, 21*, 178–186.

Deykin, E. Y., Hsieh, C. C., Joshi, N., & McNamara, J. J. (1986). Adolescent suicidal and self-destructive behavior: Results of an intervention study. *Journal of Adolescent Health Care, 77*, 88–95.

Egan, J. (1988). Treatment of borderline conditions in adolescence. *Journal of Clinical Psychiatry, 49*, 9(Suppl.), 32–35.

Elkind, D. (1980). Egocentrism in adolescence. In R. E. Muuss (Ed.), *Adolescent behavior and society: A book of readings* (3rd ed., pp. 79–88). New York: Random House. (Original work published 1967.)

Feindler, E. L., & Ecton, R. B. (1986). *Adolescent anger control: Cognitive–behavioral techniques.* New York: Pergamon Press.

Fishman, H. C. (1988). *Treating troubled adolescents.* New York: Basic Books.

Frederick, C. J. (1978). Current trends in suicidal behavior in the United States. *American Journal of Psychotherapy, 32,* 172–200.

Glaser, K. (1978). The treatment of depressed and suicidal adolescents. *American Journal of Psychotherapy, 32,* 252–269.

Goldfried, M. R. (Ed.). (1980). Some views on effective principles of psychotherapy. *Cognitive Therapy and Research, 4,* 269–306.

Goldney, R. D., & Burvill, P. W. (1980). Trends in suicidal behavior and its management. *Australian and New Zealand Journal of Psychiatry, 14,* 1–15.

Gross, A. E., Piliavin, I. M., Wallston, B. S., & Broll, L. (1972, Sept.). *When humanitarianism is not humane: Helping—the recipient's view.* Paper presented at the annual convention of the American Psychological Association, Honolulu, HI.

Gutheil, T. G. (1989, October). Physician liability in suicide. In R. S. Brown (Chair), *Forensic issues in suicide.* Symposium conducted at the meeting of the American Academy of Psychiatry and the Law, Washington, DC.

Hamilton, J. D., Decker, N., & Rumbaut, R. D. (1986). The manipulative patient. *American Journal of Psychotherapy, 40,* 189–200.

Hansen, D. J., Watson-Perczel, M., & Christopher, J. S. (1989). Clinical issues in social-skills training with adolescents. *Clinical Psychology Review, 9,* 365–391.

Hatton, C. L., Valente, S. M., & Rink, A. (1977). *Suicide: Assessment & intervention.* New York: Appelton-Century-Crofts.

Hendin, H. (1982). *Suicide in America.* New York: W. W. Norton.

Hoff, L. A. (1984). *People in crisis: Understanding and helping.* Menlo Park, CA: Addison-Wesley Publishing.

Hynes, P. (1989, April). *Principles of long-term psychotherapy with chronically suicidal patients.* Paper presented at the annual meeting of the American Association of Suicidology, San Diego, CA.

Jobes, D. A., & Berman, A. L. (1991). Crisis intervention and brief treatment for suicidal youth. In A. Roberts (Ed.), *Contemporary perspectives on crisis intervention and prevention* (pp. 53–69). Englewood Cliffs, NJ: Prentice-Hall.

Kendall, P. C., & Williams, C. L. (1986). Therapy with adolescents: Treating the "marginal man." *Behavior Therapy, 17,* 522–537.

Knesper, D. (1982). A study of referral failures for potentially suicidal patients: A method of medical care evaluation. *Hospital and Community Psychiatry, 33,* 49–52.

Kogan, L. S. (1957). The short-term case in a family agency. *Social Casework, 38,* 296–302.

Kolko, D. J., & Brent, D. A. (1987, May). *Cognitive–behavioral interventions for suicidal youth.* Presented at the annual meeting of the American Association of Suicidology, San Francisco, CA.

Kreitman, N. (1986). The clinical assessment and management of the suicidal patient. In A. Roy (Ed.), *Suicide* (pp. 181–195). Baltimore, MD: Williams and Wilkins.

Landau-Stanton, J. L., & Stanton, M. D. (1985). Treating suicidal adolescents and their families. In M. P. Mirkin & S. L. Koman (Eds.), *Handbook of adolescents and family therapy,* (pp. 309–328). New York: Gardner Press.

Lerner, S., & Lerner, H. E. (1983). A systematic approach to resistance: Theoretical and technical considerations. *American Journal of Psychotherapy, 37,* 387–399.

Lester, D. (1989). Restricting methods of suicide as a means of preventing suicide: The case of drugs. *Perceptual and Motor Skills, 68,* 273–274.

Lewinsohn, P. M., Antonuccio, D., Steinmetz, J., & Teri, L. (1984). *The coping with depression course: A psychoeducational intervention for unipolar depression.* Eugene, OR: Castalia.

Liberman, R., & Eckman, T. (1981). Behavior therapy vs. insight oriented therapy for repeated suicide attempters. *Archives of General Psychiatry, 38,* 1126–1130.

Lindsay, W. R. (1987). Social skills training with adolescents. In J. C. Coleman (Ed.), *Working with troubled adolescents: A handbook* (pp. 107–122). London: Academic Press.

Linehan, M. (1984). *Dialectial behavior therapy for treatment of parasuicidal women treatment manual.* Unpublished manuscript, University of Washington, Seattle.

Litman, R. E. (1982). Hospital suicides: Lawsuits and standards. *Suicide and Life-Threatening Behavior, 12,* 212–220.

Litman, R. E. (1987, May). *Responsibility and liability for suicide.* Paper presented at the annual meeting of the American Association of Suicidology, San Francisco, CA.

Litt, I. F., Cuskey, W. R., & Rudd, S. (1983). Emergency room evaluation of the adolescent who attempts suicide: Compliance with follow-up. *Journal of Adolescent Health Care, 4,* 106–108.

Lochman, J. E., & Curry, J. F. (1986). Effects of social problem-solving training and self-instruction training with aggressive boys. *Journal of Clinical Psychology, 15,* 159–164.

Maltsberger, J. T. (1986). *Suicide risk: The formulation of clinical judgment.* New York: New York University Press.

Maltsberger, J. T., & Buie, D. H. (1974). Countertransference hate in the treatment of suicidal patients. *Archives of General Psychiatry, 30,* 625–633.

McCarthy, B. W., Wasserman, C. W., & Ferree, F. H. (1975). The growth and development of a university companion program. *Journal of Counseling Psychology, 22,* 66–69.

Miller, D. (1986). *Attack on the self.* Northvale, NJ: Jason Aronson.

Mintz, R. S. (1971). Basic considerations in the psychotherapy of the suicidal patient. *American Journal of Psychotherapy, 25,* 56–73.

Modestin, J. (1987). Counter-transference reactions contributing to completed suicide. *British Journal of Medical Psychology, 60,* 379–385.

Morris, W. (Ed.). (1973). *The American heritage dictionary of the english language.* Boston, MA: Houghton Mifflin.

Motto, J. A. (1983). Clinical implications of moral theory regarding suicide. *Suicide and Life-Threatening Behavior, 13,* 304–312.

Novaco, R. (1979). The cognitive–behavioral regulation of anger. In P. C. Kendall & S. D. Hollon (Eds), *Cognitive–behavioral interventions: Theory, research and procedures* (pp. 241–286). New York: Academic Press.

O'Farrell, T. J., Goodenough, D. S., & Cutter, H. S. G. (1981). Behavioral contracting for repeated suicide attempts. *Behavior Modification, 5,* 255–272.

Pope, K. S. (1989). Malpractice suits, licensing disciplinary actions, and ethics cases: Frequencies, causes, and costs. *The Independent Practitioner, 9,* 22–26.

Rehm, L. (1987). Approaches to the prevention of depression with children: A self-management perspective. In R. F. Munoz (Ed.), *Depression prevention: Research directions* (pp. 79–91). Washington, DC: Hemisphere Publishing.

Reubin, R. H. (1973). A study of factors involved in the decision to treat suicidal clients. *Dissertation Abstracts International, 34,* 296B–297B. (University Microfilms No. 73-16, 696, 284)

Reynolds, W. M., & Coats, K. I. (1986). A comparison of cognitive–behavioral therapy and relaxation training for the treatment of depression. *Journal of Consulting and Clinical Psychology, 54,* 653–660.

Richman, J. (1986). *Family therapy for suicidal people.* New York: Springer Publishing.

Rinsley, D. B. (1980). *Treatment of the severely disturbed adolescent.* New York: Jason Aronson.

Rogawski, A. B., & Edmundson, B. (1971). Factors affecting the outcome of psychiatry interagency referral. *American Journal of Psychiatry, 127,* 925–934.

Ross, C. P., & Motto, J. A. (1984). Group counseling for suicidal adolescents. In H. S. Sudak, A. B. Ford, & N. B. Rushforth (Eds.), *Suicide in the young* (pp. 367–392). Boston: John Wright PSG, Inc.

Roy, A., & Glaister, J. (1984). Suicide in psychiatric patients. *Psychiatric Journal of the University of Ottawa, 9,* 42–44.

Schopler, J., & Matthews, M. W. (1965). The influence of the perceived locus of partner's dependence on the use of interpersonal power. *Journal of Personality and Social Psychology, 2,* 609–612.

Shneidman, E. S. (1985). *Definition of suicide.* New York: John Wiley & Sons.

Shure, M. B., & Spivack, G. (1978). *Problem-solving techniques in childrearing.* San Francisco, CA: Jossey-Bass.

Spivack, G., & Shure, M. B. (1974). *Social adjustment of young children: A cognitive approach to solving real-life problems.* San Francisco, CA: Jossey-Bass.

Strupp, H. (1980). Some views on effective principles of psychotherapy. *Cognitive Therapy and Research, 4,* 269–306.

Taylor, E. A., & Stansfeld, S. A. (1984). Children who poison themselves: II. Prediction of attendance for treatment. *British Journal of Psychiatry, 145,* 127–132.

Taylor, L., & Adelman, H. S. (1989). Reframing the confidentiality dilemma to work in children's best interests. *Professional Psychology: Research and Practice, 20,* 79–83.

Tessler, R. C., & Schwartz, S. H. (1972). Help seeking, self-esteem, and achievement motivation: An attributional analysis. *Journal of Personality and Social Psychology, 21,* 318–326.

Trautman, P. D. (1989). Specific treatment modalities for adolescent suicide attempters. In Alcohol, Drug Abuse, and Mental Health Administration, *Report of the Secretary's Task Force on Youth Suicide: Volume 3. Prevention and interventions in youth suicide* (pp. 253–263). (DHHS Publication. No. ADM 89-1623. Washington, DC: U.S. Government Printing Office.

Trautman, P. D., & Shaffer, D. (1984). Treatment of child and adolescent suicide attempters. In H. S. Sudak, A. B. Ford, & N. B. Rushforth (Eds.), *Suicide in the young* (pp. 307–323). Boston, MA: John Wright PSG, Inc.

VandeCreek, L., & Young, J. (1989). Malpractice risks with suicidal patients. *The Psychotherapy Bulletin, 24,* 18–21.

Vlasak, G. J. (1975). Medical sociology. In S. Perlin (Ed.), *A handbook for the study of suicide.* New York: Oxford Press.

Wheat, W. D. (1960). Motivational aspects of suicide in patients during and after psychiatric treatment. *Southern Medical Journal, 53,* 273–277.

Young, J. E. (1982). Loneliness, depression and cognitive therapy: Theory and application. In L. A. Peplau & D. Perlman (Eds.), *Loneliness: A sourcebook of current theory, research and therapy* (pp. 379–405). New York: John Wiley & Sons.

Zuroff, D. C. (1981). Depression and attribution: Some new data and a review of old data. *Cognitive Therapy and Research, 5,* 273–281.

Chapter

6

Prevention and Postvention

In March 1987, Bergenfield, New Jersey gained instant celebrity, no doubt one it neither desired nor appreciated. Four
teenagers, two males and two sisters ranging in age from 16 to
19, died in a group suicide pact by carbon monoxide poisoning
in a car in a closed garage. While waiting to die, each took turns
writing notes on a brown paper bag.

In published reports of their deaths, these four teens were
variously described as "deeply troubled," "losers," and "pain-
in-the-ass type kids" (Martz, 1987). Indeed, all had significant
histories of alcohol and drug abuse, all were estranged from
their conflict-ridden families, three had dropped out from school
and the fourth had recently been suspended, and all four advocated punk styles and were into heavy-metal music. Perhaps
of most profound importance, all had been friendly with another school dropout, an 18-year-old male who in an alcohol
related incident, either fell or jumped to his death off the New
Jersey Palisades along the Hudson River the year before. One
of the girls had dated this boy. One of the male suicide victims
had witnessed that death. The other male had seen his father
kill himself four years earlier.

During the prior year, three other Bergenfield youths had
died equivocal deaths, each certified by the coroner as an accident. Two of these youngsters, best friends, were hit by freight
trains, in alcohol-related incidents within 3 weeks of each other

227

(Cantor, 1990). In the days immediately succeeding the "Bergenfield Four" deaths, a 20-year-old male died by carbon monoxide in his family car at home, 20 miles southwest of Bergenfield; and within hours of this death, a psychiatrically disturbed 20-year-old female, with three prior attempts, and her 17-year-old boyfriend were interrupted and rescued in the midst of their carbon monoxide suicide attempt in the same garage as the Bergenfield Four!

In Chicago on the day after the first Bergenfield suicide incident, two females ages 17 and 19, described as "inseparable," carried out their planned suicide pact. This occurred also by carbon monoxide poisoning, under the influence of alcohol and, apparently, the publicity from Bergenfield (Martz, 1987). As many as a dozen other "copycat suicides" were alleged to have occurred over the following several months (Diegmuller, 1987).

The phenomenological experience of a suicide cluster in a community or school typically will mobilize active steps among responsible persons in the community to initiate preventive programming. Such crisis-initiated problem-solving behavior probably has reinforced the unfortunate use of the word "contagion" to describe the process of clustering, as if anyone and everyone in the community were now susceptible to catching the suicide bug!

Although these youths may have had in common what we know now to be risk factors for completed suicide, the commonality in their method and in the apparent suggestibility of their suicidal actions is most striking to us. What mechanisms might underlie such a rash of suicidal actions? Shared delusions, a magical belief that in death one can appreciate the attention of the media to such events, or simply a legitimizing—a permission giving to an action otherwise still latent—stirred by the model of another?

Some adolescents are symbiotically bonded with another. The death of the one therefore compels the death act of the other. This is done to avoid an unwanted separation. Others are compelled to suicide as penance, because they feel overwhelming guilt and responsibility for not preventing the death of the first. Each of these mechanisms is apparent in the Bergenfield suicide pact and the influencing deaths that preceded the pact.

There is little dispute that clusters do occur and that suicidal youths within a cluster have known risk factors that can identify them with some precision. By identifying adolescents at risk for an imitative suicide and those closely bonded with suicidal others, interventive steps can be taken to interrupt pathways of influence. Community-wide models for the prevention and containment of suicide clusters have been proposed by the Centers for Disease Control (1988), and recommendations for the media response to suicidal events have been developed (Staff, *Newslink*, 1989) to minimize the potential for imitative suicides.

Youth Suicide Prevention: Federal and Public Health Initiatives

The Centers for Disease Control (CDC) is the United States government's public health overseer. Since 1986, with the publication of a report by the National Academy of Sciences (Committee on Trauma Research, 1985), the CDC has been charged by the U.S. Congress with a leadership role in developing preventive foci for both unintentional and intentional injuries. As part of this role, the CDC has helped articulate the priority goals and objectives for the nation's public health. In 1991 the CDC is expected to publish its "Year 2000 National Health Objectives to Reduce Violence and Abusive Behavior," in which is a clearly stated objective to reverse the rising trend in suicidal deaths for youth ages 15–19.

An earlier set of objectives established as a goal for the year 1990 a rate of suicide among people ages 15–24 below 11 in 100,000. As noted in chapter 1, progress toward that goal appears insubstantial. Recognizing the probability by mid-decade that this goal would not be reached, then-Secretary of the Department of Health and Human Services (DHHS) Margaret Heckler established the Task Force on Youth Suicide to integrate and synthesize available knowledge and recommend strategies, in both public and private sectors, for the prevention of youth suicide. Work groups commissioned papers and held national conferences during 1986. The final set of recommendations and supporting papers were finally published as a four-volume report in January 1989 and, where relevant, have been referenced frequently throughout this book.

The Task Force made 33 recommendations in six broad categories: data development, research into risk factors, intervention effectiveness evaluation, increased support for suicide prevention services, public information and education, and broadening the involvement of both public and private sectors in the prevention of youth suicide. Each recommendation was supported by an "action plan," suggested steps for implementation. To its credit, the Task Force acknowledged the complexity of the problem of prevention and the necessity for a long-term and cooperative strategy, elements almost impossible to accomplish at the federal level when dealing with shifting administrations, priorities, and personalities.

In addition, one of the Task Force's own commissioned papers (Eddy, Wolpert, & Rosenberg, 1989) concluded that uncertainty about the cost and effectiveness of several proposed interventions made it inappropriate (i.e., lacking a rational basis) to implement any one. These authors surveyed a group of 15 experts about the possible effectiveness of six interventions for decreasing youth suicides: affective education, early identification and treatment, school-based screening, crisis centers and hotlines, improved health care professional training, and restriction of access to lethal means of suicide. No single intervention proposed had sufficient support to recommend it as an intelligent choice among the alternatives, and the most by which any one intervention was expected to reduce the number of youth suicides was an averaged estimate of only 16%.

Community Approaches to Prevention

Restricting Access to Lethal Means

Restricting access to firearms (particularly handguns) was estimated by Holinger (1984) to reduce youth suicide by about 20%. Given the frequency with which firearms, particularly handguns, are used among youth who commit suicide (approximately 65% of completions), their increasing rate of use in completions, their lethality, and their correlated use by high-risk, substance-abusing youth (Brent, Perper, & Allman, 1987), controlling access and availability of guns, particularly to high-risk youth, has compelling logic as a preventive measure.

Logic also suggests that restricting access to highly lethal means would allow the impulse to commit suicide to wane or would force the potential youth suicide to consider and locate an alternative means, one most likely to be less immediately lethal, therefore allowing opportunity for intervention. Support for this approach has come principally from two areas. In 1970 Great Britain changed the source of its domestic heating gas to one containing one sixth the carbon monoxide content of the earlier supplies. Suicide by carbon monoxide asphyxiation, which had accounted for over 40% of all British suicides before this transitional detoxification, now accounted for fewer than 10%, with no appreciable increase in the use of alternative methods (Shaffer, Garland, Gould, Fisher, & Trautman, 1988). Secondly, the mandated introduction of automobile emission control systems in the United States allowed for a similar naturalistic experiment. In examining before and after rates of suicide by carbon monoxide asphyxiation, Clarke and Lester (1987) reported a notable decline after installation of these systems.

Cantor (1989) has outlined a number of specific interventions regarding firearms. These range from the politically sensitive and possibly unattainable goal of outright gun control to more limited and feasible measures such as mandatory safety training and mandatory waiting periods for and background checks on those who purchase guns.

Similar proposals have been made regarding other commonly available means. Jumping from heights, although accounting for only a small proportion of youth suicides, has been observed to be a most preventable method. One such case example is discussed in Berman (1990a), with experts proposing a number of strategies to restrict access to high places. Restricting access to drugs, the most common method of suicide attempt among adolescents, has been proposed by Eddy et al. (1989) and Cantor (1989). One means to reduce the ease of overdose, for example,

might be to limit prescription dosages of potentially lethal medications such as antidepressants to a 7-day supply. Another
suggestion (Holinger, 1984) is to sell prescription antidepressants along with an emetic or antidote, available for immediate
administration should the overdosing adolescent change his or
her mind or be found in the midst of an attempt.

Crisis Intervention and Telephone Hotline Services

In 1985 Franklin, Comstock, Simmons, and Mason (1989) surveyed almost 400 suicide prevention and intervention programs
in the United States, about one third of those identified. The
majority of these programs were crisis telephone services and
mental health centers having a crisis component. Although reported proportions were considered conservative, suicide-related crisis telephone contacts were estimated at only 6% per
year, 8% of these being adolescents. Of walk-in clinics, only
an estimated 11% of annual clients were considered suicidal,
8% of which were adolescents.

Crisis centers and telephone hotlines offer immediate help, with
24-hour availability to resolve crises of a suicidal or potentially
suicidogenic nature through active interventive efforts. For teenagers, the anonymity and comfortableness of the telephone and
the typically nonprofessional staffing of these services theoretically make this form of entry to the help-giving system more
acceptable than direct, face-to-face contact with an office-based
professional. With this entry, either crises may be resolved without the need for professional treatment, or referrals for more
intensive care can be accomplished when needed.

How effective are these services in preventing suicide? Most
studies have been methodologically unsound and lacking in
direct evidence of usage, comparing communities before and
after the establishment of a program or communities with versus without a program, thus risking the "ecological fallacy"
(Shaffer, Garland, Gould, et al., 1988).

Quantitative methods of meta-analysis were applied by Dew,
Bromet, Brent, and Greenhouse (1987) to a series of published
evaluation studies to determine whether suicide prevention services work. They found that center clients were at higher risk

for suicide than those members of the general population and that completed suicides were more likely than members of the general population to have contacted a program. However, taking the series of studies as a set, the establishment of a center had no demonstrable effect on a community's suicide rate. One of the studies in this set (Miller, Coombs, Leeper, & Barton, 1984) was the only to report data for specific race, sex, and age cohorts. In contrast to other cohorts, and of special interest to our focus on youth, this study found the suicide rate for white women and girls under age 25 to show a large and significant decrease in communities with versus without a center. Since young white women are the most frequent clients of such programs, the Miller et al. study is especially encouraging regarding the impact of suicide prevention services should their utilization by youth be increased.

The relatively low rates of utilization by suicidal teenagers noted here begs the question of how to encourage increased contact between those in need and those who provide needed services. The answer appears to be in public relations. As the majority of adolescent suicides are males, targeted advertising of these programs to males would be imperative (Shaffer, Garland, Gould, et al., 1988). As it is well known that teens typically share problems first with other teens, raising the consciousness of teenagers in general to the existence of these programs, particularly their anonymity and confidentiality and their specific services, should have some effect on increasing referrals to them. Until such gatekeeper services attain the level of support necessary to accomplish a sustained marketing of services to the community of adolescents in general as well as those specifically at risk, little significant impact on the overall suicide rate can be expected.

School-Based Prevention

In recent years the schools have increasingly become sites for a variety of educational prevention models designed to combat a range of public health concerns facing today's youth. Programs in drug abuse prevention, AIDS prevention, child abuse prevention, and sex education have proliferated and compete for time with basic education demands. The school is a logical and natural site for such preventive effort, given this is where student attention is held relatively captive, where teaching and learning are normative tasks, and where peer interaction can be mobilized around a common theme. With increasing public and community awareness of the reality of adolescent suicide, it is not surprising that suicide prevention education programs have joined the growing list of pressing public health education foci.

The typical school-based suicide prevention program is a three-to-six-class, classroom-centered, curriculum-based, lecture–discussion program using, to a lesser extent, experiential exercises or films. Goals typically include heightening awareness about the problem of adolescent suicide and informing (facts and "myths") about suicide; increasing recognition of signs and symptoms (risk factors) in order to facilitate case identification; changing attitudes about suicide and about help receiving; and resource identification. Additionally, programs often attempt pragmatic skill building in the areas of affect recognition, listening, communication, crisis and stress management, problem solving, and referral making (Smith, Eyman, Dyck, & Ryerson, 1990). One common focus is on encouraging "secret sharing" with a responsible and trusted adult, as when a suicidal teen confides to a peer his or her suicidal ideation or plan but only with the caveat that the confidant will "tell no one!"

To a lesser extent, some school-based programs focus principally on gatekeeper education, increasing awareness among teachers, administrators, and other school personnel of warning signs and teaching referral skills. Others have encouraged the development of peer counseling programs, emphasizing the natural communication patterns and help-giving system common to the student culture.

In order to make more normative the notions of "problem solving" as a treatment and peers as caregivers, these programs attempt to destigmatize suicide by deemphasizing the relation between suicide and psychopathology (e.g., suicide is a "problem in living"). Hoberman and Garfinkel (1988) have expressed some concern that such attempts to normalize the experiences of suicidal youth invalidate what we know about youth suicide and psychopathology, thereby directly countering the goal of increasing recognition (case finding) of those in need of treatment (psychotherapy). Shaffer, Garland, Gould, et al. (1988) argue furthermore that by so misrepresenting the facts, these programs may heighten the risk of imitation. In their view, the likelihood of suicide being imitated would be lessened if suicide were depicted "as a deviant act by someone with a mental disturbance" (p. 681).

Other criticisms of school-based models have questioned the implicit assumption in these programs that education is synonymous with prevention. Citing unflattering evaluations of attempts in the United States to stem the prevalence of unwanted pregnancy, AIDS, smoking, and drug abuse through school-based prevention models, Berman (1990b) has questioned whether there is any reason to believe that knowledge alone is sufficient to change behavior. In addition, Berman notes that those teens most at risk for these health-endangering behaviors are those who are least likely to attend to preventative education programs.

Shaffer, Garland, and Whittle (1988), in their systematic evaluation of three high school programs in New Jersey, confirm that identified high-risk students may be "turned off" by these programs and that behavioral preferences (e.g., what the student would do and to whom the student would talk if depressed) and attitudes about the management of a suicidal problem did not change. On the more positive side, they found no evidence that these programs caused harm and, in contrast, many students reported that the prevention training served as a source of comfort (confidence boosting) regarding their attempts to help other students.

Whether the focus of changing attitudes and knowledge and the attempt to impart skill building in relatively short periods of training can impact on the ultimate goal of these models, that of decreasing the incidence of suicidal behavior, has yet to be established. Moreover, given the relative infrequency of suicidal behavior, evidence of decreased rates of attempt or completion requires long-term evaluative outcome research. The call for such evaluation research was one of the six recommendations made by the Task Force on Youth Suicide (Alcohol, Drug Abuse, and Mental Health Administration, 1989).

Issues in Prevention

The rush to develop school-based programs perhaps speaks more to our humanitarian spirit than to a reasoned approach to suicide prevention. It is therefore probable that these first-generation models will change dramatically as outcome studies of their relative effectiveness are reported.

The great majority of these programs are targeted school- or grade-wide and have multiple goals ranging from attitude change to knowledge and skill acquisition. On a broader level, these school-based programs pose unanswered questions as to the best use of limited resources in developing future models. What strategy of intervention makes the most sense? Should targets of interventions be limited, for instance, to those most at risk or to parents most in position to observe their children? Should efforts be geared toward primary prevention (e.g., skill development beginning in primary grades and continued through booster trainings thereafter), or case finding, or improving response capabilities of caregivers? Should efforts be directed not at education but perhaps toward changing suicidogenic conditions in the environment or effecting legislation, for example to deal with issues of gun control or drug abuse? We need a theory of change and an effective public health model with which to define what targets should be approached best by whom and when—and all this at an affordable cost.

These questions are not particular to suicide prevention but apply to a number of pressing public health concerns such as AIDS prevention and drug abuse prevention (Berman, 1990b). But the pressing need to respond to these problems does not allow us the luxury of awaiting research data before we attempt to implement well-planned, rational interventions (cf. Eddy et al., 1989).

It is our belief that the schools are appropriate sites for preventive programming. Furthermore, we believe that clinicians trained in suicidology and understanding of youth suicide should initiate training models with the enlisted cooperation of school personnel. In particular, we believe that the emphasis should be given to the school- and community-based models of intervention that follow. Each of these suggestions focuses on behavioral change achievable through educational efforts. Each has a somewhat limited scope and target and therefore, a measurable goal. Together these models promote the idea of the school as a community resource, placing education in a broad frame including the teaching of skills to children, their parents, and the community as a whole.

A Menu of Approaches

1. Early detection and referral-making skills. It is appropriate that both faculty and students be taught to be observers of self and others. Specific behaviors associated with suicide risk, particularly signs of psychopathology common to depression and substance abuse as co-related risk conditions, might be widely posted as easily as have been "the warning signs of cancer." Students and faculty should not be expected to intervene directly, but rather to refer a student believed to be at risk to a professional competent to evaluate and treat that student. Referral-making skills are teachable.

2. Resource identification. An effective referral rests on having competent professionals in the community to whom referrals can be made. Community resources, agencies and private practitioners, can be evaluated to ensure the competencies of those to whom students at risk may be sent. Students themselves could be trained to serve on consumer investigative teams, sent with appropriate evaluative criteria, to establish a dynamic system, updated annually, of those professionals so identified. In this way also, chances are greater that students would understand and demystify the professional community, thereby increasing probable access and utilization.

3. Help-seeking behavior. One of the side benefits to resource identification by students is making more normative the idea of help seeking and help receiving. When the community as a whole is perceived as engaged in showing concern for the quality of its services and resources, public awareness of these resources increases as does destigmatization, that is, there is a greater acceptance of resource utilization. It is possible that compliance with referred treatments might also increase, thereby reducing the frequency of repeat suicide attempts.

4. Professional education. Also related to resource identification is the evaluation of the specific training of professionals dealing with youth suicide. When a community's schools view their mission to be the education of the community as a whole, particularly when that education serves to impact positively on the educability of students by enhancing their health and minimizing their distress, the upgrading of professional skills becomes part of the school's function.

5. Parent education. Again, if the broad view of the school's role is that of educating all segments of the community, parents should be alerted to be observant of risk factors and available resources to whom they might bring their questions and seek counsel. Outreach programs can be developed to teach responsible gun ownership, particularly to parents of high-risk children. Drug abuse awareness programs are available to teach parental awareness of signs of potential drug use by youth. Parent training classes might be encouraged, even required, of new parents.

6. Primary prevention. Taking the long view, the most effective and probably the most *cost-effective* strategy is that of primary prevention, incorporating any number of programs designed to teach health-enhancing behavior through teaching behavioral skills. These programs must begin in the primary grades, be reinforced through follow-up training, and focus on adaptive skills and competencies. A number of models, relevant to mental health goals, are in the literature related to self-esteem training, problem-solving training, social skill training, anxiety management training, and assertiveness training. Additionally, time-limited, structured educational models for training youth to manage negative affect states such as anger and depression are available (see chapter 5).

Given that a sizable proportion of suicide-prone youngsters display their impending risk through decreased attention to their academics, thereby increasing their likelihood of dropping out of school; and that many suicidal adolescents have already dropped out or been expelled from school, school-based programs that identify such youth well before they leave school and attempt to attach them more positively to the school environment should be encouraged. Programs designed to enhance the school environment for all students, irrespective of academic skills, increase the likelihood of positive role model identifications and alternative skill attainment.

7. School-based postvention. Preventive functions are served through appropriate interventions after the fact of suicidal behavior. For example, a student hospitalized for a suicide attempt and treated may now need help successfully reintegrating into the academic and social environment of the school without risk of repeat attempt or ultimate completion.

Considerations for an ongoing therapeutic plan and coordination between therapist and school counselor or other liaison are essential. A number of questions need to be adequately addressed. Among these are: What initial and longer term academic load should the student carry in order to minimize stress and maximize a successful reentry? How should parents be involved in planning reintegration? What attention needs to be given the peer community into which the student will reenter? Suicide attempters may be viewed with contempt or avoided by others. Attention must be given to sensitizing the peer environment, dealing with fears and anxieties, and smoothing the path of reentry for the returning student.

Should the school suffer the completed suicide of one of its constituents, bereaved survivors must be attended to in order to reduce the likelihood that survivor vulnerability (e.g., guilt, self-blame, depression) will turn into either imitative suicidal behavior or self-destructive penance.

A Model School Suicide Prevention Plan

The Centers for Disease Control has published recommendations (Centers for Disease Control, 1988) for preventing and containing suicide clusters. These should serve as a template for a school or community plan.

The 10 CDC recommendations describe the need for anticipatory planning *before* the onset of a suicide cluster and the coordinated involvement of concerned sectors of the community. Day-to-day crisis management would be the responsibility of a coordinating committee, housed in and called to meeting by a host agency that would also monitor the incidence of suicidal behaviors.

The response plan would be implemented when either a suicide cluster occurred or when one or more traumatic deaths occurred in the community, particularly among the young or of someone of potential influence. Pre-identified community resources would be contacted and groups who would play key roles in the response prepared. The CDC directives express a caution to avoid glorification of the suicide victims and to minimize sensationalism, while providing a timely flow of accurate, appropriate information to the media. The plan calls for early identification of those at high risk for suicide, a screening interview with a trained counselor, and referral for further counseling or services as needed. Environmental interventions, where necessary to change an identified condition likely to stimulate further suicidal behavior, are recommended, as are interventions in long-term issues suggested by the nature of the cluster. These recommendations might be translated by a school interested in establishing a coordinated response plan as follows:

Anticipatory procedures. A Trauma Response Team, available to respond to all school crises (from a student suicide to a teacher death to the disappearance of a student), should be established. Among the first tasks of the team would be the development of procedural flow charts and an emergency contact telephone tree. Additionally, they would lobby for the establishment of an in-school "crisis room" for drop-in group or individual crisis counseling. Training procedures necessary for the implementation of the response plan would have to be developed; and all personnel having roles appropriate to the response procedures would then be identified and trained. Significant to the flow and control of information would be the designation of gatekeeper and liaison personnel to deal with media relations, police, and parents. A "school spokesperson" should be the only one to speak for the school during the crisis and a secretary designated to screen and channel calls to the spokesperson.

Crisis (suicide completion) response plan. The team coordinator would have the role of verifying information regarding the suicide with police and the medical examiner's office and secondarily, to contact and offer support to parents and determine needs of relevance to the school. A faculty or staff meeting should be called as soon as possible (before school?) to present pertinent information: what is and is not known and what is being done or planned. Participants at this meeting would have an opportunity to ask questions, ventilate affect, or opt out of the response plan. This meeting would afford opportunity to review assessment procedures (for at-risk youth), establish appropriate responses to expected student reactions, and identify community resources and referral agents. A meeting at day's end should be scheduled at this time with an agenda to process events and plan next steps.

As deemed necessary, scheduled school activities should be adjusted (e.g., field trips postponed). At the same time, as much as possible, the order of the day would be "business as usual." As necessary, activities could be added (e.g., an open meeting for parents), but no special activities, unless these were standard operating procedures (s.o.p.) in response to any trauma or death, would be scheduled (e.g., a memorial service would be appropriate only if this were s.o.p.).

All communications to students should be given in class, not through the public address system or in large assembly. In this way, students identified as at-risk can be observed and receive a response. Also, the location and availability of the designated crisis room and counselor contact could be announced. This room and designated personnel, including peer counselors if appropriate, should be kept available for several days, with students given liberal classroom leave to visit.

In a more informal manner, it would be helpful to designate someone to "walk the halls" to monitor common areas (including bathrooms, parking lots, eateries) to observe and connect with students in need or at risk who are not in classrooms. Similarly, a school designee would walk the decedent's scheduled classrooms in succession, helping students in those classes particularly affected by the "empty chair."

Consistent with general school policies, funeral attendance should be facilitated (e.g., there should be no penality for absence; car pools could be organized) and supported with parental permission for any student to attend. Some students might need directives and anticipatory guidance about what to expect at a funeral. For many, this would be their first close experience with surviving a death.

Procedures for contact–communication with parents would need to be implemented. These should include procedures for parents to have access to school services, privacy considerations for the decedent's family, notification and follow-through for parents of students noted to be at high risk, and approaches for dealing with the decedent's siblings, if any, in school.

Procedures also would need to be implemented to channel the media to a predesignated media spokesperson as well as to minimize contact between the media and students on school grounds during school hours. These procedures would be designed to minimize disruption of school activity while maximizing dissemination of accurate information.

In-class postvention: teacher guidelines. Teachers would have the front-line responsibility in class to deal with student reactions to the suicide. They should be pretrained for a number of tasks that would allow a healthy refocusing and restabilization of the school environment. Their roles would involve replacing rumor with immediately disseminated, current, and accurate information. They would have to encourage and give opportunity for the ventilation of feeling in an accepting environment, all the time reinforcing the normality of grief and stress responses. They would need to discourage student notions to romanticize the suicide. With criteria for observation in mind, they would have to identify those at risk for destabilized and imitative responses to the suicide, facilitating the referral of identified students through predeveloped triage procedures to receive needed help.

A large number of schools and school districts have developed coordinated crisis response procedures available as models for implementing the above guidelines. A network of individuals representing these programs has been established through the American Association of Suicidology[1] and is available to the reader.

School-based suicide prevention models are excellent examples of how postvention procedures effectively complete the loop to become prevention procedures. Each suicide in a defined community becomes the potential stimulus for another suicidal event, which in turn may be prevented through effective postvention procedures. To that end, it is essential that we adequately understand what is known about suicide survivorhood and bereavement, particularly as distinguished from the survivorhood of other manners of death.

Survivors of Suicide and Postvention

Case Illustration

> As a high school freshman, Steve was a popular and active 15-year-old, the pride and joy of his loving parents. Outstanding academically, a starter on the varsity baseball team, Steve had a girlfriend and a network of good friends. Hoping to gain entrance to an Ivy League college, Steve transferred to a private school his sophomore year. That was the year everything turned bad.
>
> Inexplicably, Steve had trouble adjusting to the new school environment; his grades began to slip as he began to withdraw into himself. He made few new friends and eventually lost touch with old friends. His girlfriend broke up with him over Christmas, and Steve appeared to become more and more depressed, withdrawn, and hostile to his parent's attempts to help. When spring approached, he refused to try out for baseball. His parents thought it was just a phase and had planned to transfer him back to his old school in the fall. But Steve would not live that long. One Friday night his parents came home from a movie to find Steve lying dead

---

[1]American Association of Suicidology, 2459 So. Ash St., Denver, CO 80222.

after shooting himself in the head with his father's favorite hunting rifle.

His parents were shocked and utterly devastated. Their loss inexplicable, they felt they had no one to whom they could turn. Their mourning was filled with confusing feelings of guilt, hurt, anger, loss, and embarrassment. Steve's two younger sisters were devastated as well. Ashamed about Steve's suicide, his parents hurriedly arranged a brief memorial service and cremated his body within a few short days.

Steve's parents found it difficult to talk about the death with their friends and withdrew from the active involvement in the community. In the year following Steve's death, his father began to drink heavily, stayed out late, and engaged in frequent arguments with his wife. As the year anniversary of Steve's death approached, the situation had further deteriorated. Steve's sisters were acting out in school, his mother remained distraught and depressed, his father's drinking had resulted in two arrests for driving while intoxicated, and the marriage was on the verge of collapsing. Upon a recommendation from their priest, the family went to see a family therapist to begin to sort out what had happened to them as individuals and as a family.

Overview

Suicidology as a field of study is perhaps most fundamentally rooted in, and oriented to, the prevention and intervention of suicidal behaviors. Yet despite our best efforts as clinicians, parents, teachers, or friends, we can never ultimately protect a determined individual from himself or herself. One of the most devastating outcomes that exists with virtually any suicide is therefore the pain experienced by the "survivors"—those who are left behind in the aftermath of a suicide. As adolescent suicide rates climb, so climb the numbers of survivors of suicide who must deal with lives suddenly left empty. Over the past decade, suicide survivorship and healing work conducted with survivors, referred to as "postvention" (see Shneidman, 1967), have emerged as major areas of interest within the field of suicidology.

The History of Suicide Survivorship

In his discussion of the history of the suicide survivor, Colt (1987) graphically describes the desecration of the corpse of a young man "convicted" of suicide in Paris during the 18th century. The victim's body was dragged by his heels through the city streets and subsequently hung upside-down in the public square as an example to all who would consider such a crime—a crude form of suicide prevention indeed. His body would be denied a proper burial and would be tossed in the sewer or the town dump. Property, title, and goods of the deceased would all be forfeited to the King, and law would decree that there be no memory of him. Wife and children would leave the town humiliated, hoping to start a new life while always hiding the secret shame of being suicide survivors.

There is a long history to the stigma of suicide and the litany of acts and rituals practiced throughout the world to mark the shameful act (Colt, 1987). To prevent the suicide's ghost from wandering, corpses have been decapitated, buried outside city limits or tribal territories, burned, beaten with chains, thrown to wild beasts, or buried at a crossroads with a stake through the heart. In years past, survivors of suicide were often directly punished as accessories to the crime of suicide (since the guilty party was not available). As mentioned above, survivors in Britain and France were frequently forced to forfeit both the goods and property of the victim as well as their own. On occasion, family survivors of the victim were required to pay a fine to the suicide's in-laws in redemption for the shame brought to their name.

In England during the 18th century, automatic forfeiture of property to the crown and desecration of the corpse began to be replaced by crude invesitgations into the cause of death. Trials were held posthumously in a Coroner's Court to determine if the victim had been insane and therefore innocent (*non compos mentis*), or a criminal against himself or herself (*felo de se*), guilty of crime, and subject to subsequent forfeiture of property and desecration of the body (Colt, 1987). The determination of insanity was thus central to civil disposition of a suspected suicide, and survivors were thereby afforded a modicum of relief from some of the direct blame and punishment. However, rewritten laws did not release the survivor of the societal stigma of suicide or the superstitions and prejudices associated with madness and insanity.

During the 19th century, there was a distinct shift away from the view of suicide as a crime or sin toward a more medical perspective. A major line of research emerged in the area of genetic influences on suicide. Various theories of heredity were proposed that placed survivors at risk of succumbing to genetically influenced suicide (Winslow, 1840). By the mid-20th century, these theories were largely disregarded (Kallman & Anastasia, 1947).

While researchers attempted to take a more empirical perspective on the topic, a new kind of social stigma for the suicide survivor was ushered in by the Victorian era of respectability (Colt, 1987). Although suicide was no longer directly punished in a civil sense, the act nevertheless marked a family's name, lowered property values, and generally tainted the reputations of the survivors. In response, survivors attempted to conceal the suicide, hastily arranged funerals, and kept the truth from children. Suicide became the family secret, the neighbor's gossip, and a source of blame and public shunning. Survivors were thus doomed to their own private shame—trapped with their feelings of hurt, loss, and anger.

It is striking to note that even with the increased interest in the study of suicide in the last 30 years, suicide survivorship long remained a largely unexamined topic. Slowly, however, interest in suicide survivorship began to emerge during the 1960s as members of the Los Angeles Suicide Prevention Center in coordination with the Coroner's office of Los Angeles began to conduct "psychological autopsies" (i.e, investigatory interviews conducted with survivors of suicide to help determine the medicolegal manner of death). As an unexpected outgrowth of this technique, there was an emerging awareness of the unique psychological needs of survivors. In response to this awareness, Shneidman (1967) coined the term *postvention*, referring to efforts to assist grieving suicide survivors. Since that time, a growing body of clinical and empirical literature has begun to emerge. But clearly, much more study and work are needed to help us better work with the living who survive a death by suicide.

Bereavement

Normal Versus Suicidal Death

Hauser (1983) defines bereavement as the physiological, psychological, behavioral, and social response patterns displayed by an individual following the loss (usually through a death) of a significant person or thing. Grief and mourning are two distinct components to bereavement. Grief refers to the specific feelings and emotional responses related to bereavement, whereas mourning refers to the social customs and rituals that help the bereaved to grieve, expressing thoughts, feelings, and memories related to the loss of the loved one (Hauser, 1987). Although mourning rituals tend to vary widely, mourning as a means to express grief is common to most cultures (Averill, 1968; Rosenblatt, Jackson, & Walsh, 1972). Culturally based rituals of mourning that facilitate the expression of grief and provide support for the bereaved appear to lead adaptive patterns of bereavement and healing (Hauser, 1987).

There appears to be a fairly consistent bereavement process that is virtually universal in nature. Bowlby and Parkes (1970) have described the phases of "normal" bereavement in terms of initial shock, followed by yearning and protest, which lead to disorganization, and ultimately leading to a working-through and reorganization phase. Although most people work through the phases in a fairly predictable manner, a death by suicide may cause the survivor to become "stuck" in one phase and unable to move on to successful reorganization (Hauser, 1987). As discussed by van der Wal (1989–1990) there is a popular notion that survivors of suicide have more pathological reactions and a more complicated and prolonged grief process than other survivor groups. While there is evidence of qualitative differences in the bereavement of suicide, there is no empirical evidence of a quantitative difference between suicide survivors and survivors of other deaths in terms of length of bereavement or degree of pathology in grief reactions (van der Wal, 1989–1990).

Hauser (1983) has found a variety of specific factors that may affect the normal bereavement process. For example, sudden or unexpected deaths, especially those that are violent or traumatic, appear to make integration and grief resolution more difficult. Felt responsibility for the death or the presence of various stressors (e.g., economic or legal difficulties) may impair the process of grieving as well. Poor bereavement outcome has also been associated with absence of funeral rites, difficult relations or distorted communications with the victim prior to his or her death, and lack of role models and social support. Finally, the age of the deceased also greatly influences the unexpectedness of the death (i.e., the death of a child is more stressful than the death of an adult). Notably, many of these factors are directly implicated in the survivorship of an adolescent suicide and may therefore account for the unique hardships associated with this type of loss.

Suicide

Beyond characteristics that are common to all forms of death bereavement, there are some unique aspects that are specific to suicide bereavement. These include volitional aspects of the death, the suddenness of the death, the potential violence of the death, shame among survivors, guilt among survivors, the compromise of mourning rituals, distorted communication patterns, and the withdrawal of social support systems. As alluded to earlier, many of these factors are further complicated or intensified when the victim of the suicide is a young person.

Volitional aspects of suicide. One of the most confusing and upsetting aspects of a suicide loss is the volitional nature of the suicide act. Feelings of rejection, helplessness, and anger may be engendered in the survivor by the fact that the deceased fundamentally *chose* to die. When the suicide is an adolescent, there is often a particular sense of despair and futility—young people are not supposed to die, they hardly know what it means to live. The volitional aspect of suicide leaves the survivor with questions, the "whys," which will never be answered.

The suddenness of suicide. Despite the common occurrence of direct or veiled warnings of an imminent suicide, survivors are virtually never prepared for such a devastating event. In contrast to an elderly person's natural death, there is little cause or impetus to anticipate the premature death of a young person. Suicide survivors are therefore unable to perform preparatory grief work. While different from natural death, the effects related to the suddenness of suicide are often similar to effects seen in cases of homicidal and accidental death. It appears that sudden deaths cause an accelerated rate of change in the environment that may be emotionally and physically devastating (Rabkin & Struening, 1976). Empirical data strongly indicate a range of pathological grief reactions that can be associated with sudden deaths (Flesch, 1977; Glick, Weiss, & Parkes, 1974; Lehrman, 1973; Parkes, 1975a, 1975b).

The potential violence of suicide. Suicides may often be very violent acts, particularly in those cases where highly lethal means are used (e.g., guns, hangings, or jumps from tall buildings). If indeed suicide may be conceptualized as murder in the 180th degree, there is then an element of violence against the self as well as against others. For example, what interpersonal communication could be more hostile and angry than a shotgun suicide of a youth lying on the white spread of his parents' bed? The visual impact of such a grisly scene could be devastating to a parent or sibling survivor who discovers the body. Violent and ugly images of such a scene may linger and torment a suicide survivor for years to come.

The shame of suicide. As discussed previously, a sense of shame has always been closely associated with suicide survivorship. The negative views so commonly held by various cultures place a special and unwelcome burden on the suicide survivor. Social castigation and stigma make an already painful and tragic loss that much more difficult. Commonly, the suicide of a loved one reflects negatively on the survivors, leaving a mark of shame that is unique among various forms of bereavement.

The guilt of suicide. Closely linked to shame is the guilt which is often experienced by suicide survivors. Although feelings of guilt are common to the grieving process of any death, the guilt experience of suicide survivors may be particularly more frequent, intense, and persistent (Sheskin & Wallace, 1976). Survivors often feel that they could or should have done something to foresee and prevent the death. Alternatively, a survivor may feel directly responsible for the suicide, that he or she personally caused the tragic death. While various forms of guilt emerge in the suicide aftermath, it appears that suicide guilt lingers an especially long time, thereby preventing the survivor from gaining a sense of closure (Henslin, 1970; Rudestam, 1977). Indeed, feelings of guilt and reponsibility may haunt the survivor for years, particularly when the reality of suicide is avoided or denied and not worked through more directly.

The compromise of mourning rituals. Families may circumvent traditional mourning rituals in hopes of avoiding public shame and scrutiny (Hauser, 1987). The avoidance or limiting of mourning rituals can directly compromise the support and healing these traditions potentially offer to the bereaved and may further foster the denial and avoidance commonly associated with suicide deaths. Moreover, attempts to play down the death limit the potential for wider social support—for the survivor, the suicide becomes a secret, and feelings of guilt, anger, and loss cannot be discussed with others who could help.

Distorted communication patterns. Feelings of rejection and abandonment are virtually unavoidable for the suicide survivor. Denial is often a major defense used against the feelings of rejection and anger (which may feel particularly unacceptable) toward the victim. The unconscious expression of these intense feelings may take the form of projection, scapegoating, and blaming (Hauser, 1987). Blaming, especially in the family context, can be intensely expressed and profoundly hurtful to people who may be sharing similar feelings of rejection and anger. Accordingly, family patterns of communication may become both selective and distorted in such a way that family myths and secrets may arise, impeding relationships inside and outside the family and further complicating the painful process of grieving a death by suicide (Hauser, 1987).

Withdrawal of social supports. The quality of social support has been shown to have an enormous effect on the bereavement process, in both a positive and negative sense (Lindemann, 1944). As Hauser (1987) suggests, members of the social network have the ability to augment or negate a survivor's perceptions and labeling of events. They may comfort and support the bereaved, or else increase the felt stress by not providing the support and reassurance which is so desperately needed. Data suggest that members of a survivor's social network often respond with avoidance, gossip, and cloaked communication (Calhoun, Selby, & Selby, 1982). Experimental subjects asked to consider the parents of a child who commits suicide found them to be less respectable and likable. The parents were further perceived as more disturbed, more worthy of blame, and more responsible for their child's death than parents of children who die by other causes (Calhoun, Selby, & Faulstich, 1980). Similar findings of negative reactions to survivors have been widely replicated in other studies (Range & Kastner, 1988; Reynolds & Cimbolic, 1988–1989; Rudestam & Imbroll, 1983). Alternatively, Calhoun, Selby, and Abernathy (1984) have found that when family survivors are actually known to the respondents, the previously described blaming effect may be diminished. With few guidelines in our society of "how to be," it appears that the social response to suicide survivors may vary widely and, unfortunately, be less than supportive.

Therapeutic Approaches to Survivorship

Helping Others

Having reviewed and highlighted the history of suicide survivorship, various aspects of general bereavement, and unique aspects of suicide bereavement, we are prepared to examine therapeutic responses to survivors. Before considering some of the specific approaches, however, it is important to consider who we mean when we refer to "suicide survivors."

Identifying survivors. Perhaps the most obvious survivors are the suicide's immediate family—the parents and siblings of the victim. Additional survivors of suicide may include others who are not so obviously identified. Extended family such as grandparents, aunts, uncles, and cousins are often deeply affected by a suicide, and their grief may not be as readily recognized as that of the immediate kin. Friends of the deceased represent another group of survivors who may be profoundly devastated, especially when the victim is an adolescent peer. Mental health professionals, who may have worked heroically to prevent a suicide, are frequently neglected as legitimate survivors. Formal groups or organizations—a sports team, a church, a school—can be seen as survivors of suicide. Zinner's (1985) notion of "group survivorship" conceptualizes groups as extended families (with their own mores, symptoms, goals, hierarchies, and communication networks) that must mourn the loss of a member. In truth, virtually anyone touched by the death of suicide may be considered a survivor.

Interventions with survivors. Survivors of suicide have special treatment and support needs that can be met in various modalities and settings. For our purposes, we will briefly examine the two main areas of survivor intervention, namely various forms of psychotherapy and survivor support groups.

Psychotherapy. As Dunne (1987) has noted, survivors of suicide often do not seek assistance from mental health professionals, possibly due to anger toward the profession for not preventing a death or to fear of the stigma of mental illness. Unfortunately, those who do seek treatment may often encounter a therapist who may be unfamiliar with those aspects of suicide survivor grief that uniquely differentiate from other forms of grief. In his review of working with survivors in therapy, Dunne (1987) examines both general considerations and specific clinical themes that are relevant to treatment.

Effective work with survivors requires that the therapist be aware of his or her own attitudes about suicide and guard against countertransference responses—especially blaming the client or family. Moreover, therapists should be knowledgable about normal grief processes and respectful of the time that grief work can require. It may be necessary to work in different modalities, depending on the needs of the survivor. In many cases, family therapy may be particularly useful to work through systemic issues such as blaming, scapegoating, and isolation of family members. Individual or couples therapy may be the treatment of choice for survivors working with alternative sets of issues. Dunne (1987) suggests that often the client is the best barometer of which specific treatment strategy may be most useful.

In terms of clinical themes relevant to working with survivors, Dunne (1987) cites six major themes commonly seen:

1. Surviving suicide often establishes a perpetual need to search for both physical and psychological clues to the reason for the suicide.

2. Whether irrational or appropriate, suicide survivorship often leaves a legacy of profound guilt.

3. Survivorship often profoundly alters one's social relationships as a consequence of real or imagined stigma.

4. Grief following a suicide is often complex and likely to be incomplete.

5. The idea of suicide as a solution to a problem becomes implanted in the survivor's mind.

6. Suicide erodes the survivor's capacity to trust others.

Although these general considerations and themes are by no means exhaustive, they do suggest that there are special considerations relevant to working with suicide survivors. Central to this work is the need for clinicians to be aware of their own attitudes about suicide and the special issues that suicide survivors bring to the therapeutic setting.

Survivor support groups. There has been a virtual explosion in suicide survivor support groups in recent years, possibly due to a general decrease in social taboos related to suicide (Heilig, 1985) and the growing public awareness of adolescent suicide (McIntosh, 1987). As Appel and Wrobleski (1987) suggest, survivors increasingly appear to be less secretive and more prepared to seek help. The self-help survivor support group by its very nature appears to draw many to seek help who might otherwise avoid traditional mental health modalities (Maxim & Brooks, 1985). As with other self-help movements, the involvement of mental health professionals, who are not themselves survivors, in self-help support groups has sparked its share of controversy (see Heilig, 1985; Appel & Wrobleski, 1987). Although undoubtedly each side of the argument has legitimate perspectives and concerns, we would support Silverman (1978), who has advocated a nonadversarial stance between professionals and self-help programs in order to create a partnership in providing compassionate help to survivors of suicide.

Recent empirical data are beginning to confirm that survivor groups seem to be helpful to survivors of suicide. In her study of multiple family support groups for survivors, Billow (1987) notes three major implications of the function of these groups. First, survivors clearly have a need to be with other survivors, a key aspect of engaging survivors in treatment. Second, they found that open-ended groups were particularly effective in working with survivors who may move away from the group and subsequently return (possibly around significant holidays and anniversaries). A third implication was the way in which members used the group to resolve their feelings of hopelessness through political action and consumer advocacy. Many survivors have been actively involved in gun-control legislation as well as in petitioning the media in relation to their coverage of suicide or the use of the topic in entertainment mediums (e.g., heavy-metal rock music). Overall, these researchers found that support groups are beneficial in their capacity to provide mutual support and reassurance. Perhaps one of the most notable aspects of suicide survivor support groups is that they provide assistance to individuals who may be inclined to avoid traditional modes of mental health care (Maxim & Brooks, 1985). While support groups are inherently and intuitively appealing, additional research is needed to determine more specifically how and why they are helpful to survivors of suicide.

Surviving the Suicide of a Patient

Case Illustration

> Stephanie is a 35-year-old clinical psychologist who works at a large university counseling center. As a staff psychologist, she sees a wide range of undergraduate and graduate patients. Stephanie received her PhD about 5 years ago and is licensed in her state of practice. She enjoys her work at the counseling center, has a small private practice on the side, and dabbles in some ongoing research projects. She

has worked with many depressed and suicidal patients and believes she has a fairly good working knowledge of suicide.

One afternoon Stephanie conducted an intake with a 19-year-old sophomore political science major. Her patient, Mike, was a pleasant but emotionally immature young man who appeared to be very depressed. During the course of their first interview, Mike tearfully revealed to Stephanie that he had been in a homosexual relationship with a distant cousin who was 20 years his elder.

The relationship had begun rather innocently when they met for the first time at a large family reunion the summer after Mike's freshman year at college. Mike, a self-described social introvert, came to idolize his cousin, a schoolteacher who happened to live in the university town where Mike went to college. During the fall of his sophomore year, Mike became quite close to his cousin as they spent hours together talking and going to movies and sporting events. By the end of the fall semester, Mike's cousin had became the entire focus of Mike's social life.

Upon his return from Christmas break, Mike eagerly went to visit his cousin. His cousin received him warmly and through the course of the evening became quite intoxicated. When Mike got up to leave, his cousin made a sexual advance. Simultaneously terrified and exhilarated by his idol's sexual interest, Mike capitulated.

Thereafter, an ongoing sexual relationship evolved over the following weeks. While Mike felt confused, he was also flattered and excited by this new development, until one fateful night. Shortly after mid-term exams, Mike's cousin took him to a gay bar, an experience that was very upsetting to Mike. Upon their return home, his cousin initiated sex and Mike refused. After his refusal, Mike's cousin brutally raped him.

This event occurred about two weeks prior to seeking treatment at the counseling center. Since that night, Mike had become quite depressed and unable to go to classes. The incident left Mike with a sickening feeling, and he felt profoundly guilty and "dirty" about the entire relationship. His cousin repeatedly attempted to call and visit him, but Mike refused to have any contact with him. Each phone call or attempted contact brought a cycle of depression and acute agitation.

Stephanie quickly recognized the depth of injury, the degree of betrayal, and the fragility of Mike's emotional world. She empathically listened to his story and began to focus her assessment around the cycles of depression and upset that followed his cousin's attempts to contact Mike. She astutely asked whether Mike ever felt suicidal in this cycle of depression. Mike quietly confirmed that indeed he thought about suicide a great deal and how he would like to end the pain. When Stephanie appropriately inquired about a plan, Mike said he thought of shooting himself, but he did not have a gun.

Stephanie, concerned about Mike's imminent safety, conducted a thorough assessment of suicide risk and received clear commitments from Mike that he would remain safe and would call her if he felt unsafe. Mike seemed greatly relieved to finally tell his story, and Stephanie sensed a good connection with Mike. She scheduled their next session for later that week and felt fairly confident about his safety. She carefully documented her assessment and consulted with the director of the agency about the case.

Stephanie met with Mike for another 2 weeks and felt that they were making good headway. She continued to assess his suicidality and felt that the alliance was forming quite well. Mike had been able to maintain the boundary with his cousin, who had begun to leave him alone. Stephanie was cautiously encouraged about Mike's progress.

About a month after she had begun to work with Mike, Stephanie received a call from the director of the agency in the early hours of a Monday morning. It seemed that the resident director of Mike's dormitory had called—Mike had been found by his roommate hanging by a belt in his closet. Two notes had been left, one for his parents and one for Stephanie.

Her note read:

> Dear Stephanie,
>   I'm so sorry, I know I've let you down. I broke my promise to you, but I had no choice. I can't live with him and I can't live without him—I tried but it hurt too much. You did the best you could, please don't be mad at me. I appreciate all that you tried to do, but it's my life and my choice. Now my pain will end, but his will begin.
>
>   Mike

Despite all her best efforts, her skill and knowledge, her thorough assessment and treatment, Stephanie was unable to save Mike from his own pain and anger. The story of Mike's death serves to remind us of our most fundamental limitations as therapists and as human beings—we can never ultimately predict and prevent a patient's suicide. Such a realization strikes at the very heart of our own narcissism and grandiosity as psychotherapists.

Having applied a number of different lenses through which we have broadly examined the epidemiology, theory, research, assessment, treatment, and prevention of suicide, we apply yet one more lens. This final lens brings the topic of suicide into a narrow and sharp focus, a focus that is most personal and perhaps most threatening. Therein, our final consideration centers on the therapist's survivorship of an adolescent patient's suicide.

A personal and professional crisis. Jones (1987) asserts that the suicide of a patient in therapy is the most difficult bereavement crisis that therapists may encounter and endure. Litman (1965) has noted that the crisis is compounded because the patient's suicide often presents a personal as well as a professional crisis. The differentiation of personal versus professional issues as it relates to a patient's suicide often becomes quite fuzzy.

Skilled therapists tend to develop very intense and intimate relationships with their patients. While for the competent and ethical therapist, these relationships remain fundamentally professional and appropriate, they do invariably touch the therapist personally as well. Therapists often come to care sincerely for the patient and, moreover, may become quite invested in their progress. Unarguably, therapists become quite invested in their patients' remaining alive. We have found that the personal investment may become especially intense in the case of youthful suicidal patients—"They have so much living yet to do." In our perceived omnipotence and grandiosity, we may be professionally, and personally, drawn to take it upon ourselves to be the savior of a particular young patient. Such a natural and seductive pull may set up a traumatic personal loss for the therapist should the child choose death over life.

The various and confusing boundaries between professional and personal issues related to working with suicidal patients are further complicated by the specific demands and responsibilities of the professional role. For better or worse, therapists are society's watchdogs, legally bound to protect patients from themselves and others. Thus, the professional role may require breaking the patient's fundamental right to confidentiality or may require hospitalizing a patient against his or her will, limiting personal liberty. The failure to uphold the standards of the profession may result in malpractice litigation that may fundamentally threaten the therapist's continued professional existence.

Thus, the personal and professional issues inherent in a patient's suicide provide a complex matrix of various manifestations and consequences (see Table 5).

Fundamentally, the survivorship of a patient's suicide generates a number of essential questions that speak to issues of both personal and professional competence and responsibility: "What could I have done that I did not do? Was it my fault? What did I do that I should not have done?" Readers may find the personal account of Jones (1987) helpful in gaining some perspective on the therapist's personal and professional survival of a patient's suicide.

Resources for therapists. Little has been written in the professional literature about therapist survivorhood, what Litman (1965) has referred to as a "taboo" topic within psychology. Not surprisingly, however, what is written tends to focus on the enlistment of others to provide personal and professional support. Marshall (1980) has made some useful recommendations to facilitate the survivorship at the professional group level (e.g., the professional staff of an interdisciplinary team working in an inpatient psychiatric setting). Marshall describes three basic conditions for helping a professional staff to survive a patient's loss: (a) a supportive and nonblaming staff atmosphere that ensures that a range of feelings can be expressed and understood; (b) the availability of a neutral consultant or consultation group; and (c) training to supplement prior training and experience with suicidal people. This training should include discussions of personal philosophies concerning suicide, clarification of personal responsibilities, an awareness of limits of responsibility, and knowledge of agency policies relevant to actions

Table 5

Therapist Reactions to Suicide

Manifestations	Consequences
I. *Personal*	
A. *Affective*	
Anger (deceased, family, supervisor)	Blame ? suicide rate
Sadness/depression/hopelessness	Fuels guilt, denial, anger
Relief	
B. *Cognitive*	
Denial/Repression	Myth-making
Guilt	Obsessive reviewing, fuels professional fears Search for meaning
Shame	Fuels professional fears
One-way communications:	
"I won't let you help me"	Anger toward decreased
"You can't help me"	Feelings of inadequacy
C. *Behavioral*	
Loss of patterns of conduct	Impaired professional and personal performance
Partial identification	? suicide rate
II. *Professional*	
Fears—Blame by the family/Lawsuit	Avoid contact with family, avoid attending funeral
—Censure by colleagues	Secrecy and isolation, personally and professionally
—Damage to reputation/publicity	
Doubts regarding adequacy/competence	Conservatism to avoid repeat Decline in suicidal patients Professional shift or leaving profession altogether

table continues

Table 5   (*continued*)

Manifestations	Consequences
Reorganization: What can I learn?	Formal case review Enhanced skills, competence Owning responsibility for "mistakes"

Note. Reprinted from "Therapists as Survivors of Client Suicide" by Frank A. Jones, Jr., from *Suicide and its aftermath: Understanding and counseling the survivors* (p. 131), edited by Edward J. Dunne, John L. McIntosh, and Karen Dunne-Maxim, Copyright 1987 by Edward J. Dunne, John L. McIntosh, and Karen Dunne-Maxim. Used by permission of the publisher, W. W. Norton & Company, Inc.

taken before and after suicides. For individual therapist-survivors, Marshall (1980) similarly recommends outside consultation to provide objectivity and support.

In a somewhat different vein, self-help support groups of therapists who have survived patient suicides have been cited in the literature as being particularly helpful (Binder, 1978; Goldstein & Buongiorno, 1984; Kolodny, Binder, Bronstein, & Friend, 1979). As described by Jones (1987), therapist-survivor support groups provide (a) a place to acknowledge and work through personal loss; (b) an opportunity to practice what they preach, in terms of dealing with and talking about their emotions; and (c) the opportunity to talk to other professionals who have been through a similar experience.

Conclusion

The prevention of adolescent suicide is the business of all of a community's constituent members. Given both its preventability and the enormous cost to society caused by the premature loss of life, it is encouraging that the federal government has become involved in partnership with the mental health community in addressing the problem of adolescent suicide. Given both the concentrated time the adolescent spends at school and the role of the school in fostering skill attainment and increasing awareness, it is encouraging that our schools have assumed a role in and have become a logical site for preventive education models.

It is the clinician, however, who has a pivotal role in prevention, as a translator to others of what is known (empirical risk factors), as a direct, early interventionist (secondary prevention), and as a researcher–evaluator of programmatic interventions. To date, program evaluations of large-scale prevention interventions have yielded perhaps but one significant conclusion, that the problem of adolescent suicide is complex and its resolution is not simple. We should not be discouraged. It is the nature of science to continuously raise and test refined hypotheses based on tests of prior hypotheses that were not confirmed. We must and will eventually get enough of it right to make a significant difference.

Irrespective of the success of our efforts, there always will be suicides. And as long as therapists engage the suicidal patient, there will be suicides among these patients.

Much more research and literature are needed to provide additional perspectives and useful responses for therapists who survive the suicide death of a patient. The open discussion of the inherent issues has only begun rather recently, as therapists are coming to be recognized as legitimate survivors of a patient's suicide death. In closing, Jones (1987) has eloquently summarized the topic as follows:

> The tragedy of patient suicide can also be an opportunity for us as therapists to grow in our skills at assessing and intervening in suicidal crisis, to broaden and deepen the connection and support we give and receive, to grow in our appreciation of the precious gift that life is, and to help each other live it more fully. All of us who work with significantly troubled individuals shoulder the potential burden of be-

coming survivors of a patient's suicide. The burden, should it come, is better carried with support. (p. 141)

References

Alcohol, Drug Abuse, and Mental Health Administration. (1989). *Report of the Secretary's Task Force on Youth Suicide: Volume 1. Overview and recommendations.* (DHHS Publication No. ADM 89-1621). Washington, DC: U.S. Government Printing Office.

Appel, Y. H., & Wrobleski, A. (1987). Self-help and support groups: Mutual aid for survivors. In E. J. Dunne, J. L. McIntosh, & K. Dunne-Maxim (Eds.), *Suicide and its aftermath* (pp. 215–233). New York: W. W. Norton.

Averill, J. R. (1968). Grief: Its nature and significance. *Psychological Bulletin, 70*, 721–748.

Berman, A. L. (Ed.). (1990a). *Suicide prevention: Case consultations.* New York: Springer Press.

Berman, A. L. (1990b). Suicide interventions in schools: Critical reflections. In A. A. Leenaars & S. Wenckstern (Eds.), *Suicide prevention in schools* (pp. 243–255), Washington, DC: Hemisphere Publishing.

Billow, C. J. (1987). A multiple family support group for survivors of suicide. In E. J. Dunne, J. L. McIntosh, & K. Dunne-Maxim (Eds.), *Suicide and its aftermath* (pp. 208–214). New York: W. W. Norton.

Binder, R. (1978). Dealing with patients' suicides [Letter to the editor]. *American Journal of Psychiatry, 135*, 1113.

Bowlby, J., & Parkes, C. M. (1970). Separation and loss within the family. In E. J. Anthony & C. Koupernik (Eds.), *The child in his family* (Vol. 1, pp. 197–216). New York: Wiley Interscience.

Brent, D. A., Perper, J. A., & Allman, C. J. (1987). Alcohol, firearms and suicide among youth. *Journal of the American Medical Association, 257*, 3369–3372.

Calhoun, L. G., Selby, J. W., & Abernathy, C. B. (1984). Suicidal death: Social reactions to bereaved survivors. *Journal of Psychology, 116*, 255–261.

Calhoun, L. G., Selby, J. W., & Faulstich, M. E. (1980). Reactions to the parents of the child suicide: A study of social impressions. *Journal of Consulting and Clinical Psychology, 48*, 535–536.

Calhoun, L. G., Selby, J. W., & Selby, L. E. (1982). The psychological aftermath of suicide: An analysis of current evidence. *Clinical Psychology Review, 2*, 409–420.

Cantor, P. C. (1989). Intervention strategies: Environmental risk reduction for youth suicide. In Alcohol, Drug Abuse, and Mental Health Administration, *Report of the Secretary's Task Force on Youth Suicide: Volume 3. Prevention and interventions in youth suicide* (pp. 285–293). (DHHS Publication No. ADM 89-1623. Washington, DC: U.S. Government Printing Office.

Cantor, P. C. (1990). Commentary: Suicide prevention: Clusters and contagion. In Berman, A. L. (Ed.). *Suicide Prevention: Case consultations* (pp. 42–55). New York: Springer Press.

Centers for Disease Control (1988). Centers for Disease Control recommendations for a community plan for the prevention and containment of suicide clusters. *Morbidity and Mortality Weekly Report, 37*(Suppl. S-6), 1–12.

Clarke, R. V., & Lester, D. (1987). Toxicity of car exhausts and opportunity for suicide. *Journal of Epidemiology and Community Health, 41*, 114–120.

Colt, G. W. (1987). The history of the suicide survivor: The mark of Cain. In E. J. Dunne, J. L. McIntosh, & K. Dunne-Maxim (Eds.), *Suicide and its aftermath.* New York: W. W. Norton.

Committee on Trauma Research (1985). *Injury in America.* Washington, DC: National Academy Press.

Dew, M. A., Bromet, E. J., Brent, D., & Greenhouse, J. B. (1987). A quantitative literature review of the effectiveness of suicide prevention centers. *Journal of Consulting and Clinical Psychology, 55*, 239–244.

Diegmuller, K. (1987, August 10). The violent killing of youths: Adolescent fact of death. "Insight," *The Washington Times,* pp. 18–20.

Eddy, D. M., Wolpert, R. L., & Rosenberg, M. L. (1989). Interventions to prevent youth suicides. In Alcohol, Drug Abuse, and Mental Health Administration. *Report of the Secretary's Task Force on Youth Suicide: Volume 4. Strategies for the prevention of youth suicide* (pp. 37–81). (DHHS Publication No. ADM 89-1624). Washington, DC: U.S. Government Printing Office.

Flesch, R. (1977). Mental health and bereavement by accident or suicide: A preliminary report. In B. L. Danto & A. H. Kutscher (Eds.), *Suicide and bereavement* (pp. 128–137). New York: MSS Information Corporation.

Franklin, J. L., Comstock, B. S., Simmons, J. T., & Mason, M. (1989). Characteristics of suicide prevention/intervention programs: Analysis of a survey. In Alcohol, Drug Abuse, and Mental Health Administration. *Report of the Secretary's Task Force on Youth Suicide: Volume 3. Prevention and interventions in youth suicide* (pp. 93–102). (DHHS Publication No. ADM 89-1623). Washington, DC: U.S. Government Printing Office.

Glick, I. O., Weiss, R. S., & Parkes, C. M. (1974). *The first year of bereavement.* New York: John Wiley & Sons.

Goldstein, L. S., & Buongiorno, P. A. (1984). Psychotherapists as suicide survivors. *American Journal of Psychotherapy, 38*, 392–398.

Hauser, M. J. (1983). Bereavement outcomes for widows. *Journal of Psychosocial Nursing and Mental Health Services, 21*, 22–31.

Hauser, M. J. (1987). Special aspects of grief after suicide. In E. J. Dunne, J. L. McIntosh, & K. Dunne-Maxim (Eds.), *Suicide and its aftermath.* New York: W. W. Norton.

Heilig, S. M. (1985, April). Survey of 41 survivor groups [Abstract]. In R. Cohen-Sandler (Ed.), *Proceedings of the 18th Annual Meeting of the American*

Association of Suicidology (pp. 110–113). Denver, CO: American Association of Suicidology.

Henslin, J. M. (1970). Guilt and guilt neutralization: Response and adjustment to suicide. In J. D. Douglas (Ed.), *Deviance and respectability: The social construction of moral meaning* (pp. 192–228). New York: Basic Books.

Hoberman, H. M., & Garfinkel B. D. (1988). Completed suicide in children and adolescents. *Journal of the American Academy of Child and Adolescent Psychiatry, 27,* 689–695.

Holinger, P. C. (1984). Suicide prevention and intervention. In Carter Center, *Closing the Gap Project.* Atlanta, GA: Centers for Disease Control.

Jones, F. A. (1987). Therapists as survivors of client suicide. In E. J. Dunne, J. L. McIntosh, & K. Dunne-Maxim (Eds.), *Suicide and its aftermath* (pp. 126–141). New York: W. W. Norton.

Kallman, F. J., & Anastasia, M. M. (1947). Twin studies on the psychopathology of suicide. *Journal of Nervous and Mental Diseases, 105,* 40–50.

Kolodny, S., Binder, R., Bronstein, A., & Friend, R. (1979). The working through of patients' suicides by four therapists. *Suicide and Life-Threatening Behavior, 9,* 33–46.

Lehrman, S. R. (1973). Reactions to untimely death. In H. M. Ruitenbeek (Ed.), *The interpretation of death* (pp. 222–236). New York: Jason Aronson.

Lindemann, E. (1944). Symptomatology and management of acute grief. *American Journal of Psychiatry, 101,* 141–148.

Litman, R. (1965). When patients commit suicide. *American Journal of Psychotherapy, 19,* 570–576.

Marshall, K. (1980). When a patient commits suicide. *Suicide and Life-Threatening Behavior, 10,* 29–40.

Martz, L. (1987, March 23). The copycat suicides. *Newsweek,* pp. 28–29.

Maxim, K., & Brooks, C. (1985, April). Multi-impact family therapy: A therapeutic approach following a client's suicide [Abstract]. In R. Cohen-Sandler (Ed.), *Proceedings of the 18th Annual Meeting of the American Association of Suicidology* (pp. 106–109). Denver, CO: American Association of Suicidology.

McIntosh, J. L. (1987). Suicide as a mental health problem: Epidemiologic aspects. In E. K. Dunne, J. L. McIntosh, & K. Dunne-Maxim (Eds.), *Suicide and its aftermath* (pp . 19–30). New York: W. W. Norton.

Miller, H. L., Coombs, D. W., Leeper, J. D., & Barton, S. N. (1984). An analysis of the effect of suicide prevention facilities on suicide rates in the United States. *American Journal of Public Health, 74,* 340–343.

Parkes, C. M. (1975a). Determinants of outcome following bereavement. *Psychiatry, 33,* 444–467.

Parkes, C. M. (1975b). Unexpected and untimely bereavement: A statistical study of young Boston widows. In B. Schoenberg, I. Gerber, A. Weiner, A. H. Kutscher, D. Peretz, & A. C. Carr (Eds.), *Bereavement: Its psychosocial aspects* (pp. 119–138). New York: Columbia University Press.

Rabkin, J., & Struening, E. (1976). Life events, stress, and illness. *Science, 194,* 1013–1020.

Range, L. M., & Kastner, J. W. (1988). Community reactions to attempted suicide and completed child suicide. *Journal of Applied Social Psychology, 18,* 1085–1093.

Reynolds, F. M. T., & Cimbolic, P. (1988–1989). Attitudes toward suicide survivors as a function of survivors' relationship to the victim. *Omega, 19,* 125–133.

Rosenblatt, P. C., Jackson, D. A., & Walsh, R. P. (1972). Coping with anger and aggression in mourning. *Omega, 3,* 271–284.

Rudestam, K. E. (1977). Physical and psychological responses to suicide in the family. *Journal of Consulting and Clinical Psychology, 45,* 162–170.

Rudestam, K. E., & Imbroll, D. (1983). Societal reactions to a child's death by suicide. *Journal of Consulting and Clinical Psychology, 51,* 461–462.

Shaffer, D. Garland, A., Gould, M., Fisher, P., & Trautman, P. (1988). Preventing teenage suicide: A critical review. *Journal of the American Academy of Child and Adolescent Psychiatry, 27*(6), 675–687.

Shaffer, D., Garland, A., & Whittle, B. (1988, March). An evaluation of youth suicide prevention programs. *New Jersey adolescent suicide prevention project.* Final project report, New Jersey Division of Mental Health and Hospitals, Trenton, NJ.

Sheskin, A., & Wallace, S. E. (1976). Differing bereavements: Suicide, natural, and accidental deaths. *Omega, 7,* 229–242.

Shneidman, E. S. (1967). *Bulletin of Suicidology* (No. 1). Rockville, MD: The National Institute of Mental Health Center for Studies of Suicide Prevention.

Silverman, P. R. (1978). *Mutual help groups: A guide for mental health workers.* [National Institute of Mental Health Monograph] (DHEW Publication No. ADM 78-646). Washington, DC: U.S. Government Printing Office.

Smith, K., Eyman, J.R., Dyck, R., & Ryerson, D. (1990). *School-related suicide programs.* Manuscript submitted for publication.

Staff. (1989). Suicide and media response. *Newslink* (American Association of Suicidology Newsletter), *15*(4), 1.

van der Wal, J. (1989–1990). The aftermath of suicide: A review of empirical evidence. *Omega, 20,* 149–171.

Winslow, F. (1840). *The anatomy of suicide.* London: Renshaw.

Zinner, E. S. (1985). Group survivorship: A model and case study application. In E. S. Zinner (Ed.), *Coping with Death on Campus* (pp. 51–68). San Francisco, CA: Jossey-Bass.

Index

About the Authors

Alan L. Berman has a PhD in clinical psychology from The Catholic University of America. Dr. Berman is a professor of psychology at The American University, where he has taught since 1969. He has maintained a private practice at the Washington (DC) Psychological Center since 1977. Dr. Berman is a past president (1984–1985) of the American Association of Suicidology (AAS), and he received the AAS's Shneidman Award in 1982 for outstanding contributions in research in suicidology. He is a Fellow of the American Psychological Association and a Diplomate in clinical psychology, American Board of Professional Psychology.

David A. Jobes has a PhD in clinical psychology from The American University. Dr. Jobes is an assistant professor of psychology at The Catholic University of America, where since 1987, he has held a joint appointment in the university's counseling center as a staff member and Director of Training. Dr. Jobes is an active researcher, writer, trainer, and consultant in the field of suicidology and also maintains a private practice in Washington, DC.